Experiments with EPROMS

Advanced Technology Series

Experiments with EPROMS

By Dave Prochnow
Edited by Lisa A. Doyle

Experiments in Artificial Neural Networks

By Ed Reitman
Edited by David Gauthier

Experiments with EPROMS

By Dave Prochnow

TAB BOOKS Inc.
Blue Ridge Summit, PA

Trademark List

The following trademarked products are mentioned in *Experiments with EPROMs.*

Apple Computer, Inc.: Apple *II*e
Autodesk, Inc.: AutoCAD 2
Bishop Graphics, Inc.: E-Z Circuit
Wintek Corporation: HiWIRE
smARTWORK
Borland International: Turbo BASIC
MicroPro International, Inc.: WordStar

To my patient and understanding Kathy

FIRST EDITION
FIRST PRINTING

Library of Congress Cataloging in Publication Data

Prochnow , Dave.
Experiments with EPROMS / by Dave Prochnow.

p. cm.
Includes index.
ISBN 0-8306-0362-X ISBN 0-8306-2962-9 (pbk.)
1. Computer storage devices—Experiments. I. Title.
TK7895.M4P76 1988 88-1508
621.397'3—dc19 CIP

Questions regarding the content of this book
should be addressed to:

Reader Inquiry Branch
TAB BOOKS Inc.
Blue Ridge Summit, PA 17294-0214

Contents

List of Projects

Acknowledgments

Significant contributions were made by several outstanding manufacturers during the preparation of this book. Borland International, CAD Software, Inc., Heath/Zenith, Kepro Circuit Systems, Inc., and Wintek Corporation all made generous hardware and software contributions which served as important references in developing the following text.

Introduction

EPROM programming is one of the great mysteries in advanced circuit design. Here is a discrete, dual in-line package that is capable of holding any user-supplied programming in a nonvolatile fashion. Furthermore, this silicon-housed carrier can be quickly erased at the discretion of the user and reprogrammed at a modest cost. Unfortunately, there is a fixed set of perennial problems which continually hamper the widespread usage of EPROM technology.

Basically, these EPROM restrictions can be broken down into three standard questions. How do I program an EPROM? How can I incorporate an EPROM into my circuit design? And, what are my alternatives to using an EPROM? Up until now, these questions were only answered by a select group of individuals who had braved the uncharted reaches of EPROM programming. Even their answers were far from definitive, however. Extensive pioneering work in EPROM technology has yet to be performed at the experimenter's level. This is a field that is ripe for discovery.

In actual practice, the implementation of EPROMs into digital circuits is a relatively easy task. Virtually, any design that uses microprocessor control or requires external data for its operation can be modified or adapted to accept EPROM programming. To achieve this desired digital memory goal, you will need three things: an EPROM programmer, an EPROM eraser, and an extensive guidebook. At this moment, you are holding the direct solution to the latter requirement and the indirect answer to the previous two necessary EPROM elements.

This book contains complete circuit information for building a number of EPROM programmers, erasers, and dedicated projects. Each of these circuits is based on a varying level of design need. These programmers, erasers, and projects represent working solutions to every major EPROM usage, including stand-alone and computer-based units. But this book doesn't stop at hardware answers. There is also a complete introduction into the theory of digital circuitry and digital memory devices. Therefore, not only will you learn how to construct several powerful EPROM programmers and erasers, but you also receive an education in the technology of programmable memories.

Following a brief introduction into human memory, there is a complete examination of the current state of digital memory. Once you have mastered the basics of memory fabrication, three chapters list the major types of digital memories that can be found on today's market. After you have gained the necessary background information in EPROM technology, the remainder of this book covers the actual programming and erasing of EPROMs.

Fifteen different programmers, erasers, and EPROM-based circuits are fully detailed in four valuable chapters. All of these projects are advanced in the methods that they use for their construction and operation. Therefore, beginning readers might need some background training prior to attempting the construction of these EPROM projects. There are three appendices, however, that can guide you through many of these areas. Two important considerations that you should make before attempting to build any of these projects are the purchases of both a quality soldering iron and a reliable digital logic probe. While the need for the former is obvious, you will find that the logic probe's ability to pinpoint logic status errors is invaluable when troubleshooting EPROM wiring problems.

If the construction of an EPROM programmer and/or eraser doesn't satisfy your needs, then this book's chapter dealing with commercial programmers and erasers can help you explore EPROM technology. The inclusion of this chapter expands the potential of incorporating EPROMs into your next circuit design. Thus, you have two different methods for acquiring the benefits of nonvolatile memory.

Finally, after all of your creative juices have been stimulated with the knowledge of creating your own EPROM circuits, this book's last chapter gives a thumbnail look at alternate memory technologies. So all three of the EPROM programming requirements have been met by this book. Both an EPROM programmer and an EPROM eraser can either be built from the circuits that are contained within this book or purchased from a manufacturer. Additionally, the information in this book supplies all of the reference material that is necessary for mastering EPROM technology. Therefore, the conclusion of this book leaves you with only one remaining task:

54 68 61 6E 6B 73 20
66 6F 72 20
74 68 65 20
6D 65 6D 6F 72 69 65 73 2E

1

EPROM Technology

Perform this series of three simple tests: What was the name of your kindergarten teacher? Now, what was the name of your college advisor? Finally, what is your social security number? How'd you do? Your ability to correctly recall each of these answers depends largely on your command of a relatively mysterious process which inhabits the human brain—the memory.

Memory is an ephemeral product derived from the interactions between over 15 billion neurons inside the average human brain (see Bibliography for further reference materials supporting this study). These interactions form a neurochemical change that is retained over lengthy periods of time in spite of other brain activities. There are several unknown variables in this simplified explanation of human memory, however. For example, how are these neuronal interactions initiated? What length of exposure is required for commiting a name, idea, or concept to memory? And what is the duration of a "memorized" thought?

Any study of memory must begin with the derivation of its definition. The etymology of this noun, "memory," has its origin in Latin's *memoria* and *memor*. Complementing this literary definition, the biological derivation of memory stems from the reactions within the single-celled neuron. This small grayish cell is the basis for all neurological activity. Unfortunately, the action of these neurons in the formation of memory is far more complicated.

There are two general schools of thought on the structure of the neuronal biology of the brain. The first is the *net theory* of neuron placement. As espoused by Camillo Golgi, this net theory concluded that the brain's neurons were all interconnected in dense, multiple layers of vast nerve cell networks. Golgi further stated that impulses, ideas, and memory traveled this enormous neuronal network similar to trains through a railway system. The complicated mechanics of this type of structure made this theory difficult for some biologists to swallow and alternate theories were quickly formulated.

One of these opposing views came from Ramon y Cajal of Spain. Cajal's theory stated that neurons were discrete individual cells with no distinct point of articulation. In this theory, an impulse or idea travels from neuron to neuron through a proximate space known as a *synaptic cleft* or *synapse* (see Fig. 1-1). Therefore, Cajal's synapse serves as a communication point between individual neurons with impulses able to travel in any direction to any nearby neuron. The flexible concept of synaptic communication between neurons has made Cajal's theory more widely accepted than Golgi's nerve cell network theory. Support in the scientific community can be fickle, however.

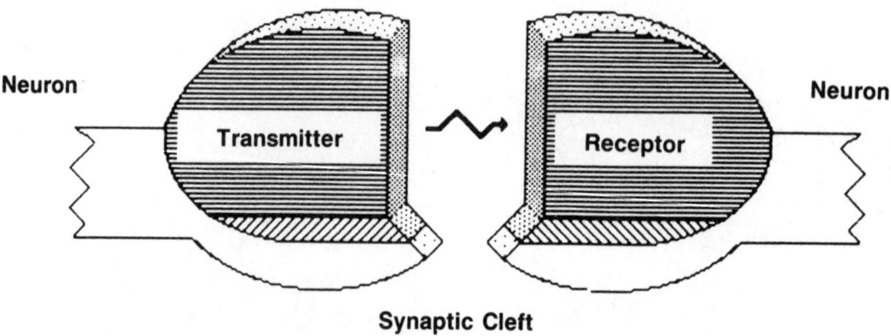

Fig. 1-1. Diagram of a neuronal synapse in the human brain.

This point is illustrated by the 1906 Nobel Prize awards ceremony. In 1906, the Nobel Prize Committee couldn't make a definitive decision on the "best" neuronal theory. Therefore, the Nobel Prize in Medicine was awarded to both Cajal and Golgi. In spite of this dual selection, Cajal's theory was quickly adopted by the medical world as the most sound explanation of impulse and idea transmission within the human brain. An interesting footnote to this widespread refutation of nerve network impulse conveyance is that several new studies are now lending a degree of credence to Golgi's theory (see Bibliography). Who knows, maybe the Nobel Prize Committee was correct after all in dividing the 1906 award between both Cajal and Golgi?

Restricting our neurological study to the more generally accepted Cajal theory, there are three main components of a neuron: the cell *body*, the *axon*, and the *dendrite* (see Fig. 1-2). Each of these neuronal parts serves a key role in sending an impulse through the brain. Basically, an impulse travels from one neuron's axon to another cell's dendrite. This process is carried out between any neuron across any synapse. The resultant impulse can culminate in an action, a reflex, or an idea. But what exactly is an impulse?

Neuronal impulses are electrochemical signals that are carried along neurons through the various axon/dendrite synaptic joints. The nature of these

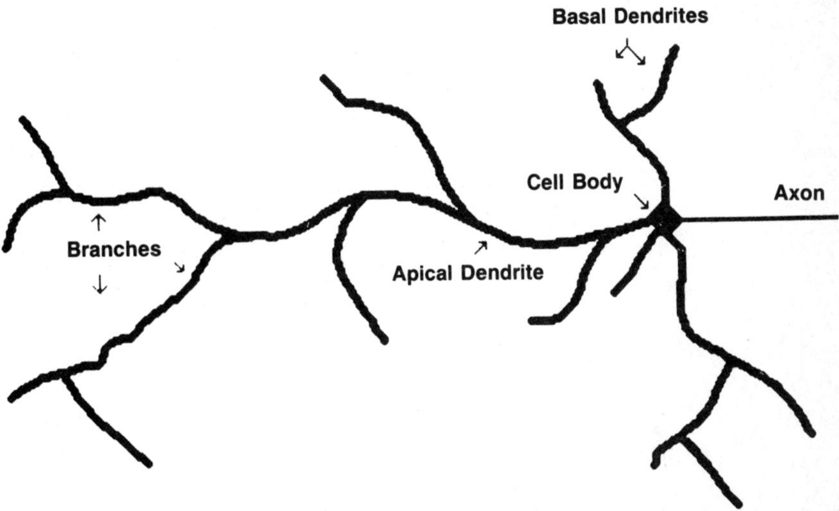

Fig. 1-2. The cellular parts of a human neuron.

impulses can be demonstrated through a simple biological experiment. By sending a low-voltage electrical charge through the exposed nerve fibers of a dissected frog leg, the inert leg can be made to twitch. Furthermore, the fluid that is produced from these electrically charged nerves will cause another muscular contraction when applied directly to the leg muscle. Therefore, the sequence of events during impulse transmission consists of:

1. An electrical charge.
2. The production of a neuronal chemical.
3. The transmission of the neuronal chemical.
4. The absorption of the chemical by another neuron.
5. The production of an electrical charge.

This process is repeated thousands of times until the final neuron causes the muscle to contract.

In terms of a single neuron, this sequence is initiated in the cell body through the production of a weak electrical current. Once this electrical charge has been generated, the signal travels down the neuron's axon to the synapse. At this junction, the impulse releases special compounds in the transmitting neuron's cell membrane and the electrical signal is changed into a chemical signal.

A neuron's chemical signal is composed of neurotransmitters that float across the synaptic cleft and latch onto another neuron's dendrite. This dendritic attachment selectively alters the receiving neuron's cell membrane and forms an electrical potential. Once again, this electrical potential travels through the neuron, along the axon, and the entire process is repeated thousands, millions, or billions of times for each and every impulse.

This elementary introduction into the biology of memory has some interesting parallels in the electronics of digital memory. Like its neuronal equivalent, digital memory can be either *volatile* or *nonvolatile* (i.e., permanent). Similarly, memory is conveyed as an electrical impulse in both systems. One sharp difference between human memory and digital memory, however, is that digital memory will never forget the name of your kindergarten teacher; that is, not unless you erase it.

DIGITAL MEMORY

Any discussion of digital memory must begin with a solid introduction to digital logic. By definition, digital logic is the sequence of events within a digital circuit. This sequencing is governed by a strict application of mathematics. Entering into this mathematical logic scheme are the two possible conditions or states that can be present in a digital circuit: OFF or ON.

Several different names are given to this dual state depending on their circumstances of occurrence. For example, the two conditions of a digital signal are labeled as LOW and HIGH for the OFF and ON states, respectively. Alternatively, in a graphics system like a computer video display, the digital representation used for indicating the OFF and ON status of the individual pixels found on a monitor screen is either dark or light, respectively. Finally, in a microcomputer's MPU (Microprocessing Unit), these OFF and ON conditions are interpreted numerically as a 0 and a 1. This final numeric symbolic definition is used throughout the ensuing discussions of digital logic and introduction to digital memory.

These 0's and 1's of digital logic are manipulated with the *binary* or base-2 number system. Like other number systems, the selective combination of the binary number system's 0 and 1 can be used for expressing any numeric value. Table 1-1 compares the same sequence of values for four different number systems. One unfortunate side effect to writing numbers in binary notation is their unwieldy dimensions. For example, consider the following decimal value along with its binary equivalent:

222 (decimal) = 11011110 (binary)

In this example, the binary value is a lengthy eight digits versus three digits for the decimal representation. Therefore, a more practical means for dealing with the binary states of digital logic is through a higher-level number system.

While the decimal or base-10 number system is more comprehensible to the human user, the *octal* (base-8) and *hexadecimal* (base-16) number systems mesh more easily with the digital circuit's multiples-of-four data and address requirements. The handling of these data and address conditions is

Table 1-1. Four Different Numbering Systems.

Decimal	Binary	Octal	Hexadecimal
0	0	0	0
1	1	1	1
2	10	2	2
3	11	3	3
4	100	4	4
5	101	5	5
6	110	6	6
7	111	7	7
8	1000	10	8
9	1001	11	9
10	1010	12	A
11	1011	13	B
12	1100	14	C
13	1101	15	D
14	1110	16	E
15	1111	17	F
16	10000	20	10

principally executed by several single-binary-digit switching circuits or through a single multi-binary digit register. In an average digital circuit, these registers range in size from 4 to 64 binary digits. This dependence on factors of four makes translating between octal and hexadecimal values and binary digits a necessary talent that must be acquired by the digital circuit designer. Even so, the use of octal programming has recently fallen into disfavor and the hexadecimal number system has become a veritable standard in the standard-less microcomputer industry.

As an exercise in number system manipulation, perform the following experiment:

Purpose: Write a decimal-to-binary conversion program.

Materials: Any microcomputer system with a high-level language interface (e.g., BASIC, FORTRAN).

Procedure:

- Make your program short with a limited number of jumps or GOTO statements.
- Your program should be able to calculate any bit-size binary value.
- Test your final program with known binary numbers and compare your achieved results with your acquired results.

Results:

✤ This is one possible solution to this experiment in BASIC:

```
5 REM BINARY CALCULATOR PROGRAM
10 INPUT ''HOW MANY DIGITS '',A
20 B=0:C=0:D=0:Z=0:PRINT ''ENTER YOUR'';A;''-DIGIT
BINARY NUMBER'':INPUT QB$
30 D=A-1
40 FOR B=1 TO A
50 IF MID$(QB$,B,1)=''1'' THEN LET C=2^D:Z=Z+C:D=D-1
60 IF MID$(QB$,B,1)=''0'' THEN LET C=0:Z=Z+C:D=D-1
70 NEXT B
80 PRINT QB$;''=''
90 PRINT TAB(A+1) Z
100 INPUT ''DO ANOTHER: Y OR N ? '',X$
110 IF X$=''Y'' THEN GOTO 10
120 IF X$=''N'' THEN END
130 IF X$<>''Y'' OR X$<>''N'' THEN GOTO 100
```

✤ After you have completed this experiment, add an octal and hexadecimal conversion option to your final program.

Referring to a register size as multi-binary digit can be almost as cumbersome as writing large binary numbers. Therefore, another means for expressing binary digits is with bits. A bit can equal either a 0 or a 1. Applying this definition to the previously mentioned 8-digit binary number example 11011110 yields an 8-bit number. When dealing with register bit size, however, the final register value can represent the computational strength of a microcomputer.

At the heart (or brain) of every microcomputer is the MPU. This single chip or IC (integrated circuit) is the repository of the CPU's registers. Based on the bit width of these registers, the data handling ability of the MPU can be fairly judged (or can it?). Unfortunately, not all registers are created equal and many MPUs are difficult to pigeonhole into an accurate statement of their true computing power.

Take the Motorola MC68000 MPU, for example. The MC68000 has 32-bit internal registers, but this same MPU also has a 16-bit data bus, a 23-bit address bus, and a 16-bit ALU (arithmetic logic unit). Furthermore, this IC is able to address 16M bytes of unsegmented memory with a 32-bit program counter. So where does this mixed bag of bit width leave us? Granted, the MC68000 can handle 32-bit-sized instructions, internally. On the other hand, it can only receive data in 16-bit slices. Therefore, the MC68000 is best classified as a 16/32-bit MPU.

Another MPU that falls into this dual personality mold is the Intel 8088. The 8088 is best labeled an 8/16-bit MPU. In this case, there are 16-bit internal registers with an 8-bit data bus, a 20-bit address bus, and 16-bit instruction pointer (the function of the instruction pointer is similar to the role of the program counter in the MC68000). Additionally, the ALU is 16 bits wide. Once again, however, the 16-bit 8088's ability to receive data in 8-bit pieces mandates the 8/16-bit qualifier in describing its computational strength.

In addition to describing the amount of data that can be processed, the bit size of a register also indicates the number of logical states that are possible. All possible logic states for two different registers are listed in Table 1-2. Based on the states listed in these two examples, an X-bit register will contain 2^X logic states.

Table 1-2. Register Logic States.

2-bit Register

bit 1	bit 0
0	0
0	1
1	0
1	1

3-bit Register

bit 2	bit 1	bit 0
0	0	0
0	0	1
0	1	0
0	1	1
1	0	0
1	0	1
1	1	0
1	1	1

Yet another means for expressing the computational strength of a microcomputer is in its CPU's (central processing unit) memory size. Memory size is usually measured in 8-bit segments. Each 8-bit chunk is defined as a *byte*. Bytes, in turn, are frequently described in terms of kilobytes (K bytes), megabytes (M bytes), and gigabytes (G bytes). A 1K-byte CPU memory is equal to 2^{10} or 1024 bytes. This same 1K-byte CPU memory also contains 8192 bits (8 X 1024 bytes). Continuing with these equivalencies:

1M bytes = 2^{100} or 1,048,576 bytes
1G bytes = 2^{1000} or 1,073,741,824 bytes

In turn, these same values equal:

1M bytes = 8,388,608 bits
1G bytes = 8,589,934,592 bits

Bit strings of a byte's width are also useful for indicating the CPU's status. Depending on its register location, a byte can have a variety of different meanings.

For example,

00111111

is equal to,

63 (decimal)

3F (hexadecimal)

77 (octal)

and can represent the 8088 instruction code AAS. This code is a mnemonic representation of "ASCII adjust for subtraction." The use of the term *ASCII* points to another possible interpretation of this byte. ASCII (American Standard Code for Information Interchange) is a coding system that uses 7 bits of data for describing alphabetic, numeric, and punctuation characters in a digital circuit. Continuing with our previously mentioned byte,

00111111

represents the ASCII character

?

Another alphanumeric character description code is *EBCDIC* (Extended Binary Coded Decimal Interchange Code). This code is used primarily on mainframe IBM systems such as the IBM 360/370. In addition to being restricted to mainframe usage, EBCDIC data is 8 bits wide. Therefore, the byte 00111111 is equal to the EBCDIC control character SUB or substitute.

BINARY CODES

In addition to these possible interpretations of an 8-bit number, there are several binary coding schemes that are used in digital circuits. The four most popular codes are: Binary Coded Decimal, Excess 3, Gray, and 2-out-of-5. Each of these codes use a unique binary format for representing decimal numbers.

Binary Coded Decimal

Binary Coded Decimal (BCD) or *8421 codes* are used for translating any decimal number into a binary string. In BCD code, only four binary digits are used. These four bits equal the decimal values 0-9.

For example,

4 (decimal) = 0100 (BCD)

Please note that this binary value is not the same as the 7-bit ASCII code for the decimal number 4. In this case, the 7-bit ASCII code for 4 (decimal) is equal to 0110100.

Even multi-digit decimal numbers can be converted into BCD code. This conversion, however, results in some interesting number system oddities.

For example,

246 (decimal) = 0010 0100 0110 (BCD)

Likewise,

0010 0100 0110 (BCD) = 246 (hexadecimal)

In this example, both the decimal and hexadecimal numbers for the BCD code are identical. This decimal-hexadecimal equality is a peculiarity found in all BCD code. Based on this equivalence, many mathematicians claim that the BCD code is a subset of the hexadecimal number system.

Excess 3

The *Excess 3 code* shares many of the same features as BCD code. The only difference between these two binary coding schemes is that Excess 3 code has the value 3 added to each decimal digit prior to BCD code conversion.

For example,

246 (decimal) = 0010 0100 0110 (BCD)
= 0101 0111 1001 (Excess 3)

Gray

Binary strings can also be used in error detection. The *Gray code* is an error detection method where only one binary digit is changed in successive numbers.

For example,

4 (decimal) = 0110 (Gray)

and

246 (decimal) = 0011 0110 0101 (Gray)

2-out-of-5

Another error detection code is *2-out-of-5*. In this coding scheme, each decimal number is represented by 5 bits. These 5 bits must have two ones and three zeros with a different arrangement for each number. One of the most frequent error detection systems used with 2-out-of-5 code is checking for even parity; this error detection means is effected by the ever-present two 1's.

For example,

4 (decimal) = 01010 (2-out-of-5)

and

246 (decimal) = 00110 01010 10001 (2-out-of-5)

Once a binary string has been placed in an MPU's register, two basic arithmetic operations can be performed: addition or subtraction. The two states of binary numbers, 0 and 1, make the execution of these functions simpler than the comparable operation in a larger number system.

BINARY MATHEMATICS

Binary Addition

In binary addition, there are two possible outcomes: non-carry and carry. A carry in binary addition only occurs when two 1's are added together. This carry is a 1.

For example,

$$0 + 0 = 0$$
$$0 + 1 = 1$$

$$1 + 0 = 1$$
$$1 + 1 = 0 \quad \text{with a 1 carry}$$
$$0011 + 0111 = 1010$$

Binary Subtraction

Two forms of number complements are used in binary subtraction: the one's (1's) complement and the two's (2's) complement. These complements convert the negative value into a positive format so that binary addition can be used for arriving at the difference. In this manner, both binary addition and binary subtraction can be performed in the same digital circuit.

The One's-Complement. This is a simple state-reversal procedure. In other words, each 1 is changed to a 0 and each 0 is inverted to a 1.

For example,

0011 = 1100 (one's complement)
0111 = 1000 (one's complement)

Binary subtraction is performed by taking the one's complement of the negative value and adding it to the other binary number. Any carry is added to the final sum.

For example,

$$\begin{aligned} 0111 - 0011 &= 0111 + 1100 \\ &= 1\ 0011 \\ &= 0011 + 1 \\ &= 0100 \end{aligned}$$

A carry is usually represented as a separate 1 in a column to the left of the most significant digit (furthest left).

The Two's Complement. Following the one's complement inversion, a one is added to the least significant bit (furthest right). This addition follows the same carry rules used in binary addition.

For example,

0011 = 1101 (two's complement)
0111 = 1001 (two's complement)

Two conventions that are used in two's complement:

- A 0 is placed in front of positive, signed numbers.
- A 1 is placed in front of negative, signed numbers.

Once the two's complement of the negative number has been determined, binary subtraction is performed by adding the two's complement to the other binary number. In certain cases, a carry will be executed from the most significant digit (the furthest left). This carry is dropped in two's complement binary subtraction.

For example,

$$\begin{aligned} 0111 - 0011 &= 0111 + 1101 \\ &= 1\ 0100 \\ &= 0100 \end{aligned}$$

BINARY LOGIC

Taking this foundational knowledge of binary mathematics and applying it to digital circuits requires an understanding of binary logic and its associated digital component equivalents. Basically, binary logic can be broken down into four elements:

- gates
- Boolean algebra
- logic families
- logic circuits

Gates

There are three general gates in binary logic: the AND gate, the OR gate, and the NOT gate. Each of these gates duplicates a binary mathematical operation. For example,

The AND gate represents binary multiplication:

$$\text{INPUT A} \times \text{INPUT B} = \text{OUTPUT C}$$

The OR gate represents binary addition:

$$\text{INPUT A} + \text{INPUT B} = \text{OUTPUT C}$$

The NOT gate represents binary one's complement:

$$\text{INPUT A} = -\text{OUTPUT C}$$

Note: The NOT gate is sometimes referred to as the binary negation operation or the *inverter* gate and is formally represented as: INPUT A = OUTPUT $\overline{\text{C}}$ (pronounced "not C").

Special logic symbols are used to represent each of these gates (see Fig. 1-3). These symbols are particularly useful when establishing the Boolean algebra of a given logic circuit.

OR

AND

A
B
C

Fig. 1-3. OR, AND, and NOT logic gate symbols.

NOT

A
B

The inverter gate can be combined with the output of AND and OR gates to form special functions (see Fig. 1-4). These newly created gates are called the NOT AND or NAND and NOT OR or NOR gates, respectively (the negation operation of the inverter supplies the "NOT" or "N" prefix in the NAND and NOR gates). Likewise, the mathematics of these two new gates are the opposite of their positive logic counterparts.

The NAND gate represents negated binary multiplication:

INPUT A × INPUT B = −OUTPUT C

The NOR gate represents negated binary addition:

INPUT A + INPUT B = −OUTPUT C

Just as the inverter gate can be applied to the output of AND and OR gates, this logic reverser can also be combined with either or both of the gate's inputs (see Fig. 1-5).

The AND gate with negated input:

−INPUT A × INPUT B = OUTPUT C
INPUT A × −INPUT B = OUTPUT C

NAND

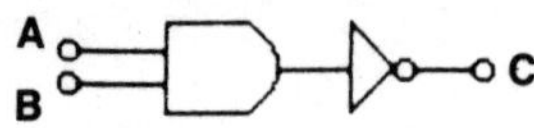

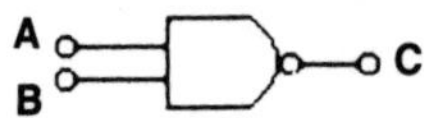

Fig. 1-4. Creating NAND and NOR logic gate symbols.

NOR

A B C

A B C

AND

A B C

A B C

Fig. 1-5. Applying NOT gates to AND and OR inputs.

OR

A B C

A B C

The OR gate with negated input:

$$-\text{INPUT A} + \text{INPUT B} = \text{OUTPUT C}$$
$$\text{INPUT A} + -\text{INPUT B} = \text{OUTPUT C}$$

More than two inputs can be attached to each of these gates and gate combinations. Even with these multiple inputs, the operation of the gate remains unchanged. For example,

The AND gate:

$$\text{INPUT A} \times \text{INPUT B} \times \text{INPUT C} = \text{OUTPUT D}$$

The NOR gate:

$$\text{INPUT A} + \text{INPUT B} + \text{INPUT C} + \text{INPUT D} = -\text{OUTPUT E}$$

One final gate that is used in binary logic is the EXCLUSIVE OR gate. Superficially, the operation of the EXCLUSIVE OR and the OR gate look identical. On further Boolean algebraic scrutiny, however, the final output value will be different for both logic functions.

The EXCLUSIVE OR gate represents exclusive binary addition:

$$\text{INPUT A} \oplus \text{INPUT B} = \text{OUTPUT C}$$

The EXCLUSIVE OR gate can also be negated by an inverter gate. This NOT gate is placed on the output of the EXCLUSIVE OR gate and forms an EXCLUSIVE NOR gate. Hence,

The EXCLUSIVE NOR gate represents negated exclusive binary addition:

$$\text{INPUT A} \oplus \text{INPUT B} = -\text{OUTPUT C}$$

Boolean Algebra

The logical combination of the two binary states is the basis for Boolean algebra. Every Boolean algebraic operation is expressed in a truth table. When combined with the logic symbols and mathematical operations formulas, the truth table forms a complete picture of the logic contained in a particular circuit. It is even possible to derive any two of these logic members given the information found in the remaining one. All of the typical gates and a few variations follow, with the schematic symbol, logic formula expression, and truth table.

NOT

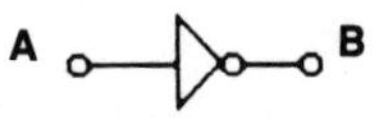

$\bar{A} = B$

A	B
0	1
1	0

AND

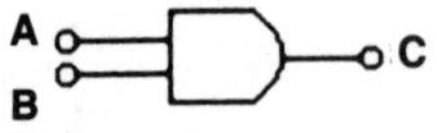

$A \times B = C$

A	B	C
0	0	0
0	1	0
1	0	0
1	1	1

OR

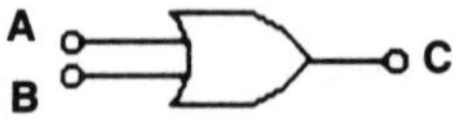

$A + B = C$

A	B	C
0	0	0
0	1	1
1	0	1
1	1	1

NAND

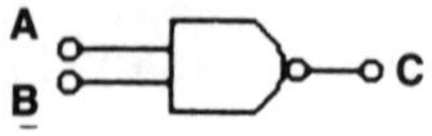

$A \times B = \bar{C}$

A	B	$\bar{C}$
0	0	1
0	1	1
1	0	1
1	1	0

NOR

$A + B = \bar{C}$

A	B	$\bar{C}$
0	0	1
0	1	0
1	0	0
1	1	0

Exclusive OR

$A + B = C$

A	B	C
0	0	0
0	1	1
1	0	1
1	1	0

Negated-Input AND

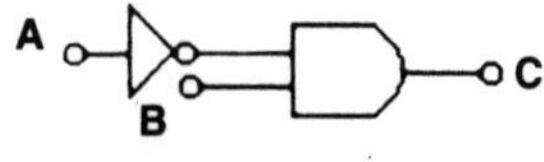

$\bar{A} \times B = C$

$\bar{A}$	B	C
0	0	0
0	1	1
1	0	0
1	1	0

Negated-Input OR

$\bar{A} + B = C$

$\bar{A}$	B	C
0	0	1
0	1	1
1	0	0
1	1	1

Multiple-Input AND

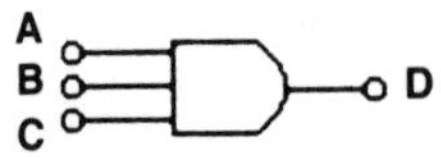

A × B × C = D

A	B	C	D
0	0	0	0
0	0	1	0
0	1	0	0
0	1	1	0
1	0	0	0
1	0	1	0
1	1	0	0
1	1	1	1

Multiple-Input OR

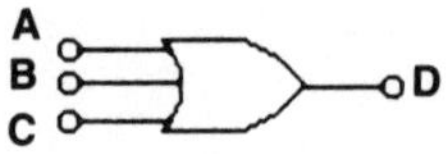

A + B + C = D

A	B	C	D
0	0	0	0
0	0	1	1
0	1	0	1
0	1	1	1
1	0	0	1
1	0	1	1
1	1	0	1
1	1	1	1

An interesting footnote to the EXCLUSIVE OR truth table is that any binary number that is EXCLUSIVE-ORed with itself will result in all zeros. In other words, a binary number of length X bits when EXCLUSIVE-ORed with itself will generate an X-bit length binary number filled with zeros. For example,

$$11011011 + 11011011 = 00000000$$

(EXCLUSIVE OR)

Once the interrelationship between the truth table, the mathematical operation formula, and the logic symbol is understood, complex multi-gate circuits can be devised. The creation of these multiple-gate circuits can be derived from any one of these binary logic members. For example, observe Figs. 1-16 through 1-19.

Based on these examples, two generalized methods of deriving the mathematical operations formula from the truth table can be easily described. In the first method, form a product on each row that has a one in the output column. A negation must be used for each zero input column. Next, add each

OR Gate

A
B
C

AND Function

A	B	C
0	0	0
0	1	0
1	0	0
1	1	1

Fig. 1-16. Multi-gate OR with an AND logic gate function.

AND Gate

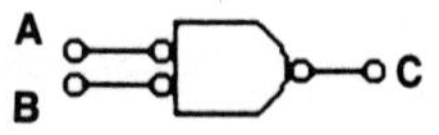

A
B
C

OR Function

A	B	C
0	0	0
0	1	1
1	0	1
1	1	1

Fig. 1-17. Multi-gate AND with an OR logic gate function.

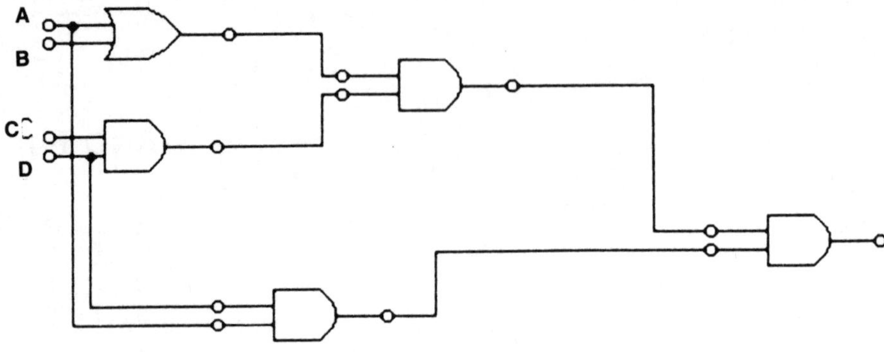

Fig. 1-18.

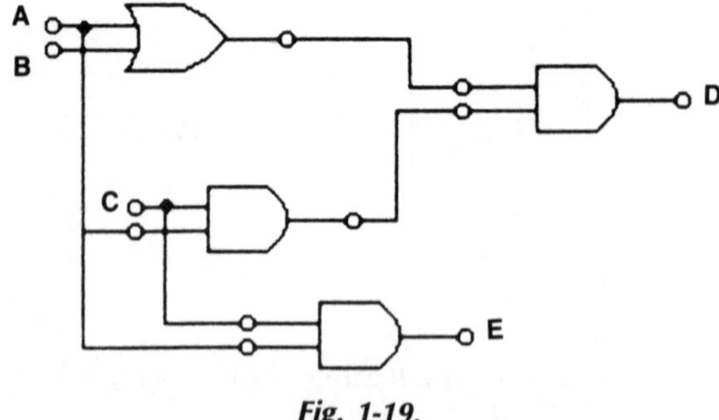

Fig. 1-19.

of these products together. The result is the mathematical operations formula for the particular truth table. This derivation method is sometimes called the sum-of-products rule. See Fig. 1-20.

The second method for learning the mathematical operations formula based on a truth table is called the product-of-sums rule. Basically, this method is just the reverse of the sum-of-products rule. In product-of-sums, form a sum on each row that has a zero in the output column. Be sure to use a negation for each one input column. Finally, multiply all of these sums together. See Fig. 1-21.

Sum-of-Products

$$\bar{A} \times \bar{B} + \bar{A} \times B + A \times \bar{B} = \bar{A}\bar{B} + \bar{A}B + A\bar{B} = C$$

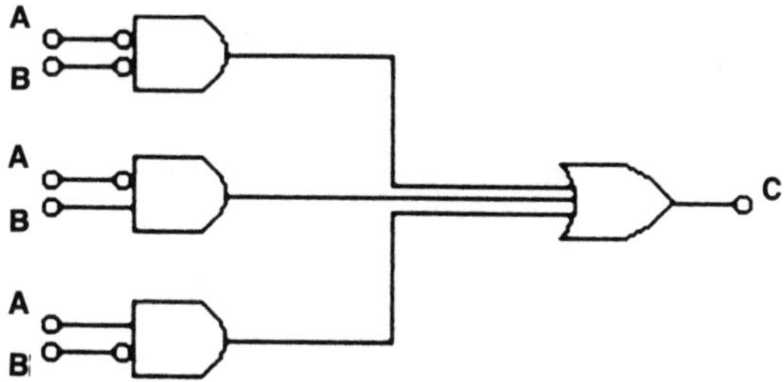

Fig. 1-20. An example of the sum-of-products rule.

Product-of-Sums

$$(\bar{A} + \bar{B}) \times (\bar{A} + B) \times (A + \bar{B}) = C$$

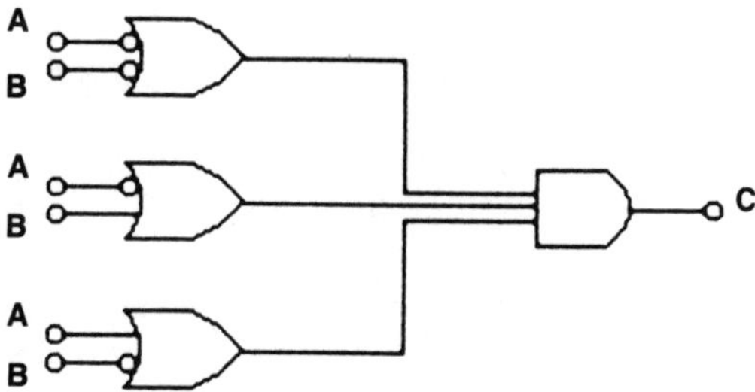

Fig. 1-21. An example of the product-of-sums rule.

As a rule, use whichever derivation method that will provide the simplest results. This determination can be based on the number of ones in the output column. In other words, if more ones than zeros are in the output column, then use product-of-sums. On the other hand, if more zeros are present in the output column, then use the sum-of-products rule.

More often than not, the mathematical operation formulas can get too large and awkward for easy translation into logic symbols. To help in minimizing this congestion, there are several Boolean rules and laws that can be used for reducing, manipulating, and simplifying these binary formulas (see Fig. 1-22).

Boolean Rules and Laws

Rule 1	$A \times 0 = 0$
Rule 2	$A \times 1 = A$
Rule 3	$A \times A = A$
Rule 4	$A \times \bar{A} = 0$
Rule 5	$\bar{\bar{A}} = A$ **(Tandem NOTs)**
Rule 6	$A + 0 = A$
Rule 7	$A + 1 = 1$
Rule 8	$A + A = A$
Rule 9	$A + \bar{A} = 1$
Rule 10	$A + AB = A$
Rule 11	$A \times (A + B) = A$
Rule 12	$(A + B)(A + C) = A + BC$
Rule 13	$A + \bar{A}B = A + B$
Commutative Law 1	$A + B = B + A$
Commutative Law 2	$AB = BA$
Associative Law 1	$A + (B + C) = (A + B) + C$
Associative Law 2	$A(BC) = (AB)C$
Distributive Law	$A(B + C) = AB + AC$
Demorgan's Law	$\overline{A + B} = \bar{A}\bar{B}$ or $\overline{AB} = \bar{A} + \bar{B}$

Fig. 1-22. The laws and rules for use with binary mathematics.

Applying Boolean algebra to actual digital circuits requires only one minor alteration. Instead of dealing with 0's and 1's, digital circuits deal with voltages. These voltages usually come in two forms: 0 volts and +5 volts. Coincidentally, these two voltage levels are ideal representatives of the two binary states. By setting 0 volts equal to a binary 0 and +5 volts equal to a binary 1, a typical positive logic circuit can be formed.

Conversely, a negative logic circuit is possible by setting 0 volts equal to a binary 1 and +5 volts equal to a binary 0. This positive-to-negative logic conversion practice also changes the function of the basic gates. In other words, a negative logic AND gate will function like an OR gate and a negative logic OR gate will function like an AND gate. Based on this information, only the function of the gate is altered and not its circuitry.

As a test of your comprehension of binary mathematics, perform the following experiment:

Purpose: Simplify a complex binary mathematical operation formula.

A	B	C
0	0	1
0	1	1
1	0	0
1	1	0

1. What is the simplest formula for this truth table?

2. What is the logic diagram for this truth table?

$$\overline{A} + B + (\overline{A}\,\overline{B}) + A + \overline{AB} = C$$

1. What is the truth table for this equation?

2. What is the logic diagram for this equation?

Fig. 1-23. Answer these questions based on the supplied logic information.

Procedure:

- Use the rules and laws of Boolean algebra to derive and simplify the binary mathematical operation formula based on the given truth table.
- Draw the logic symbols for the solved formula.
- Write a high-level language program for solving complex binary mathematical formulas.

Logic Families

Each of the binary logic gates have been duplicated in special digital ICs. These chips represent varying degrees of processing speed, power consumption, and construction material. Based on these different qualities, several large digital IC groupings can be made. These IC groupings are called logic families. In general, there are 15 logic families: primitive switch logic, switching mode logic, resistor-transistor logic, diode-transistor logic (DTL), fan-out logic, transistor-transistor logic (TTL), Schottky TTL, emitter-coupled logic (ECL), integration-injection logic, MOS logic, NMOS logic, PMOS logic, VMOS logic, CMOS logic, and QMOS logic.

Primitive Switch Logic. Early attempts at logic gates were made with analog switches. Both AND and OR gates were easily duplicated with these SPST (single-pole, single-throw) switches (see Fig. 1-24). A slight increase in the gate's switching function was made possible by substituting diodes for these switches (see Fig. 1-25). Even NPN transistors (a bipolar N-type, P-type, N-type transistor) could be added to this diode gate for generating a NOT gate (see Fig. 1-26).

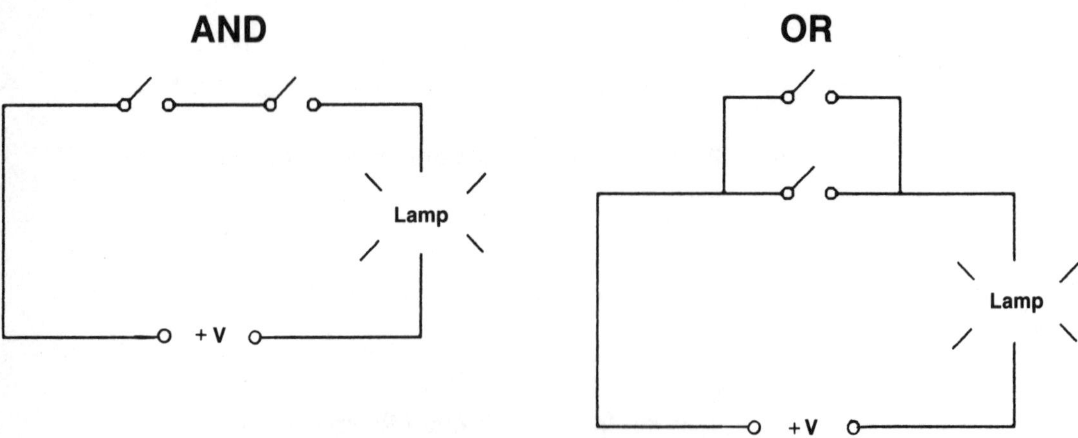

Fig. 1-24. AND and OR gates constructed from simple SPST switches.

Switching Mode Logic. Eventually, all gates were constructed from bipolar transistors. There are three types of bipolar switching mode logic gates: current sourcing, current sinking, and current mode logic.

In *current sourcing*, all subsequent gate transistor base current is derived from the previous gate's collector (see Fig. 1-27). This switching mode logic type is frequently used in resistor-transistor logic.

Current sinking, on the other hand, draws the second gate's base current from a bias resistor that is attached between its own base and collector (see Fig. 1-28). The sink for the second gate, however, is produced by the collector of the previous gate.

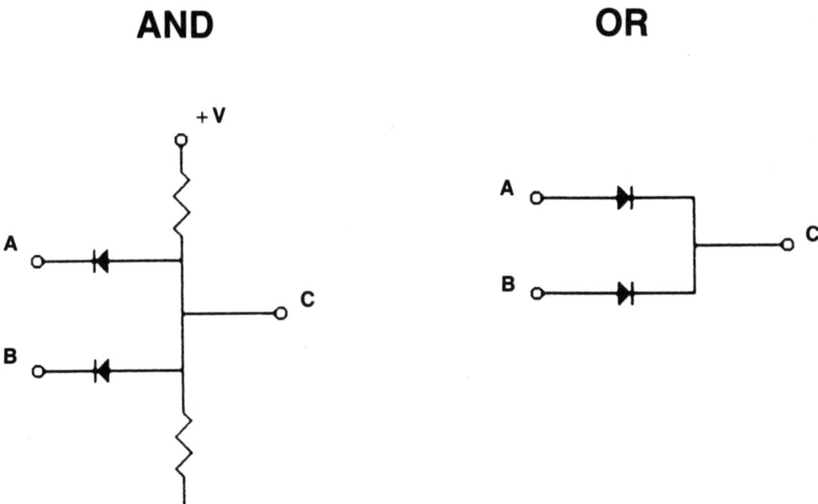

Fig. 1-25. AND and OR gates constructed from diodes.

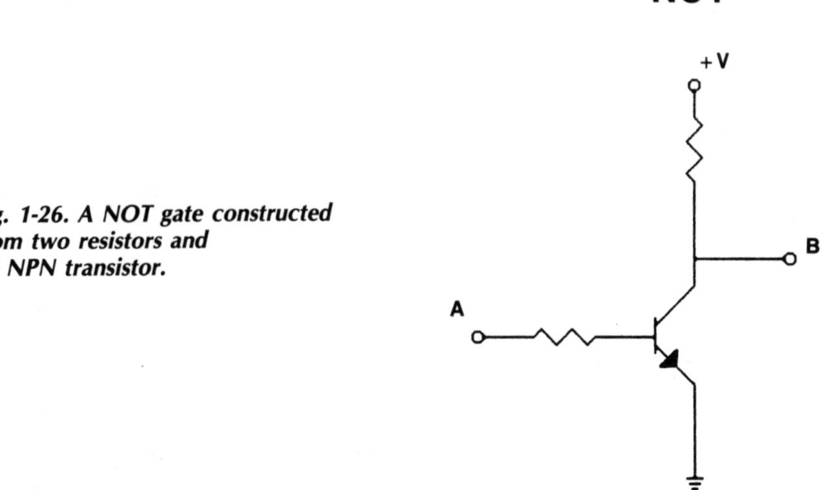

Fig. 1-26. A NOT gate constructed from two resistors and an NPN transistor.

Finally, *current mode logic* (or CML) uses a current limiting resistor to control the activation of a given bipolar transistor depending on the state of the input signal (see Fig. 1-29). CML gates operate at a higher frequency than any of the previously mentioned logic families. Even some of the later logic circuits operate at a lower frequency due to the saturation requirement of their transistors.

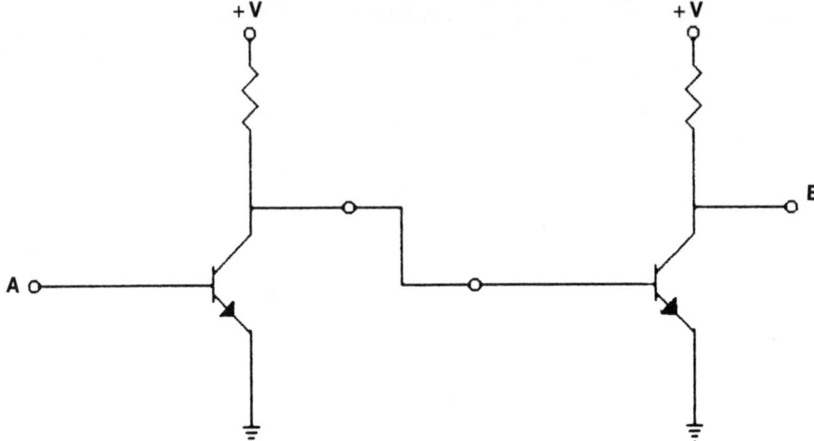

Fig. 1-27. A current-sourcing circuit.

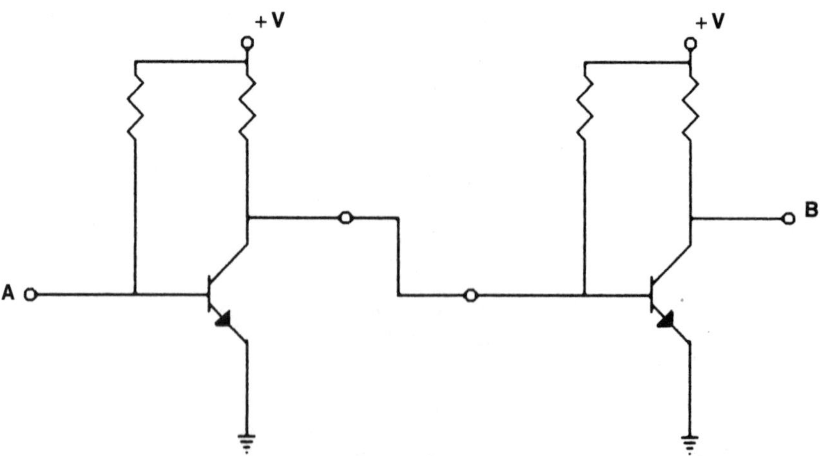

Fig. 1-28. A current-sinking circuit.

Resistor-Transistor Logic. Resistor-transistor logic (or RTL) differs from CML by placing a resistor on the gate's transistor collector, as well as a current-limiting resistor on the transistor's base (see Fig. 1-30). By adding a capacitor to the current-limiting base resistor, a resistor-capacitor-transistor logic or RCTL gate can be created (see Fig. 1-31). The advantage of the RCTL gate is an increase in the maximum operating frequency.

Diode-Transistor Logic. Controlling the voltage drop of an RTL gate through input diodes is diode-transistor logic or DTL (see Fig. 1-32). DTL is accomplished by fixing diodes to the transistor's base.

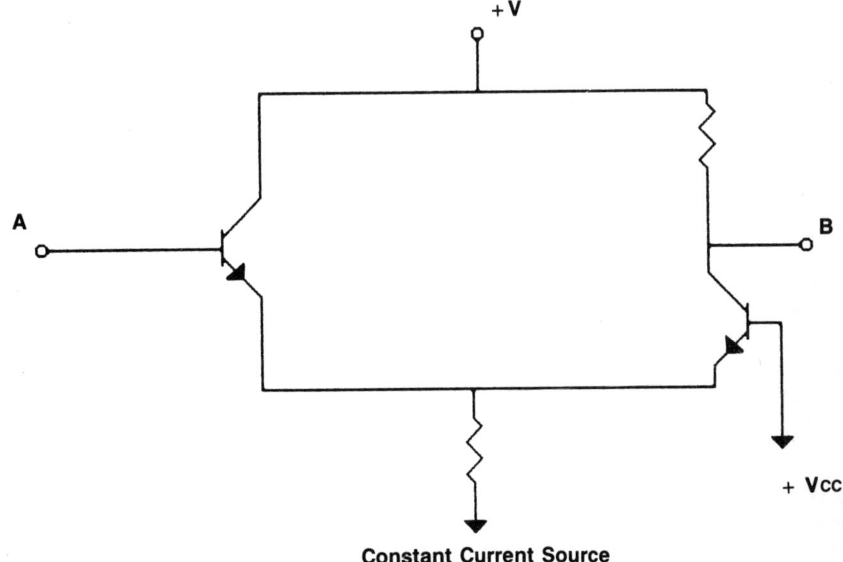

Fig. 1-29. A current-mode logic circuit.

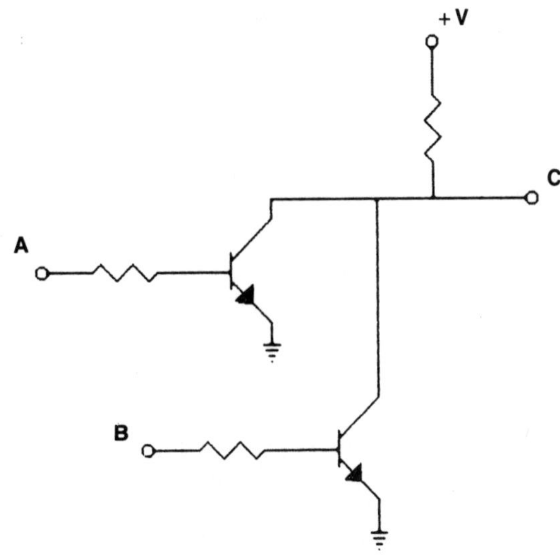

Fig. 1-30. An RTL circuit.

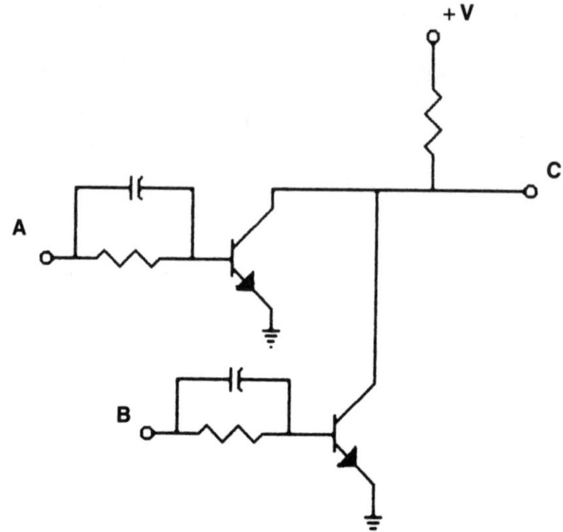

Fig. 1-31. An RCTL circuit.

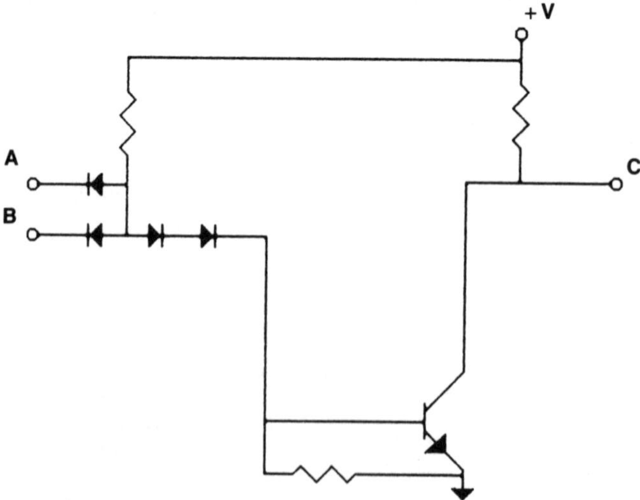

Fig. 1-32. A DTL circuit.

Fan-Out Logic. In a digital circuit, the binary states of 0 and 1 are depicted as voltage changes. Ideally, these states are 0 volts for a 0 bit and +5 volts for a 1 bit. More typically, however, these voltage variations are from 0 to +0.7 volts and from +2.0 to +5.0 volts for a binary 0 and 1, respectively. By representing these binary states with two such sweeping voltage ranges, errors in interpretation can occur. These problems can arise when adding additional digital circuitry to a gate's output. In actual operation, each added circuit lowers the output current of the gate. Once the output of the gate reaches a level lower than +2.0 volts, the logic of the gate will fail to function correctly. Usually, it takes several added digital circuits to lower a gate's output current sufficiently to destroy its logic. The number of digital circuits that is necessary to lower a gate's output current is the gate's *fan-out value*. For example, if three circuits are attached to a a gate's output and the current falls below +2.0 volts, then this gate has a fan-out of three. Understanding a gate's fan-out number is an important design specification in several of the following logic families.

Transistor-Transistor Logic. Transistor-transistor logic or TTL is one of the largest logic families (e.g., the 74XXX series of digital ICs). TTL gates use current-sinking switching logic mode in their construction (see Fig. 1-33). Another key feature in a TTL gate is the use of transistors with multiple emitters. This gives the gate high speed, low power consumption, and a degree of signal noise immunity.

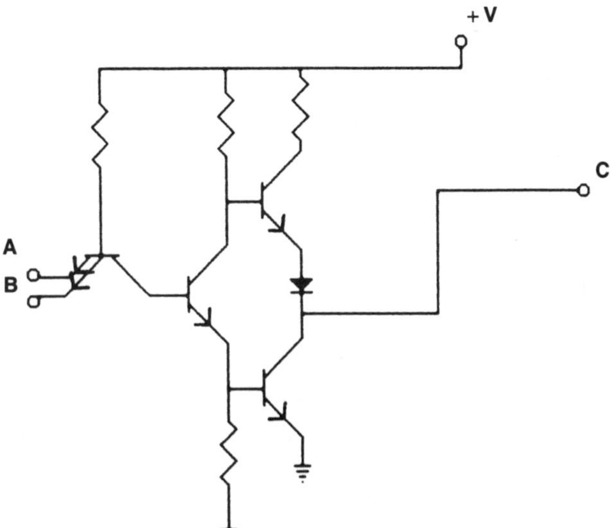

Fig. 1-33. A TTL circuit.

Schottky TTL. By adding a Schottky diode between the base and collector of every TTL transistor, an increase in operating speed and a decrease in power consumption is possible (see Fig. 1-34). Schottky TTL gates operate at a higher frequency by using the Schottky diode as conductor of bias current and, therefore, reduce the transistor's need for saturation.

Emitter-Coupled Logic. By using current switching and emitter amplifiers, the emitter-coupled logic or ECL gate is able to avoid the transistor saturation requirement (see Fig. 1-35). An unfortunate side effect of ECL gates is their constant drain on the circuit's power supply.

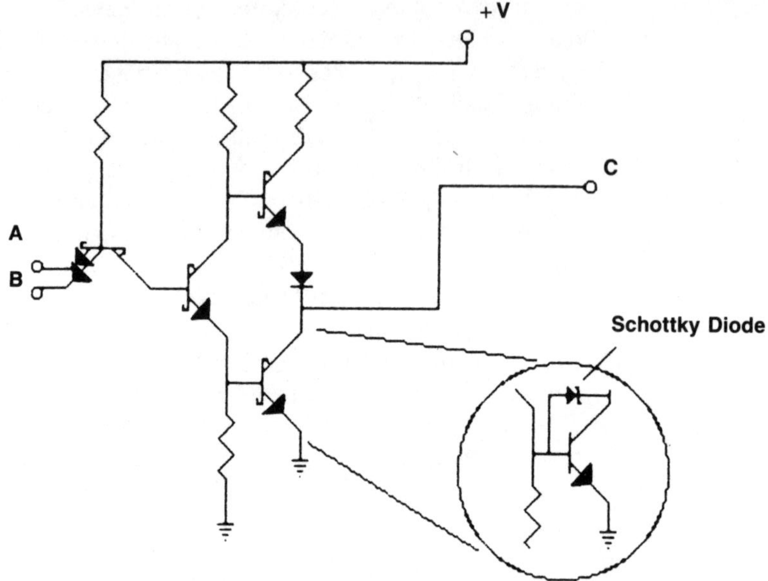

Fig. 1-34. A TTL circuit enhanced with Schottky diodes.

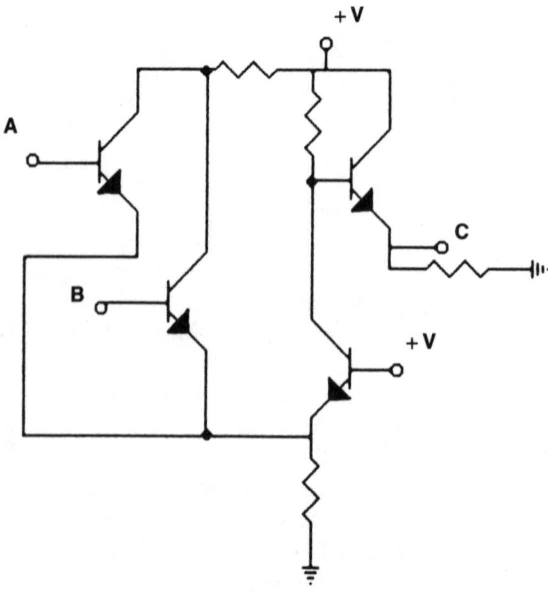

Fig. 1-35. An ECL circuit.

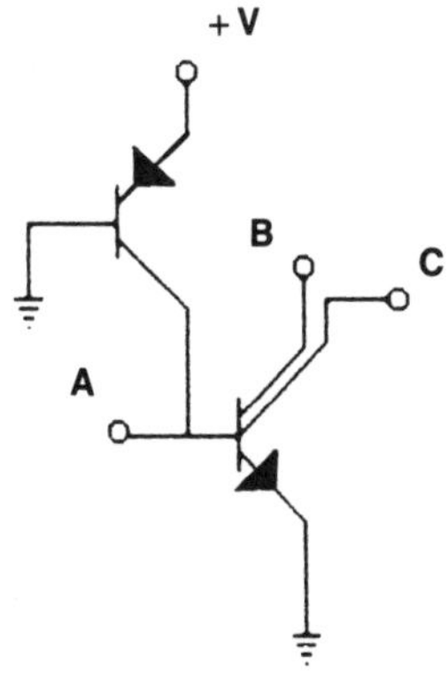

Fig. 1-36. An IIL circuit.

Integrated-Injection Logic. Integrated-injection logic or IIL transistors employ common bases, emitters, and collectors (see Fig. 1-36). Based on this combining of transistor elements, IIL is also known as MTL or merged-transistor logic. IIL gates have both a high switching speed and a high construction density. There are two construction methods, however, that enhance the performance characteristics of the IIL gate.

A Schottky diode can be added to IIL transistors for an increase in operating speed. This Schottky IIL gate offers many of the same advantages found in the Schottky TTL gate.

The other construction enhancement method is achieved through the use of an *isoplanar ion implantation process*. This Isoplanar-integrated-injection logic or IIIL gate has an oxide barrier for isolating its transistors from disruptive electron contamination.

MOS Logic. Other than bipolar transistors, metal-oxide-semiconductor field-effect transistors or MOSFETs can be used in gate construction. Basically, a MOSFET has a metal gate which is insulated from a silicon semiconductor substrate by a silicon dioxide shield (see Fig. 1-37). This is MOS (metal-oxide-semiconductor) technology. The current flows between the source and the drain. This flow is controlled by a voltage that is applied to the metal gate. There are four typical arrangements of these components within a MOSFET: N-channel, depletion mode, P-channel, depletion mode, N-channel, enhancement mode, and P-channel, enhancement mode. The major difference between a depletion mode MOSFET and an enhancement mode MOSFET is the presence of a conducting channel running between the source and the drain in the depletion mode. This channel is etched in the semiconductor substrate and it is able to conduct a 0-volt-gate state. Enhancement mode MOSFETs lack this channel.

NMOS Logic. N-channel MOSFET or NMOS gates have an N-type source and drain in a P-type substrate (see Fig. 1-38). Applying voltage to the metal gate forms a current between the source and drain.

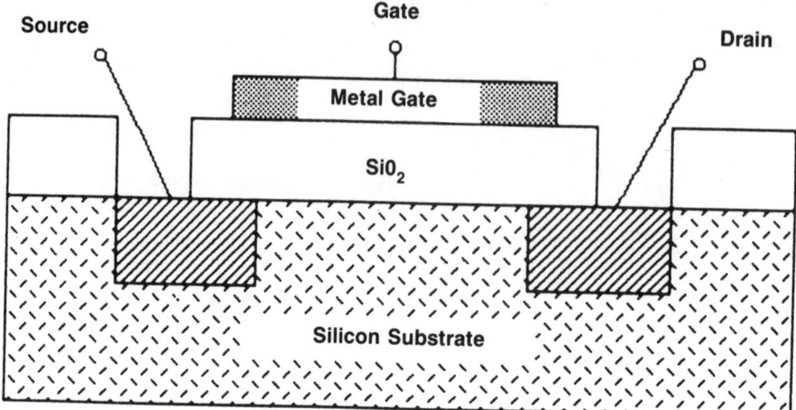

Fig. 1-37. A cross-section of a MOSFET circuit.

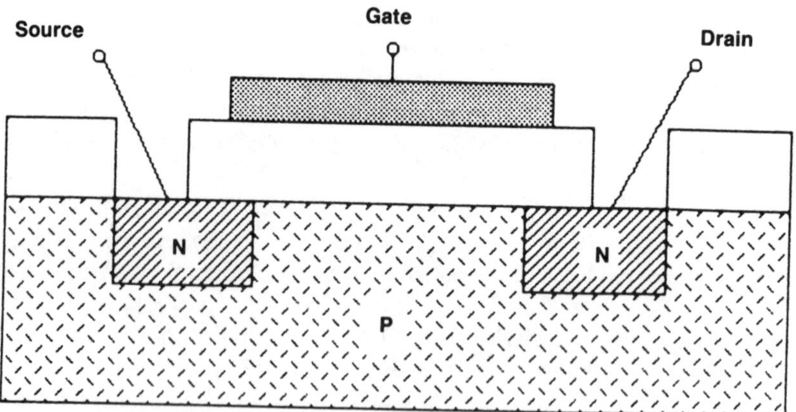

Fig. 1-38. An NMOS circuit.

PMOS Logic. Converse to an NMOS gate, P-channel MOSFET or PMOS gates have a P-type source and drain in an N-type substrate (see Fig. 1-39). A PMOS gate operates just like an NMOS one except that the PMOS has an opposite polarity.

VMOS Logic. VMOS or vertical MOSFET gates use a unique construction technique which provides the "vertical" portion of its name (see Fig. 1-40). VMOS gates have an increased power capability over NMOS and PMOS gates. This technology is frequently used in high-density RAM (random access memory) chips.

CMOS Logic. Combining both N-channel and P-channel MOSFETs into the same gate is complementary MOS or CMOS logic (see Fig. 1-41). CMOS gates have a very low power consumption with a wide range in voltage tolerance. Accompanying this reduced power consumption, however, is the

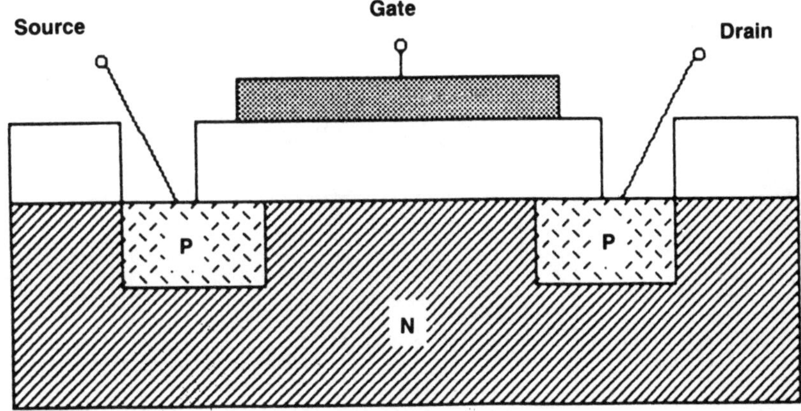

Fig. 1-39. A PMOS circuit.

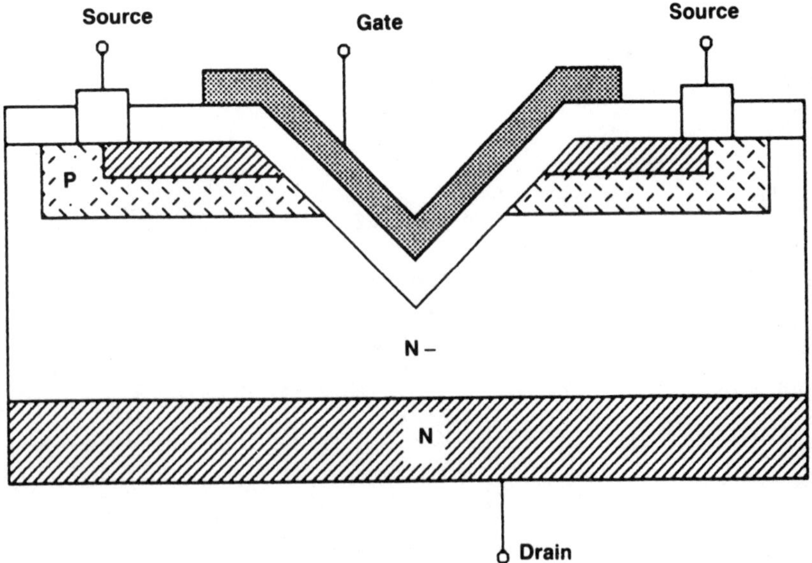

Fig. 1-40. A VMOS circuit.

lack of speed. For example, a typical CMOS gate is slower than a similar TTL gate. Furthermore, a CMOS gate has a high input impedance. A drawback to this heightened input impedance is the CMOS gate's susceptibility to static electrical discharge.

QMOS Logic. High-speed CMOS or QMOS logic is both functionally identical and pin compatible with 74XXX TTL ICs (see Fig. 1-42). QMOS gates require a slightly elevated current, but the consumption is less than that found

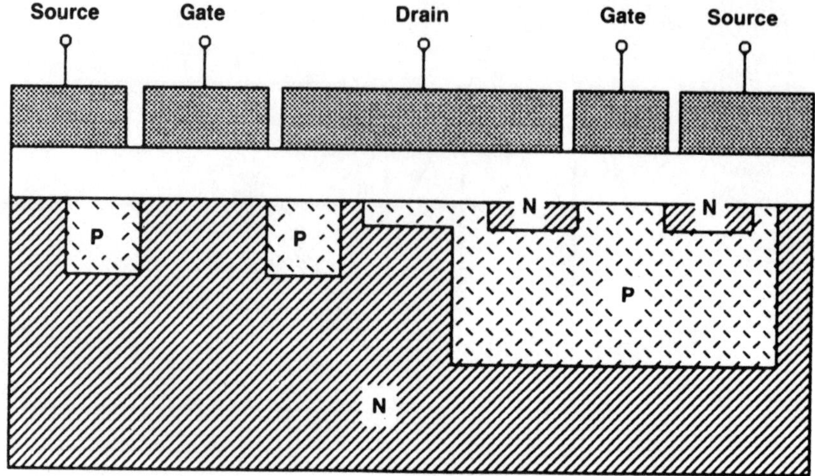

Fig. 1-41. A CMOS circuit.

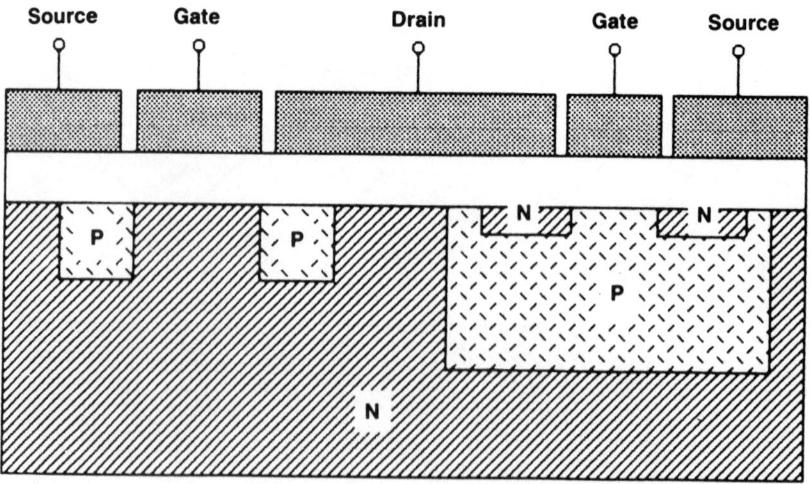

Fig. 1-42. A QMOS circuit.

in Schottky TTL gates. On the other hand, the operating speed of the QMOS gate is approximately 10 times faster than that of the comparable CMOS gate. In fact, the QMOS gate's speed is close to that of the Schottky TTL gate with less power drain.

Logic Circuits

On a practical level, a logic circuit is a direct application of all of the previously discussed gates and logic families. From this manufacturing of AND,

OR, and NOT gates with a particular logic family fabrication technique, a logic IC is created. Generally speaking, there are 12 major categories of logic circuits: arithmetic, decoders, latches, flip-flops, multivibrators, counters, shift registers, multiplexers, demultiplexers, drivers, bilateral switches, and tri-state logics.

Arithmetic. Arithmetic logic circuits perform binary addition and subtraction. There are four types of arithmetic circuits for executing this mathematics: half-adder, full-adder, half-subtractor, and full-subtractor. The addition and subtraction of two bits is carried out by a half-adder and a half-subtractor, respectively. By combining two half-adders or two half-subtractors together, a full-adder and a full-subtractor is created. A 4-bit Binary Full Adder with Fast Carry 7483 is an example of an arithmetic logic circuit (see Fig. 1-43).

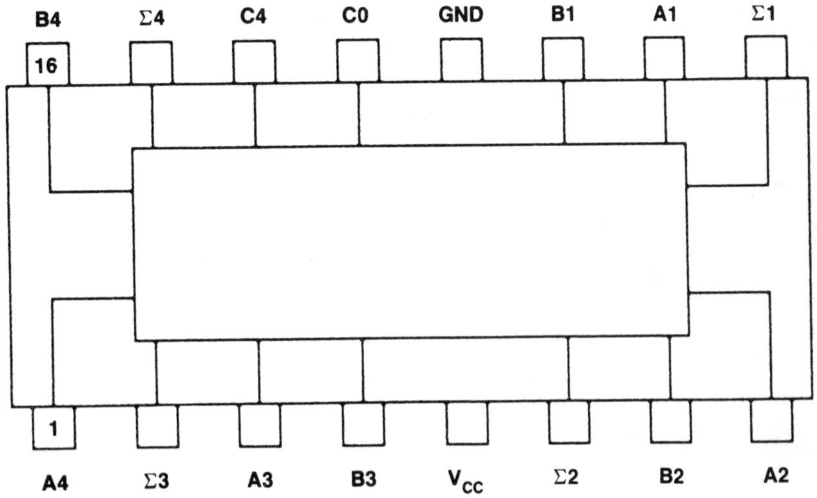

Fig. 1-43. Internal wiring logic for a 7483.

Decoders. Decoder circuits convert between number systems, coded and uncoded variables, and number representations. A decoder is able to take a given input and change it into a desired output. Some of the more common decoders can change a BCD input into a decimal output, a binary input to an octal output, or use a BCD input to drive a seven-segment LED (light-emitting diode) display. The Excess-3-to-Decimal, 4-Line-to-10-Line Decoder 7443 is a digital TTL decoder (see Fig. 1-44).

Latches. A latch is a simple memory gate with a feedback loop that toggles the gate's logic between a 0 and 1 state. An octal D-type Latch 74373 is an IC with eight separate D-type latches (see Fig. 1-45).

Flip-Flops. Combining the gates found in a latch with a circuit set and clear function is the simplest form of a flip-flop. There are four types of flip-

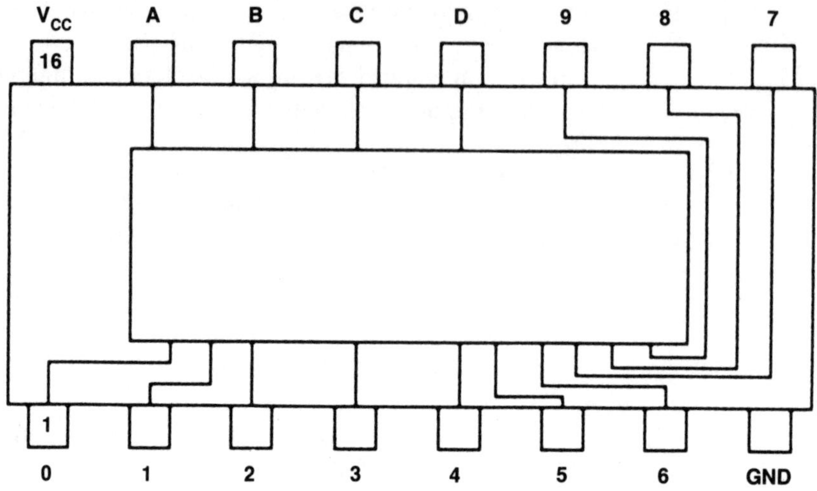

Fig. 1-44. Internal wiring logic for a 7443.

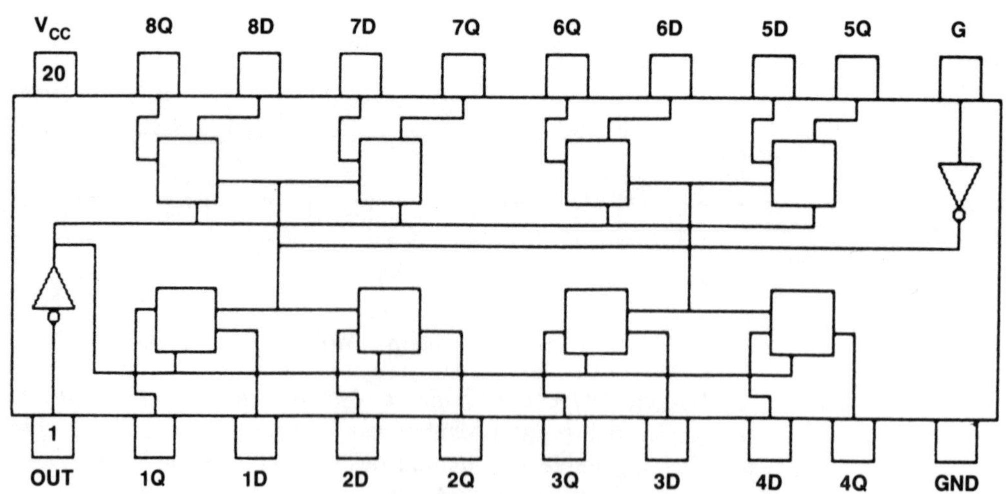

Fig. 1-45. Internal wiring logic for a 74373.

flops: S-C, clocked, J-K, and D-type. Each subsequent flip-flop type is an increase in the sophistication over the previous one. For example, by adding a clock input to a S-C (or set-clear) flip-flop, a clocked flip-flop is formed. Furthermore, the J-K (or master-slave) flip-flop can be enhanced to a D-type flip-flop by adding an inverter between the J and K inputs. The Dual J-K Flip-Flop with Clear 7473 is an example of this logic circuit (see Fig. 1-46).

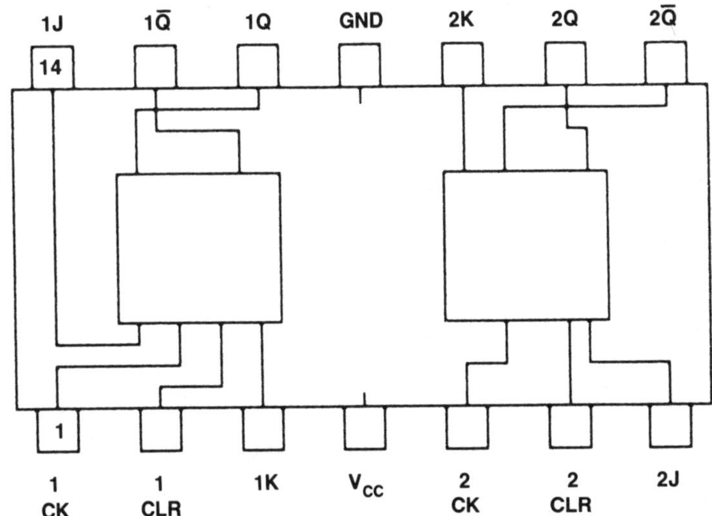

Fig. 1-46. Internal wiring logic for a 7473.

Multivibrators. The circuit's current determines the oscillating frequency of the multivibrator. This determination makes the multivibrator an excellent digital timing device. There are three types of multivibrators: monostable, bistable, and astable. A *monostable multivibrator* has a single stable output state. Similarly, the *bistable* variety has two stable outputs. Both of these multivibrators can be contrasted against the *astable* type which has no stable output states. One problem that can plague multivibrators is fluctuating or "dirty" input signals. A *Schmitt Trigger* is a logic circuit that is capable of stabilizing these inputs into solid 0 and 1 logic states. The Dual Monostable Multivibrator 74221 is a TTL example of this circuit (see Fig. 1-47).

Counters. Keeping track of the number of pulses traveling through a circuit is the job of the counter. A simple counter can be made from a series of flip-flop circuits. Dedicated counters are available, however. There are binary, BCD, divide-by-2, and divide-by-12 counter logic circuits. The Divide-by-2 and Divide-by-8 4-bit Binary Counter 7493 is a counter IC (see Fig. 1-48).

Shift Registers. A hybrid of the digital counter circuit is the shift register. In a standard shift register, a binary number (e.g., 00100101) is moved one place to the left with each clock pulse. During this move zeros are added to the right places as the openings are formed. Therefore, this binary number becomes 01001010 on the first clock pulse and 10010100 on the second pulse. Other digits movements are possible with different shift registers. A 4-bit Parallel-Access Shift Register 74195 is an example of this logic circuit (see Fig. 1-49).

Multiplexers. In a multi-signal circuit, the selective application of several control inputs can determine the nature of the final output signal. This is the

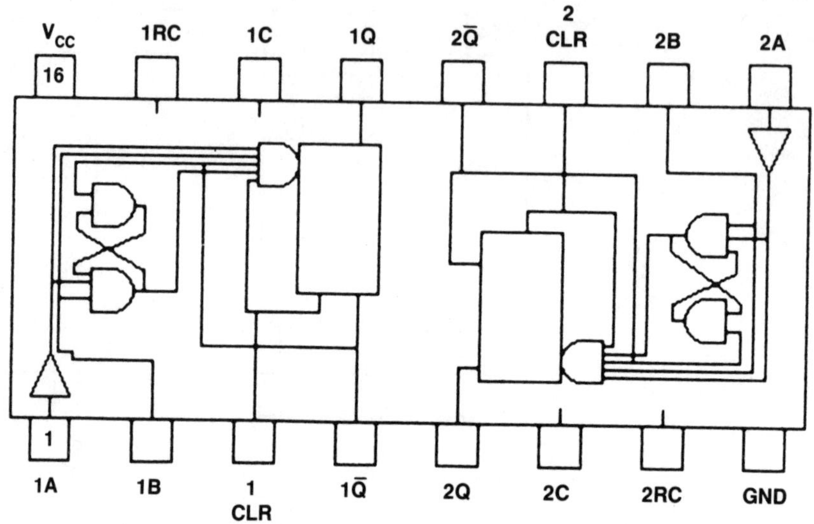

Fig. 1-47. Internal wiring logic for a 74221.

purpose of the multiplexer (or MUX) logic circuit. *Multiplexers* are described by the number of total signals that can be selected by its control inputs. In other words, a 4-of-16 multiplexer will select 4 signals from a total of 16 signals based on a given control input. The 3-to-8-Line Decoder/Multiplexer 74138 is a typical multiplexer example (see Fig. 1-50).

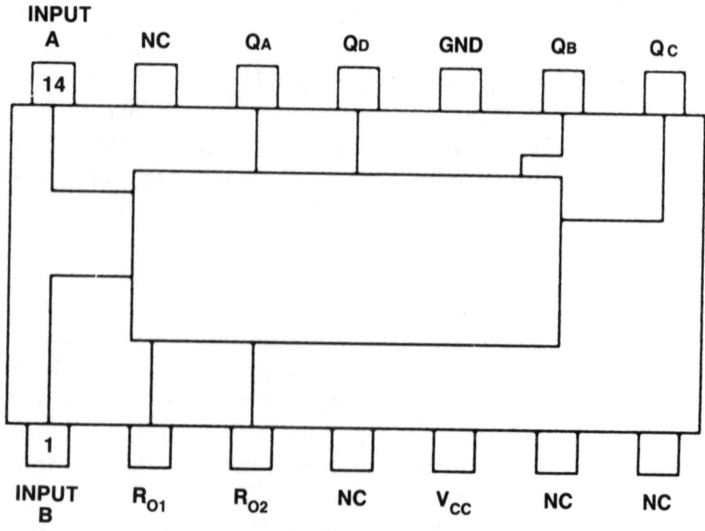

Fig. 1-48. Internal wiring logic for a 7493.

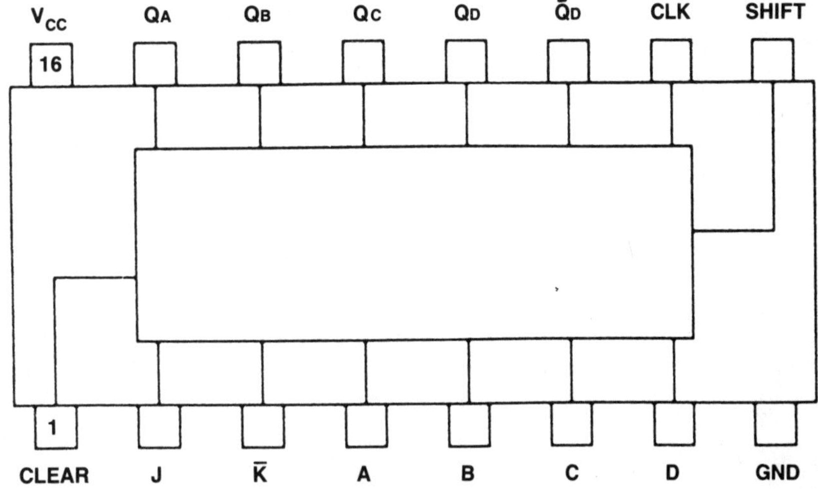

Fig. 1-49. Internal wiring logic for a 74195.

Demultiplexers. A demultiplexer is the opposite of a multiplexer. While a multiplexer established the number of signals that would be applied to a single output, a demultiplexer controls the number of outputs that will be applied to the single input. Similar to the multiplexer, the demultiplexer is named according to the number of outputs that are combined into the input. A Dual 2-to-4 Line Decoder/Demultiplexer 74139 is an example of this logic circuit (see Fig. 1-51).

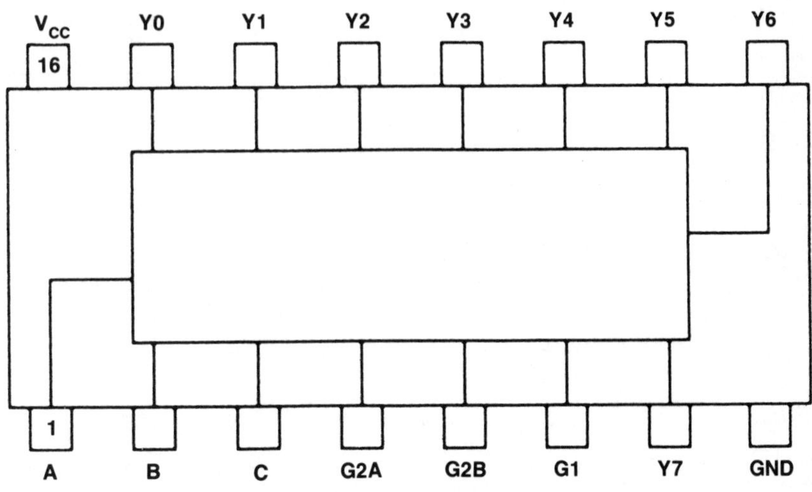

Fig. 1-50. Internal wiring logic for a 74138.

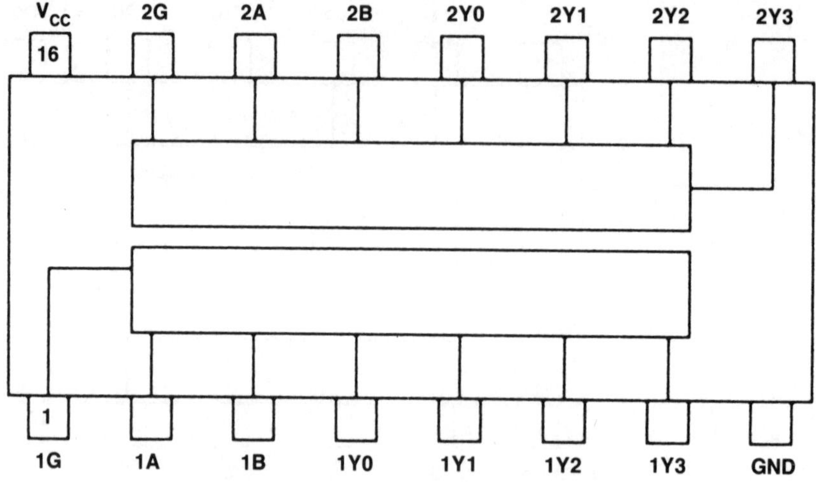

Fig. 1-51. Internal wiring logic for a 74139.

Drivers. Operating a digital display involves the conversion of the circuit's binary states into meaningful display data. This conversion usually involves the changing of 4-bit BCD nibbles into seven-segment LED display data. Frequently these display drivers are combined with BCD decoders in a single IC package. This combination makes a complete conversion and display unit inside a small space. The BCD-to-Seven-Segment Decoder/Driver 7447 is a standard digital LED driver (see Fig. 1-52).

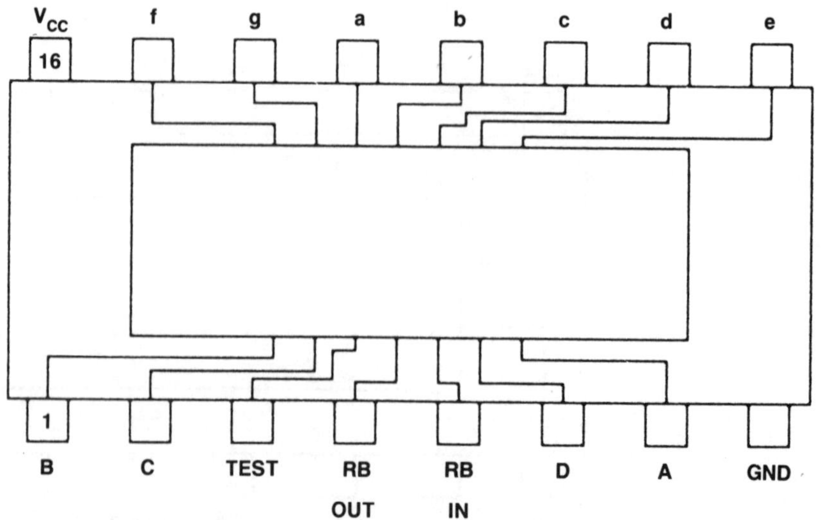

Fig. 1-52. Internal wiring logic for a 7447.

Bilateral Switches. Like the primitive analog switches that were used in early logic gates, there are digital versions available in compact ICs. Contrary to the analog variety, digital switches are controlled through the logic of the circuit. These digital switches lack a fixed polarity and are, therefore, called *bilateral switches*. In other words, each switch lacks a true input and output. A Quad Bilateral Switch for Transmission or Multiplexing of Analog or Digital Signals 4016 is a CMOS example of this logic circuit (see Fig. 1-53).

Tri-State Logics. Switching strictly digital signals is performed with tri-state logics. Tri-state logics add another output state to the binary 0 and 1. This third state is no signal or a high impedance absent signal. This special third condition is controlled by an input line. While this other input line is at a logic of 0, the output states are like that of a buffer (i.e., an input of 0, yields an output of 0, etc.). When this control input is a logic 1, however, the output is neither 0 nor 1; it is a high impedance non-signal. The Hex Bus Driver, Noninverted Data Output 74367 is a TTL tri-state logic (see Fig. 1-54).

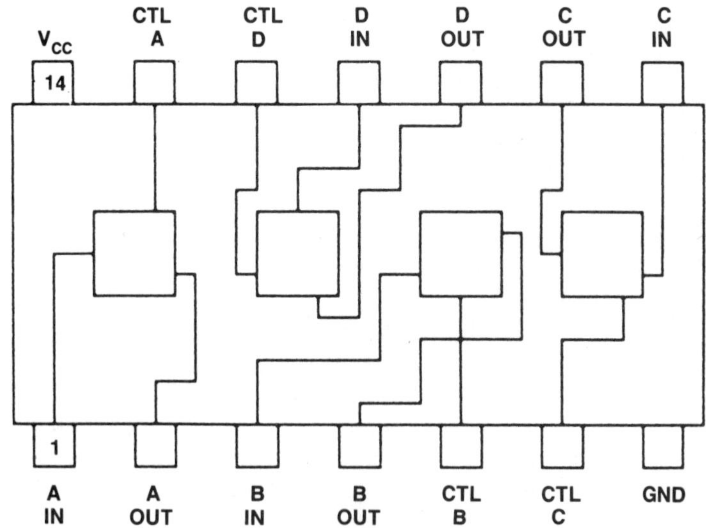

Fig. 1-53. Internal wiring logic for a 4016.

PROJECT 1: BOOLE'S BOX

The "founding father" of logic was an English mathematician named George Boole. Boole's early work with the logic of AND, OR, and NOT operators forged the basics for all digital circuitry.

Unfortunately, today's digital IC packages hide their logic inside a sterile black plastic housing. Documenting the gates and inverters that are masked into each of these components is usually obtained through the study of the

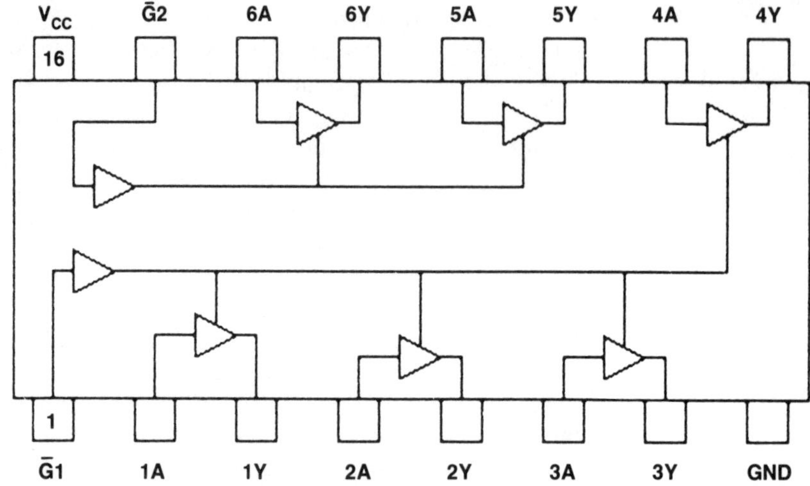

Fig. 1-54. Internal wiring logic for a 74367.

manufacturer's logic diagrams. A superior method for labeling the logic of a digital IC's pins is through the application of the Boole's Box. This simple project also provides a benefit that can't be found in a manufacturer's documentation—verification of a chips condition. In other words, the Boole's Box not only indicates the logic of each pin on a digital IC, it is also capable of determining whether or not it is functioning correctly. It is this final feature that makes the Boole's Box a valuable addition to the toolbox of every digital experimenter.

The construction of the Boole's Box is extremely simple with the parts list and wiring schematic provided in Figure 1-55. Don't underestimate the value of using a ZIF (zero insertion force) socket in this project. The use of a ZIF socket is important construction consideration in this project. ZIF sockets are used extensively in EPROM programmers. Therefore, gaining a familiarity with this fixture of EPROM experimenting at this time will prove valuable in the later chapters.

The final circuit should easily fit inside a small plastic experimenter's box. A small housing for the Boole's Box ensures the quick testing of numerous digital ICs during the construction of the subsequent projects within this book.

Testing the completed Boole's Box will require a sampling of various 14-pin digital ICs (e.g., 7400, 7402, 7406) and a set of manufacturer's logic diagrams for each of the tested chips. Begin these performance tests, by inserting the digital gate into the ZIF socket (ZIF 1 in the figure). Now begin applying both logic 1's (+5V) and logic 0's (GND) to the various pins of the target IC. Compare the results with the manufacturer's logic diagrams. Once

Parts List

LED 1 - 12 LED Light Bar
R1-R12 - 220-ohm resistor
SW1 - SPDT switch bank
SW2 - SPDT switch bank
ZIF 1 - 14-pin Zero Insertion Force Socket

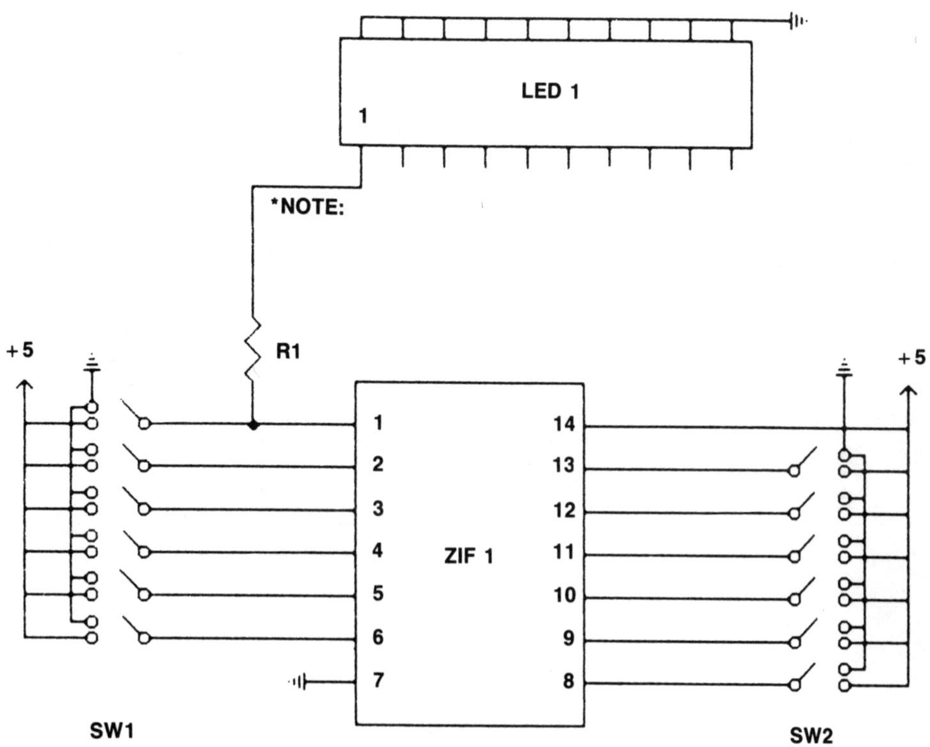

***NOTE: Repeat these connections for pins 2 through 6 and 8 through 13 of ZIF 1.**

Fig. 1-55. Schematic diagram for Boole's Box.

you have recorded the results for an AND, OR, and NOT gate, create your own logic diagram for a unknown digital IC. Mastering these initial steps during these testing stages will make the Boole's Box a valuable ally during future project construction.

While the original Boole's Box is a suitable tool for determining the logic of a given digital IC's pins, there is a certain lacking in its presentation of log-

Parts List

IC1 - 74LS00
LED 1 - Common Anode 7-segment LED
R1 - 100-ohm resistor
R2 - 1K-ohm resistor
R3 - 220-ohm resistor
R4 - 100-ohm resistor
R5 - 47-ohm resistor

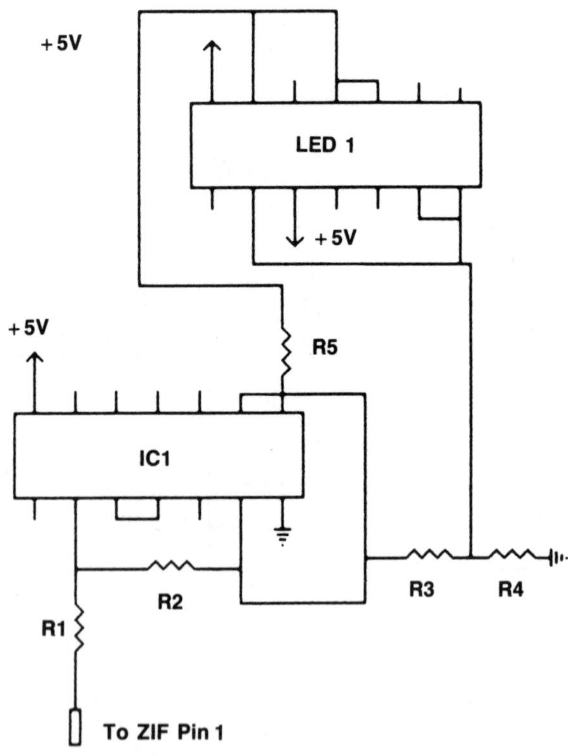

Fig. 1-56. Schematic diagram for the Boole's Box alternate logic indicator.

ic. Figure 1-56 provides an exciting enhancement to the basic Boole's Box design that will correctly indicate either a logic 1 or a logic 0 state. This elaborate indicator must be interfaced to *every* test pin of the target IC. In all, this will result in 12 different seven-segment common anode displays (one display each, for every test pin of the ZIF socket). Keep this design element in mind prior to attempting this conversion.

After this modification has been installed on the Boole's Box, repeat the same series of tests that were performed on the basic Boole's Box configuration. Contrary to the "high-only" indication that is displayed with the basic design

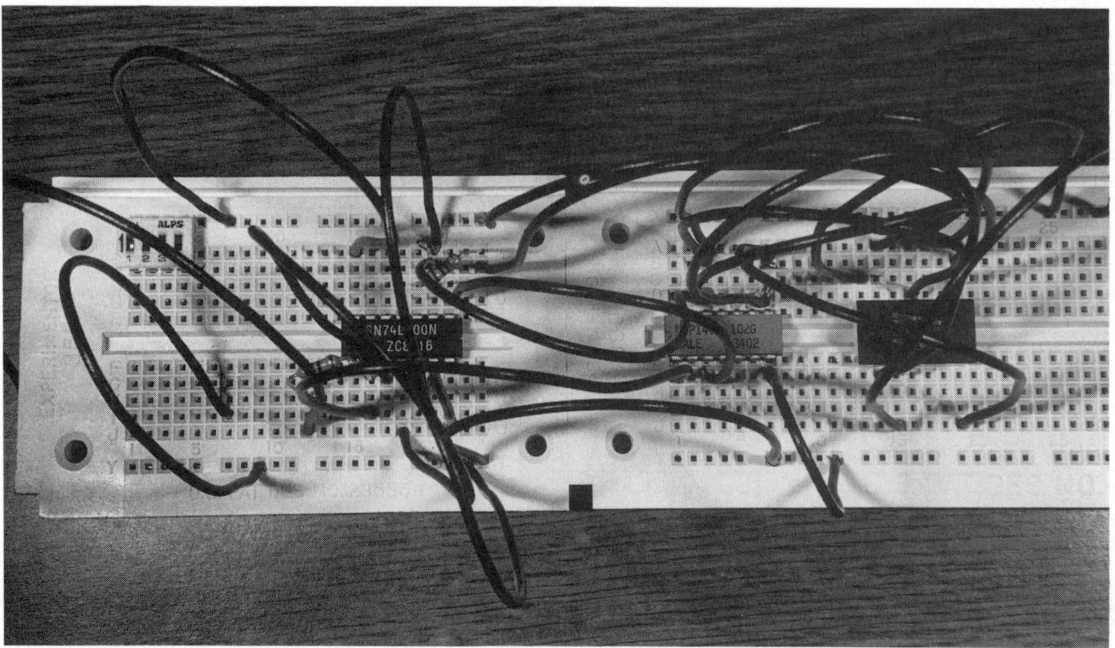

Fig. 1-57. A breadboarded Boole's Box complete with a single alternate logic indicator.

(see Fig. 1-57), this enhanced Boole's Box will display the exact logic for every pin of the target IC. The extra expense that is entailed with this modification can be justified based solely on the merit of this informative display.

PROJECT 2: KEYBOARD ENCODER

Another interesting project that utilizes many of the digital ICs that have been discussed in this chapter is a keyboard encoder. Figure 1-58 contains all of the needed information for constructing a simple BCD keyboard encoder.

This simple ten-key encoder generates a displayed digit that corresponds to the key number that is pressed. Test the final construction by pressing a key and noting the digit that is displayed. Label each key with the appropriate number according to the results of these tests. The keyboard encoder is now ready for operation.

Based on a single common anode 7-segment LED (Light Emitting Diode) display, this encoder can be easily expanded to represent a complete 64-key ASCII keyboard system. An expansion on this project that uses a programmed EPROM for generating a unique character set is discussed in Chapter 8.

Parts List

C1 - 01mF capacitor
IC1 - 7447
IC2 - 74192
IC3 - 4011
IC4 - 4049
IC5 - 4017
K1 - Keyboard
S1 - SPDT switch
R1-R7 - 220-ohm resistor
R8 - 100K-ohm resistor
R9 - 1K-ohm resistor

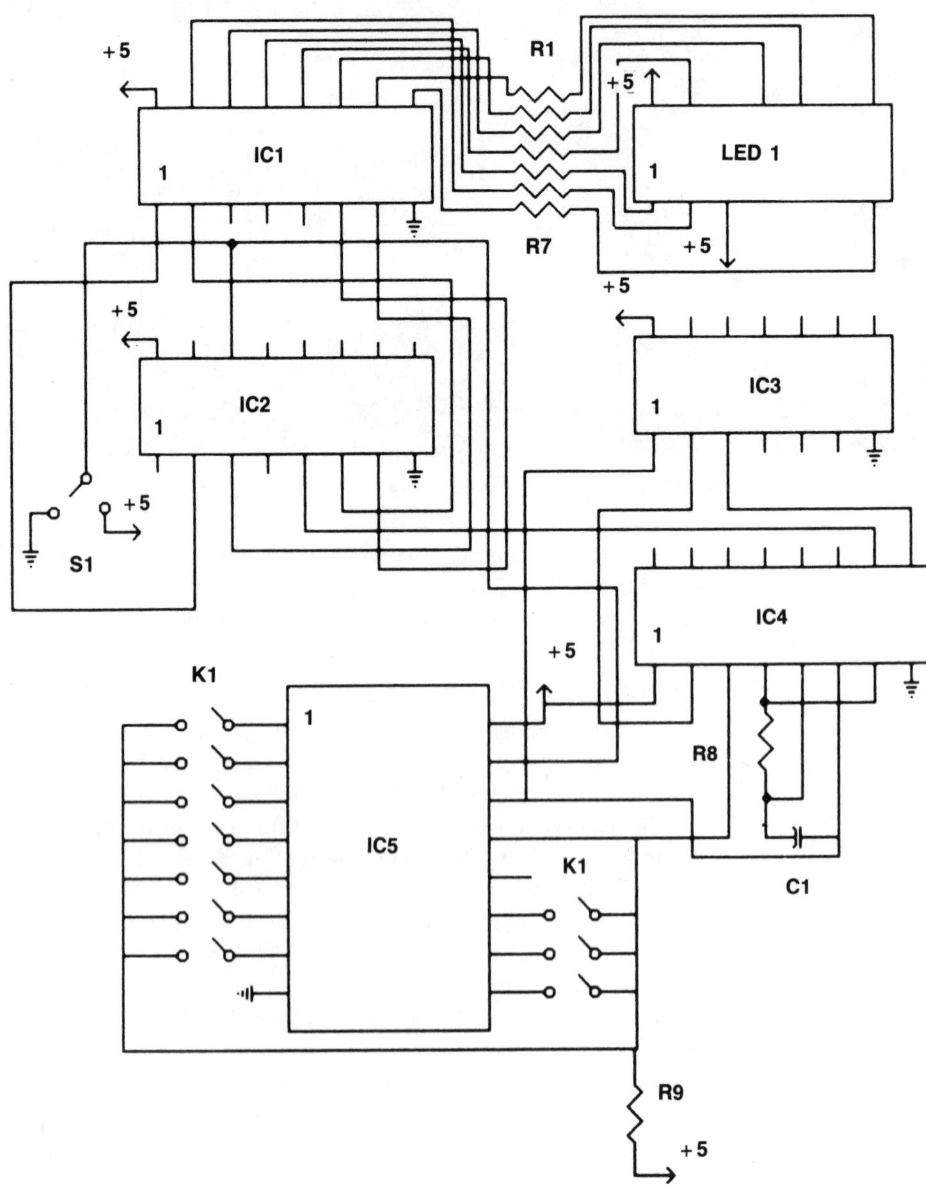

Fig. 1-58. Schematic diagram for the keyboard encoder.

2

Programmable Memory Structures

The simplest form of computer memory is the flip-flop logic circuit. A flip-flop is a 1-bit memory register that is capable of "learning" and "memorizing" either of the two binary states, 0 or 1, and altering this memory through the input of an external signal. For example, a D-type 7474 TTL flip-flop IC has a single data input and two outputs. One of these outputs is the complement of the other and is expressed as $\overline{Q}$ (see Fig. 2-1). During operation, the data bit on the 7474's input port is "memorized" or stored on the leading edge of the clock pulse CK. By receiving a binary 1 on data line D, the 7474 is *set*. Conversely, by receiving a binary 0 on data line D, the 7474 is *reset* or *cleared*. However, the exact triggering of the flip-flop's data retention is totally dependent on the nature of the clock pulse.

BASICALLY, there are two forms of clock pulses: positive and negative. A positive clock pulse has a negative-to-positive transition on the leading edge of the signal (see Fig. 2-2), while a negative clock pulse has a positive-to-negative transition on the leading edge of the clock signal (see Fig. 2-3). Each of these leading edge transitions determines the logic state of the signal during its pulse. For example, the positive transition of the positive clock pulse goes from a 0 logic to a 1 logic at the time of its pulse. On the other hand, a negative transition travels from a 1 logic to a 0 logic during its clock pulse. This difference is vital to the memory programming of a flip-flop circuit.

In the case of the 7474 flip-flop, a positive transition is necessary for changing its memory state. Furthermore, this positive transition condition is edge-triggered in the 7474. An edge-triggered flip-flop changes its memory state on either the leading or trailing edge of the clock pulse. Two factors

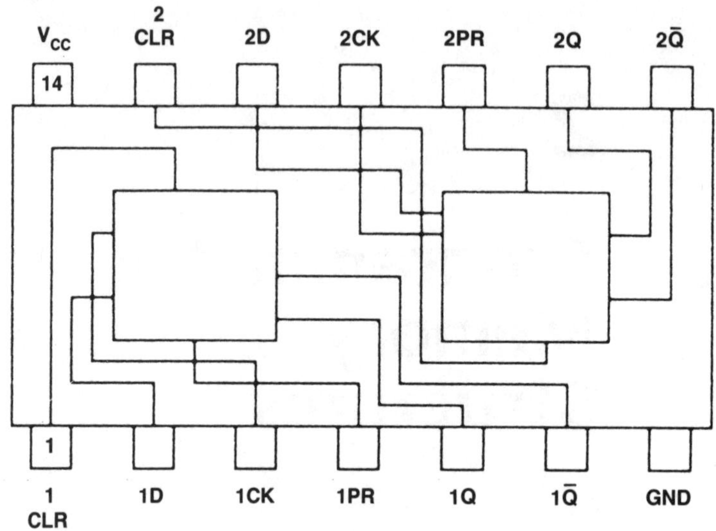

Fig. 2-1. Internal wiring diagram for a 7474 Flip-Flop.

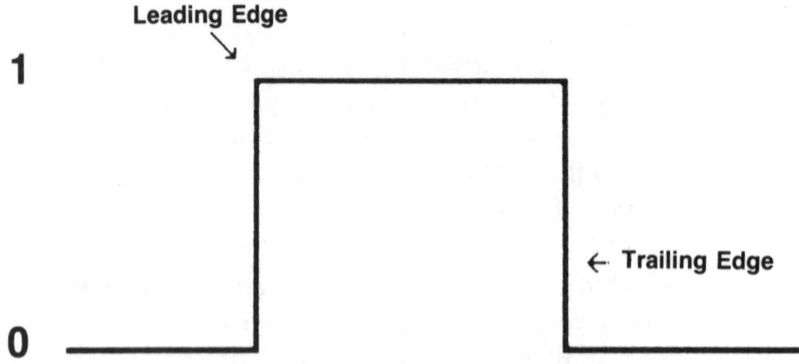

Fig. 2-2. A positive clock signal.

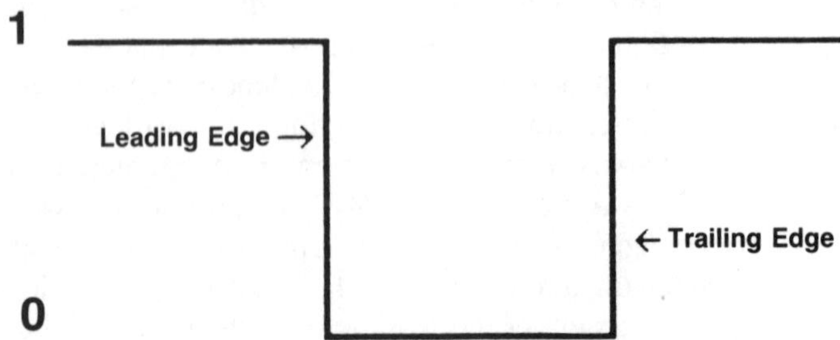

Fig. 2-3. A negative clock signal.

govern the exact time when the flip-flop's memory state will change, however. First, the input requirements of the flip-flop indicate whether a positive or a negative transition is needed for altering the register's memory. And second, the form of the clock pulse, whether it is a positive clock pulse or a negative clock pulse, will determine the actions of the flip-flop. The following example can better illustrate the interrelationship between these two factors.

A positive-edge-triggered flip-flop, like the 7474, will change its output memory state no matter whether the clock pulse is positive or negative. The only difference between the 7474's output reaction to these two clock pulses is the time when the memory state is changed. A positive clock pulse will change the 7474's state on the leading edge of the signal (i.e., during the low to high transition). A negative clock pulse, on the other hand, will cause a data latch on the trailing edge of the signal (i.e., during the low-to-high transition). Therefore, a correct interpretation of a positive-edge-triggered flip-flop is that its input data is latched during a low-to-high clock signal transition.

Another form of flip-flop is level triggered. This flip-flop latches its data input when the clock pulse makes a transition from its required state or trigger level to the resting state. The trigger level is expressed as either a positive-level trigger or a negative-level trigger. In the case of the positive-level trigger, the D input data is latched when the clock pulse changes from logic 1 to a logic of 0. The converse is true of the negative-level-triggered flip-flop (i.e., the pulse's logic changes from 0 to 1). Simply put, the input of a level triggered flip-flop will assume a logic change during the transition from its trigger level to its resting level.

There are two other control inputs on the 7474: *preset* and *clear*. Both of these inputs are normally logic 1, or high. When a low signal is applied to either of these inputs, the D input is overridden. For example, a logic 0 on the preset input sets the output Q to a logic of 1. Whereas a logic of 0 on the clear input clears output Q to logic 0. One point to remember with these two inputs, however, is that both inputs may not be a logic 0, simultaneously. This event would form a disallowed condition at output Q.

One final requirement for the proper operation of the 7474 flip-flop is the timing of the data input and clock pulse. There are three features for a usable flip-flop timing sequence: clock pulse width, setup time, and hold time. In the case of the clock pulse width, there is a minimum acceptable value. The minimal clock pulse width for the 7474 is 25 nS. The minimal stable time period for the input data is the setup time. A setup time of 25 nS is typical for the 7474. Hold time is the minimal stable time period before and after the positive transition. The 7474 uses a 5 nS hold time.

These are the fundamentals of digital memory. Granted, this discussion has centered around a 1-bit data register. But understanding the theory behind the operation of a typical flip-flop circuit will increase the application of this knowledge to more complex memory structures.

MULTI-BIT REGISTERS

Based on the above 1-bit register information, in order for a memory system to store more than one bit's worth of data, more than one flip-flop circuit must be used. The easiest means for accomplishing this feat is to link the clock inputs of multiple flip-flops together (see Fig. 2-4). This type of circuit is capable of storing X bits for X flip-flops. Additionally, this X-bit register would also have X outputs. Commonly, these multiple flip-flop combinations can be found in special interface ICs known as *latches*.

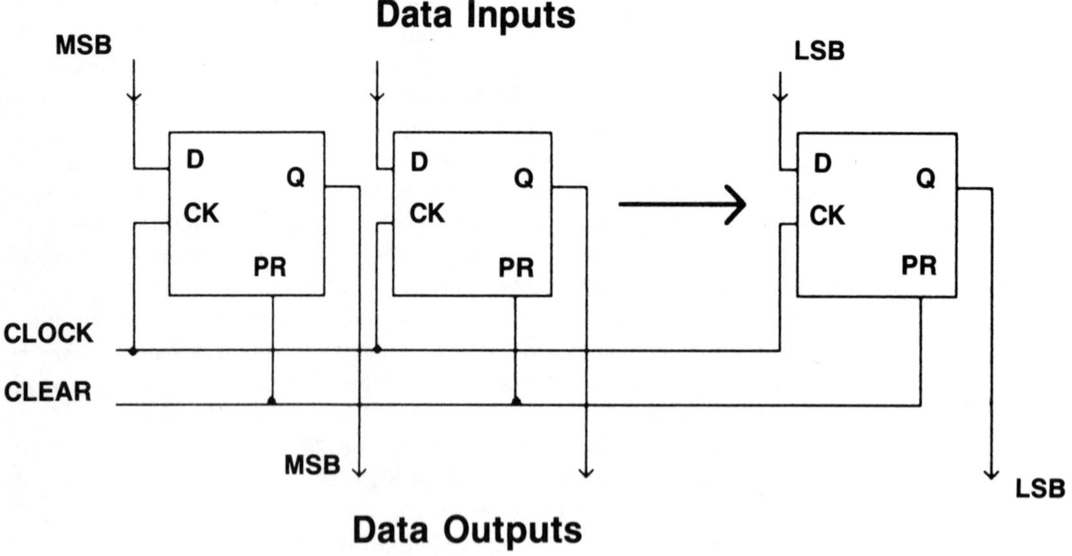

Fig. 2-4. Multiple flip-flops linked through a common bus.

One form of a latch is positive-level triggered with a common clock signal input. In this case, the clock signal serves as an enable line or device select for the entire chip.

The size of the latch is determined by the number of internal flip-flop circuits. Using the previously mentioned latch type as an example, an 8-bit latch has eight positive-level-triggered flip-flops. Selectively manipulating the output of this 8-bit latch is most easily achieved through different clock signal inputs. The control of the clock pulse over these internal flip-flops is frequently multiplexed through special external logic circuitry (see Fig. 2-5). This form of external control permits four input signals. By varying the logic on these four input lines, the data latching and level triggering condition can be controlled.

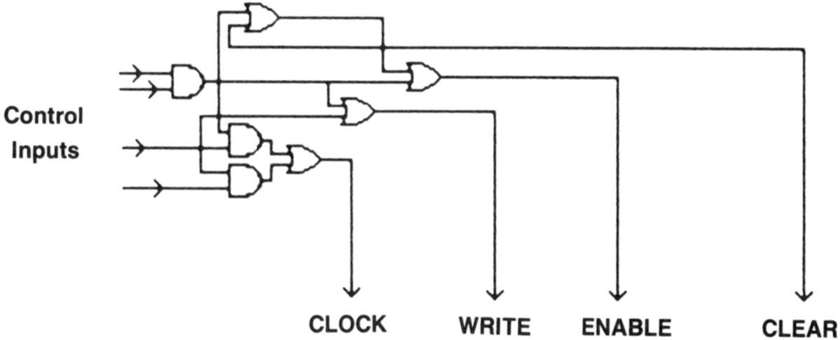

Fig. 2-5. Multiplexed decoder logic for driving multiple registers.

Just as the input of this 8-bit positive-level-triggered latch can be governed through a multi-input clock signal, so can the data output. By placing a buffer at each output, the condition or state of the output can be controlled. A common buffer for a data output is a three-state buffer. The flexible nature of this three-state buffer provides three possible outputs for each data signal. As expected, two of the possible three outputs from this buffer are the logic 0 and logic 1. The other output is possibly a high impedance. A high impedance signal is neither a logic 0 nor a logic 1. In fact, this high impedance condition's virtue is that it doesn't drive any other circuit that is connected to the output. Therefore, the high impedance state is capable of disconnecting a latch from the remainder of a circuit. This disconnected condition is known as a floating connection.

Another advantage of the three-state buffer output is that multiple circuits can be multiplexed to the same output bus. This complex connection is made possible by the latch's ability to select from three different output states. An important point to remember with selectable outputs, however, is that only one output should be enabled at a one time. This precaution will avoid circuit damage from competitive outputs.

DIGITAL MEMORY

When several registers with the same bit-addressable length are combined into an isolated circuit this unit becomes a digital memory. In contemporary microcomputer designs, this register combination is usually housed within a single IC package. There are four common features that are shared by all memory ICs: a common data bus, a common output bus, a solitary clock input, and a means for addressing each individual register. While the first three features have already been discussed, the addressing of individual registers is an important feature in digital memory technology.

Memory register addressing consists of special on-board decoding logic that enables the IC to locate a specific data byte. This decoding logic provides

Table 2-1. Decoding a $2^4 \times 8$ (16×8) Register.

Decimal Address	Binary Address	Hex Address	Binary Address	Data
0	0000	0	0000	00011000
1	0001	1	0010	11000100
2	0010	2	0100	11000000
3	0011	3	0111	00110000
4	0100	4	1010	00011100
5	0101	5	1100	00001111
6	0110	6	1111	11111100
7	0111	7		
8	1000	8		
9	1001	9		
10	1010	A		
11	1011	B		
12	1100	C		
13	1101	D		
14	1110	E		
15	1111	F		

each register location with an address assignment value (see Table 2-1). The current naming convention used in labeling register address locations is with hexadecimal notation. Each register is labeled in a sequential fashion starting with a 0H address. The size of the address bus (X) determines the final register address number. This number is equal to $2^X - 1$. Therefore, a 4-bit address bus would have registers numbered from 0 to 15 decimal or 0 to F hexadecimal.

Each register address location is capable of holding a fixed number of data bits. This data capacity is expressed in terms of the memory IC's address bus width (X) and the number of bits that each register can hold or data word length (Y). A simple form of this capacity is 2^X by Y or 2^X by Y. Applying this capacity expression to Fig. 2-6 yields a 16 by 8 memory. The following examples give a better understanding of the relationship between register address locations, the address bus width, and each register's capacity:

✤ Data Word Length = 8 bits
Address Bus Width = 4 bits
Register Locations = 0 – F
Memory Capacity = 16×8

- Data Word Length = 8 bits
  Address Bus Width = 8 bits
  Register Locations = 0 – FF
  Memory Capacity = 256 × 8

- Data Word Length = 8 bits
  Address Bus Width = 16 bits
  Register Locations = 0 – FFFF
  Memory Capacity = 65536 × 8

- Data Word Length = 16 bits
  Address Bus Width = 32 bits
  Register Locations = 0 – FFFFFFFF
  Memory Capacity = 4294967296 × 16

After the address bus width, register locations, and memory capacity have all been established, data can be written to a given register. A memory IC write is performed through a special control input usually called the read/write (R/W) signal. This write signal, when coupled with an address and input data, will store the selected data at the specified address location. During this memory write, there is a time delay. This time delay is called the *write time*. Usually, the fabrication process of the memory IC determines the write time. Other factors, like the IC's logic arrangement, can also affect the write time, however.

Once these data have been stored inside the memory IC's registers, a read signal will send the data contents of a specified address to the output bus. Once again, the R/W control signal initiates the read. Similar to the write time, there is also a read time delay. During a read, the amount of time between the input of the address and the final data's output is called the access time. For the most part, no matter which address location is accessed, the access time is virtually identical. This feature is common to the majority of digital memories. Conversely, sequential access memories (SAMs) demonstrate a dramatic shift in the access time based on the location of a given address. Examples of SAMs include: bubble memories, charge-coupled devices (CCDs), and shift registers. Refer to Chapter 11 for an introduction to SAM technology.

Based on the above discussion of digital memory writes and reads, there is a dual function for the R/W control signal. Each of these conditions is set by either a logic of 1 (the read) or with a logic of 0 (the write) on the R/W input. The derivation of this logic is indicated by the slash (/) in the control signal's name. In standard digital nomenclature, the label prior to a slash is considered the logic 1 attribute. Likewise, the label that follows the slash is active during a logic 0. This dual function input format is used frequently in digital memory circuits.

Types of Digital Memory

Generally speaking, there are three types of digital memory: read/write memory (RWM), read only memory (ROM), and programmable read only memory (PROM). Each of these memories offers a different angle of writing and reading data.

Read/Write Memory. The digital memory with the shortest write time is RWM. These memories can be written to and read from for an unlimited number of times. Typically, the name RAM (Random Access Memory) is applied to RWMs (this same practice will be followed throughout the remainder of this book). By strict definition, all non-SAM circuits are RAM circuits; including ROMs and PROMs.

RAMs are used for holding transitory data in microcomputer designs. In this application, all of the data contained in a RAM's registers will be lost once the current to the circuit is removed. Memories with this current-sensitive peculiarity are called volatile memories. Even within an active current circuit, there are two distinct classes of RAM: static and dynamic. Static RAM is a constant logic circuit that holds its memory until either the current to the IC is removed or the internal data is reprogrammed. Dynamic RAM, on the other hand, must have its registers periodically refreshed by a read and rewrite. If this refreshing cycle is not adhered to, all of the data within the dynamic RAM's registers could become disrupted.

Read Only Memory. Unlike RAM, ROM lacks any provisions for writing data. Only the preprogrammed contents of the IC's registers can be read. The programming of these registers is performed by the manufacturer during production. One of the more common programming techniques is called *mask programming*. This manufacturing method creates a digital memory register that is far simpler than the flip-flop registers that were described at the beginning of this chapter. A mask programmed ROM IC has a set of fixed, unalterable registers. This condition is particularly useful in character-generator ROMs and microcomputer "boot" ROMs.

Programmable Read Only Memory. PROMs are the more flexible cousins of ROMs. In this case, the registers of the memory IC can be programmed or fixed by the user. This process involves a lengthy write time. Unlike RAM, however, PROMs can't be written to in a conventional microcomputer system. The demands for special programming voltages and lengthy write times mandate that a *dedicated* PROM programming device be used (see Chapter 6). Another difference between RAMs and PROMs is that a PROM's registers are uneffected by the presence (or absence) of the system's power supply. This stable condition is called *nonvolatile memory*.

Under this collective PROM heading, there are five different PROMs: programmable read only memory (PROM), electrically alterable read only memory (EAROM), erasable programmable read only memory (EPROM), electrically erasable programmable read only memory (EEPROM), and programmed-logic array (PLA). Even though these five PROMs share the same general characteristics, they each represent a unique technology.

ROM TECHNOLOGY

Memory ICs, like ROMs, PROMs, and EPROMs, are manufactured with bipolar and MOS techniques. In the case of these memories, the bipolar technique uses bipolar transistors, while the MOS process uses unipolar field effect transistors (FETs) as their main component. By and large, however, the bulk of today's memories use MOS technologies (e.g., NMOS, PMOS, CMOS, etc.). Conversely, the bulk of today's support ICs (logic, counters, drivers, multiplexers, etc.), are manufactured with bipolar processes (e.g., TTL, ECL, IIL, etc.). This difference in manufacturing could lead to a conflict in circuit design.

The most frequently used method of alleviating any degree of chip conflict is through construction compatibility. In terms of memory manufacturing, this compatibility issue deals with the MOS memory ICs being compatible with bipolar support ICs. This compatibility is achieved through logic compatibility and power supply compatibility. Logic compatibility concerns the ability of the output of a MOS memory driving a bipolar logic circuit. Furthermore, power supply compatibility centers around all digital ICs, whether they are MOS or bipolar, being able to operate from a fixed +5 volts power supply. Based on these two points NMOS, CMOS, and QMOS are the three most compatible MOS technologies and TTL and ECL are the two most compatible bipolar technologies.

Both bipolar and MOS ROMs can be encountered in contemporary microcomputer designs. The major difference between these two memories is the faster access time of bipolar ROMs. Weighted against the bipolar ROM's fast access time is the small, dense size of the MOS ROM along with its low power consumption.

As their name implies, bipolar ROMs use bipolar transistors as the major component in the formation of the word and bit lines. This connection is on the emitter of each transistor. These amplifiers then sense the ROM's internal data columns in search of current patterns that represent the binary states.

MOS ROMs, on the other hand, use MOSFETs for storing the circuit's logic (see Fig. 2-6). These transistors can be placed in more complex arrangements than their bipolar counterparts. Typically, dense, highly ordered MOSFET patterns are possible in this ROM fabrication technique. When a word line is selected, the correct MOSFET is set into conduction. This is followed by the selection of an appropriate bit line. This final selection forms a connection between the transistors and the output lines. A grounded connection is a logic 0 and a high connection is a logic 1.

The same general construction steps are followed by both of these ROM technologies. This process begins with the photo masking of the overall ROM

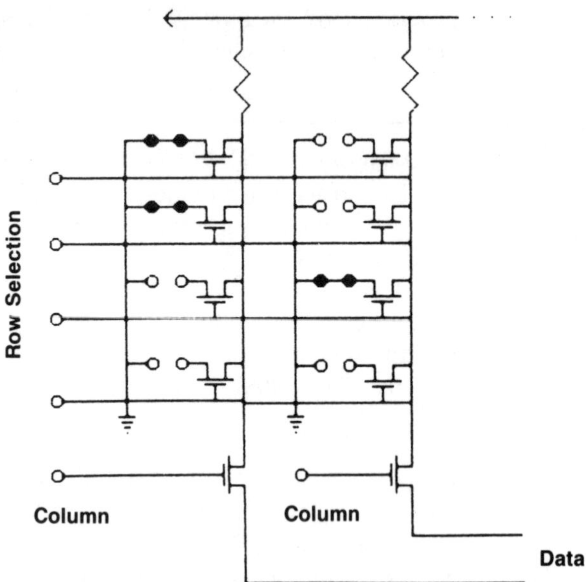

Fig. 2-6. Row and column array for a MOSFET ROM.

design. The subsequent etching and diffusion steps form the semiconductor devices which constitute the ROM's internal structure. These gates and connections are formed on a thin silicon wafer. It is during these steps that the programming of the ROM is created. Actually, a software designer must have composed the ROM's code prior to these construction steps. This code is then "translated" into the ROM's gates and junctions through the preparation of an exposure mask. Using this programming mask for the creation of a ROM is known as a mask programmed ROM. Due to the high-cost of this fabrication method, mask programmed ROMs are only practical for mass-produced circuits.

PROM TECHNOLOGY

Unlike ROMs, PROMs are field programmable memories. In other words, they can be programmed by the end user outside of the manufacturing process. This feature lends a large degree of flexibility to the PROM. Early research into field programmable memories was conducted by Frohman-Bentchkowsky with Intel Corporation in 1971.

There are two forms of PROM: the bipolar diode array and the bipolar transistor pattern. The bipolar diode array is the simplest construction form of the PROM. Conversely, the bipolar transistor pattern is similar to the mask programmed MOS ROM technique, but the bipolar PROM uses bipolar transistors instead of MOSFETs.

A PROM is constructed with deposited fusible links between the word and bit lines. This fusible link is directly attached to the base-emitter connection of a bipolar transistor (in bipolar transistor PROMs) and the P/N connection of a diode (in bipolar diode array PROMs). Each transistor and diode in their respective PROM has one of these fusible links between the word and bit lines. This link is either nichrome or polycrystalline silicon in bipolar transistor PROMs and a constriction in the interconnect metalization in bipolar diode array PROMs. Pulsing a 50-to-100-mA current for 2 mS will cause this link to fail or "blow." This programming pulse is continued until the connection is completely vaporized.

A blown link causes the connected bit line to remain open or *float*. This condition represents a logic 0. Alternatively, an intact link causes the bit line to move towards +5 volts and produce a logic 1.

If during the programming of a PROM a mistake is made, then this memory IC becomes worthless. Therefore, careful consideration and program debugging must be exercised prior to "blowing" the PROM's links. This sensitive programming requirement makes PROMs only slightly more flexible than ROMs.

EAROM TECHNOLOGY

In very broad terms, EAROMs can be thought of as RAM with long write times. Programming, reading, and erasing are all performed through selective voltage applications on an EAROM. Like RAM, all three of these functions can be performed on the EAROM without having to remove it from a circuit. Unlike RAM, an EAROM has a slower write time and also requires numerous, complex supply voltages for programming and erasing. A standard EAROM uses three voltages: +12 V, −5 V, and −30 V. This triple power requirement can seriously tax a circuit's design.

Prior to programming, an EAROM must be erased. This can be accomplished in either a word or a block mode. The *word mode* is used for erasing the data at a specific memory address location. The *block mode*, on the other hand, erases all of the EAROM's internal memory address locations.

The technology that is used for achieving the nonvolatile nature of EAROMs is called metal-nitride-oxide-semiconductor (MNOS) technology. This is a modified MOS technology that has capacitors to store the current charge. This storage technique provides a minimum memory retention of 10 years. An MNOS EAROM has a 2 mS access time with a 15 mS write time. The erase time is approximately 100 mS for this memory device.

Another EAROM construction technique is with amorphous semiconductors. In this technology, bi-state tellerium (amorphous and polycrystalline structured) is used for storing programmed data. Each of the two states possesses a unique electrical property which makes translation into 0 and 1 logics relatively easy. The application of current to an amorphous

EAROM produces these electrical differences. One fringe benefit of an amorphous EAROM is its faster access time, 15-to-20 nS. The write time, however, remains close to the MNOS EAROM, 2-to-10 mS.

The slow write time, separate erase function, and unusual voltage requirements makes the EAROM a difficult memory IC to employ in a typical microcomputer design. A static RAM IC offers several significant advantages over a comparable EAROM design. Namely, the minimal power requirements and the faster write time give this RAM IC the nod over the EAROM.

EPROM TECHNOLOGY

A major difference between EAROMs and EPROMs is that EPROMs must be removed from a circuit prior to erasure. An even greater difference is in the method that an EPROM is erased. EPROMs must be exposed to a strong UV (ultraviolet) light source (2537 Å with 6 to 15 watt-second/cm^2) for complete erasure. This UV exposure is accomplished through a small quartz window located in the dorsal side of the EPROM IC carrier. A standard erasure of 10 to 30 minutes is necessary for resetting all of the EPROM's address locations.

EPROMs are manufactured with floating avalanche injection MOS (FAMOS) technique (see Fig. 2-7). This process is also known as the *floating gate* technique. Basically, a FAMOS EPROM is a MOSFET that lacks a silicon gate connection. Similar to the construction process used in PMOS transistors, a P-channel FAMOS EPROM has the silicon gate enclosed in a silicon dioxide insulative cushion. This barrier prevents access to the silicon gate. During

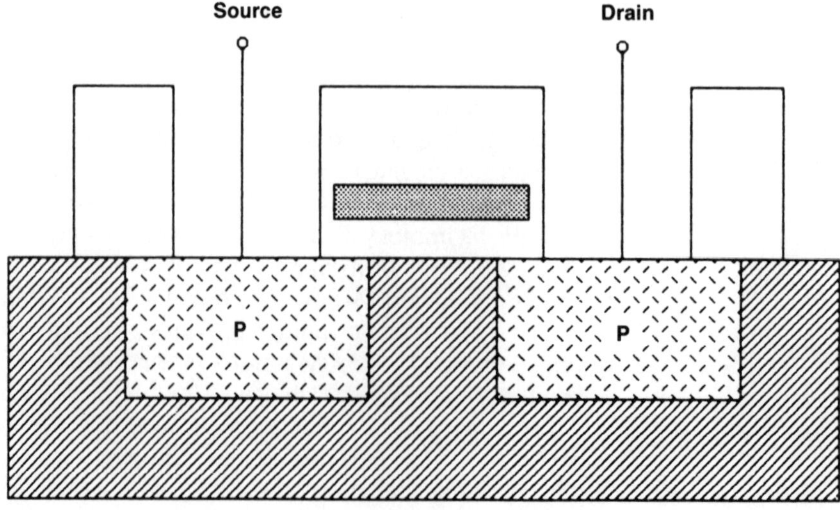

Fig. 2-7. A cross-section of a FAMOS circuit.

the programming of an EPROM, however, a negative voltage pulse of −25 to −30 volts is applied to either the source or drain of the FAMOS transistor. This pulse injects electrons into the floating gate and forms a logic 1. The insulative silicon dioxide then holds the electrons inside the floating gate. In this condition, the charge on the gate will last for approximately 10 years under normal usage.

A 3.2 eV barrier exists between the silicon substrate and the silicon dioxide. A shift of voltage threshold is required for proper programming.

$$V_T = \frac{-\Delta Q_{FG}}{C_G}$$

where:

V_T = shift of voltage threshold
Q_{FG} = change in floating gate charge
C_G = capacitance between the floating gate and the selected gate

Other EPROMs don't require such large programming voltages. These memories operate at TTL voltage levels. Programming this type of EPROM requires several steps for ensuring the accurate tranferal of data:

1. Place the address location on the EPROM's address input lines.
2. Place the program data on the EPROM's data output lines.
3. Apply the programming pulse to the EPROM's program pin for a fixed program time period.
4. Repeat the above steps for each memory address location.

Once an EPROM has been programmed, it can be used in any microcomputer design. The fast access time of a FAMOS EPROM, 450 nS to 1 mS, makes this memory device an important substitute for the more costly PROM or mask programmed ROM.

Due to the insulative silicon dioxide barrier which surrounds the floating silicon gate, an EPROM can't be erased through the application of a reverse voltage level. Only a strong UV light exposure is able to reset an EPROM to its erased state. Unfortunately, this method of erasure is not selective. Therefore, a word mode erasure is impossible. An erased EPROM usually has a logic of 1 in all of its address data locations.

A valuable virtue of the EPROM is that it is pin-compatible with mask programmable ROMs. This compatibility permits a program to be debugged on an EPROM and later transferred to a ROM for subsequent mass production. In other words, a program can be developed and tested on an EPROM before it is permanently etched into a ROM.

EEPROM TECHNOLOGY

An EEPROM is an improvement over the UV-erased EPROM. The erasure of the EEPROM is carried out inside the digital circuit through variations in supply voltages. These electrical programming and erasing functions are attributable to the construction of the EEPROM that was developed by Fowler-Nordheim in the 1960's. The most predominant EEPROMs use floating gate tunnel oxide (FLOTOX) technology.

FLOTOX technology is an improvement over the floating gate technique used in FAMOS EPROMs. Like an EPROM, a FLOTOX EEPROM has its floating gate surrounded by a silicon dioxide insulation barrier. Running underneath the floating gate is a tunnel oxide. It is this tunnel oxide that permits the EEPROM to be both programmed and erased within a circuit. This electron tunnelling is called Fowler-Nordheim EEPROM Tunnelling. Two forms of electron tunnelling are possible: over the energy barrier or through the energy barrier. In these examples, the former process is called *hot electron injection* and the latter is known as *Fowler-Nordheim tunnelling.*

During the programming of an EEPROM, the programming voltage is applied to the gate with the source and drain grounded. A small amount of the voltage is coupled across the tunnel oxide. This coupling allows electrons to flow between the drain and the floating gate. Slowly these electrons build up and reduce the flow.

This process is reversed during an erasure. In this case, the gate is grounded and the high voltage is applied to the drain. Like during the EEPROM programming step, a small amount of the voltage is coupled across the tunnel oxide. This action causes the electrons to flow from the floating gate to the drain making the gate receive a positive charge.

EEPROMs are compatible with both NMOS and CMOS technologies. This makes the incorporation of EEPROMs into digital circuits an economical, as well as high-performance design attribute. One exciting development in the fabrication of EEPROMs concerns the scaling of the electric field across the tunnel oxide. In order for the memory device to yield the highest performance possible, this field must be constant. There is a snag in scaling EEPROMs, however. Basically, the presently limited thickness of the tunnel oxide prevents much scaling. Therefore, most EEPROM designs use very large-scale integration (VLSI) techniques for beating this scaling requirement. But even this technique faces a certain compactible ceiling. The end result from this reduction in size is that EEPROMs will be able to hold more data with faster access times.

PLA TECHNOLOGY

PLAs are usually considered technical modifications of PROMs. What this means is that PLAs are programmable diode gate arrays with fusible links. Therefore, like a PROM, when a PLA has been programmed, it can't be erased.

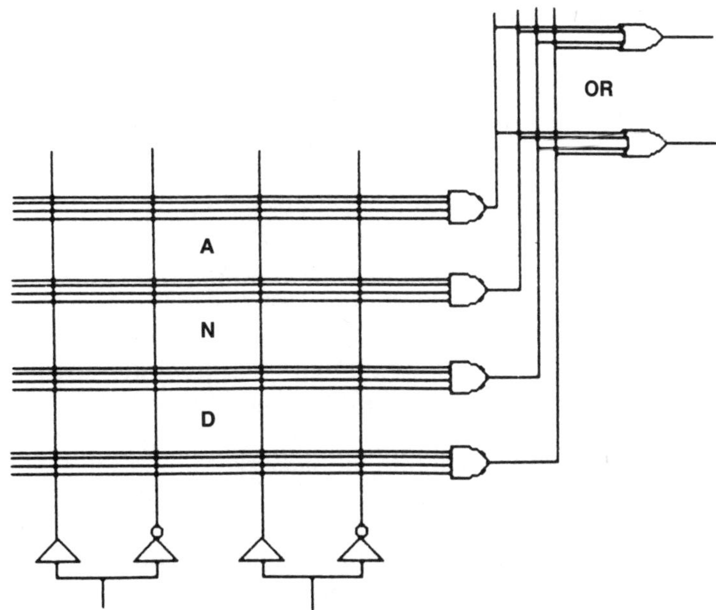

Fig. 2-8. AND and OR gate PLA pattern.

The largest difference between a PLA and a PROM is one of internal organization.

The most common PLA is the field-programmable PLA (FPLA). The diode gates of the FPLA can be programmed as multiple combinations of either AND or OR gates. A typical FPLA has a programmable AND array connected to a programmable OR array (see Fig. 2-8). This flexibility does have its problems, however. The largest problem inherent to the FPLA is the difficulty in programming it. Along with the complications in programming are a typically higher cost.

BUILDING THE X-3

A modest microcomputer system can be built around a minimal number of digital ICs. The final design will be as simple or complicated as your needs dictate. For example, a microcomputer could have the following features:

- Zilog Z-80 MPU
- 1851 Programmable I/O Interface
- Display Decoder/Driver w/LCD
- Keyboard Buffer w/Keyboard
- 1K byte EPROM
- 2K byte Dynamic RAM

Or, another microcomputer could sport these component features:

- NEC V-20 MPU
- Intel 8259A Programmable Interrupt Controller
- Terminal CRT Controller
- RS-232C Serial Port
- Parallel Centronics Port
- 64K byte EPROM
- 256K byte Static RAM
- 8272 Floppy Disk Controller

No matter which microcomputer system you design, the key to its successful operation will be the programming that is placed within its EPROM. Generally speaking, this ROM section will hold the information for booting and controlling the "housekeeping" chores of the entire system. In this case, the ROM-based boot software would load a disk-based operating system into the system's RAM for subsequent execution and reference.

There are other features that could be placed within the system's ROM, however. For example, this memory section could contain several "extras." These extras include: a monitor program for aiding in system-level programming, an operating system thereby eliminating the previously mentioned disk-intensive boot, and any other essential programming. Actually, it is this final extra which exposes the exaltation of programming your own EPROMs. By incorporating your own programming into a system's ROM, you are then able to design a dedicated computer system that is structured to your personal preferences. In other words, the age of the true personal computer is born.

Before you begin the actual digital design of your microcomputer system, you should make a "wish list" of its intended features. As an illustration of this process, the X-3 will have the following features:

- MS-DOS capability
- CP/M capability
- 64K bytes of ROM
- 256K bytes of RAM
- 5 ¼" floppy disk drive interface
- 3 ½" floppy disk drive interface
- Fixed disk drive interface
- Mathematics Coprocessor
- Expansion bus
- Serial port
- Parallel port

An ideal MPU for handling the dual MS-DOS and CP/M compatibility issue is the NEC V-20 (see Fig. 2-9). This MPU is capable of emulating both the Intel 8088, as well as the 8080 MPUs.

Figure 2-10 provides a generalized block diagram of the completed X-3 computer system.

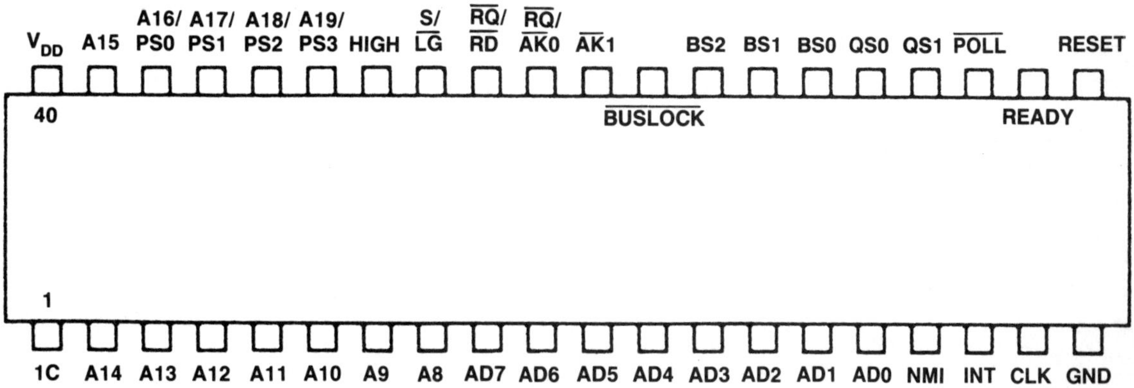

Fig. 2-9. Pin assignments for NEC V-20 MPU.

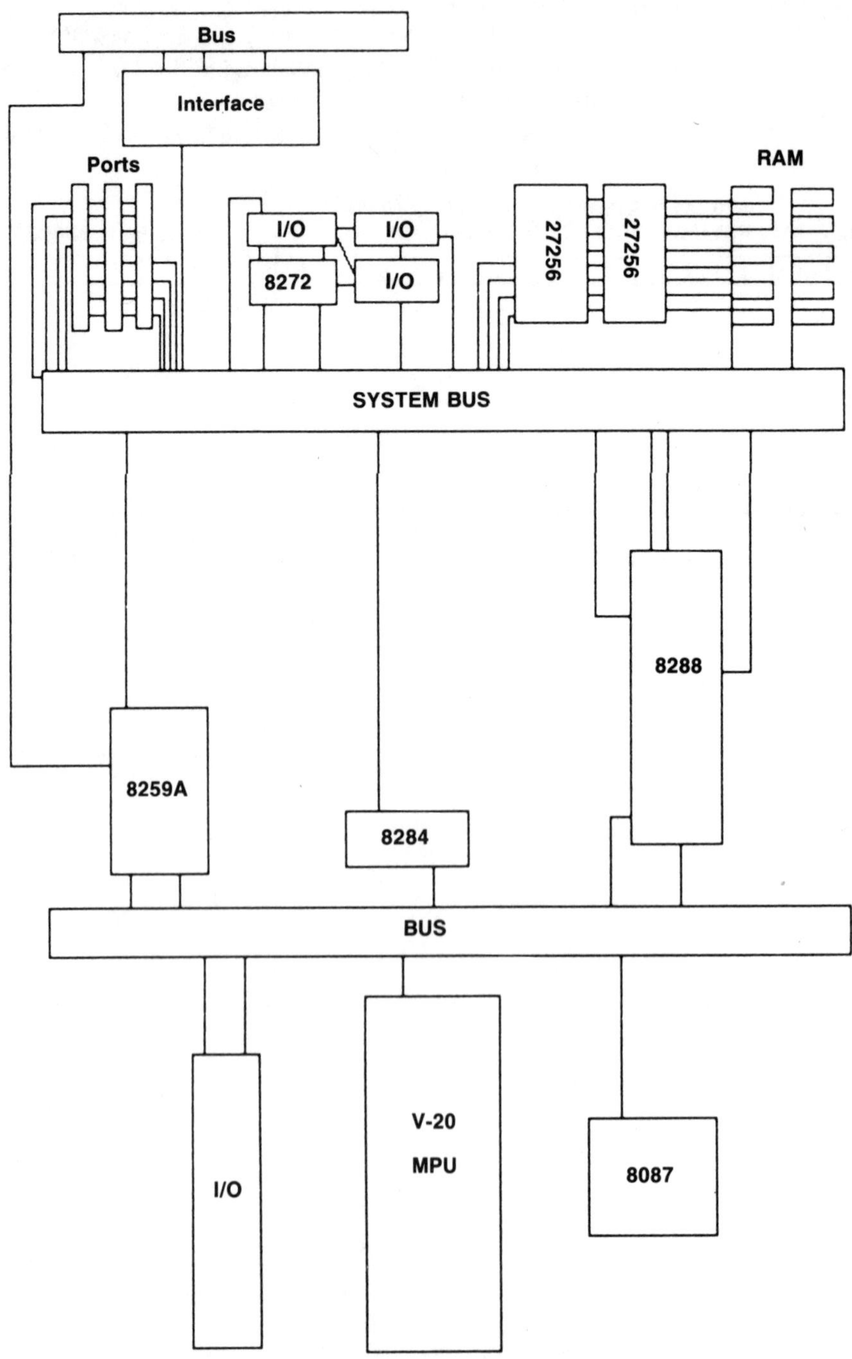

Fig. 2-10. Schematic block diagram for the X-3.

3

Popular PROMs

A typical PROM has a vast array of fusible wire links that form an elaborate network running throughout all of the PROM's memory cells. Each of these connections are intact when this memory chip is manufactured. In this condition, all of the addresses of the PROM have a logic 1.

When a PROM is programmed, a large electrical current is applied to the link at the specified memory cell location. This programming voltage causes the link to break and turns the cell's logic to a 0 binary state. Following this programming procedure, the logic of a PROM is unalterable. Granted, the memory locations that still have a logic 1 can be changed to a logic 0. For the most part, however, a PROM becomes a mask programmed ROM after its memory cell links have been broken during the programming process.

Due to the irreversible nature of a fused or broken PROM link, any programming errors that occur inside a PROM result in the discarding of the faulty memory chip. This rigid programming fact makes shoddy PROM preparation a costly venture. There are two methods for limiting the potential for creating erroneous PROMs. First, thoroughly debug or test the programming prior to "burning" the code into the PROM. These programming tests can usually be performed at the software level on a system-emulating microcomputer.

The second means for minimizing the expense of lost material is to write the required programming into an EPROM. The erasable feature of the EPROM makes the correction of programming errors both quick and inexpensive. One special precaution that must be observed with this test method, however, is pin compatibility between the production PROM and the experimental EPROM. For example, the Harris Semiconductor HM-6616 16K-bit PROM is pin compatible with the 16K-bit 2716 EPROM. If the test EPROM does not have the same pin configuration as the needed PROM, then a special test circuit will need to be constructed. This extra fabrication step increases the final circuit's cost and is of a questionable value.

One final nuance to PROM programming deals with the variations in programming requirements. Based on the numerous PROM manufacturing processes, the type of fusible link material, and the chip's pin configuration, not all PROMs program alike. In other words, a required voltage is applied to a specific pin for a fixed time period. This current, pin location, and pulse time is different for various PROMs. For example, the Fairchild 93Z667 64K-bit PROM is a 24-pin package with the programming voltage supplied on pin 20, while the Signetics 10149 1K-bit PROM is a 16-pin IC using ECL fusing. Therefore, a functional PROM programmer must be flexible enough to handle all of the current, pin, and pulse needs that are found on contemporary PROMs. This flexibility is usually provided by special personality modules which configure the PROM programmer for dealing with the special programming requirements found in the bulk of today's PROMs.

256 × 4 BIT ECL PROM

This PROM is only mentioned due to its ECL construction. Examples of this 1K-bit IC usually have some means for memory expansion. This is usually accomplished through a chip enable pin (CE or CS). The outputs from the PROM are OE or open emitter types.

Device Example: Signetics 10149

Package: 16-pin Dual In-line Package (DIP)

Pin Connections:

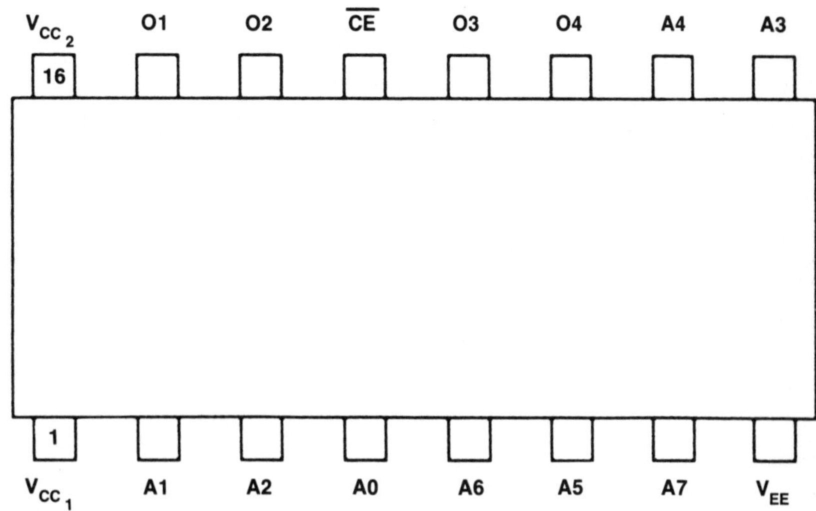

Temperature Range: Operating: 0°C to +75°C
Storage: −65°C to + 150°C

Power Requirements: Supply: +.5V to +7V
Input: −1.2V to +5.5V

Access Time: 20 nS

Logic: Supplied with all logic high or 1

512 × 8 BIT CMOS PROM

PROMs of this size are quickly falling into disfavor. Manufactured with low-power consumption techniques, this CMOS PROM is TTL compatible. Recent advances in the construction of this PROM include floating gate technology which dramatically increased the speed and significantly reduced the power usage of this memory device.

Device Example: Cypress Semiconductor 7C225

Package: 24-pin DIP

Pin Connections:

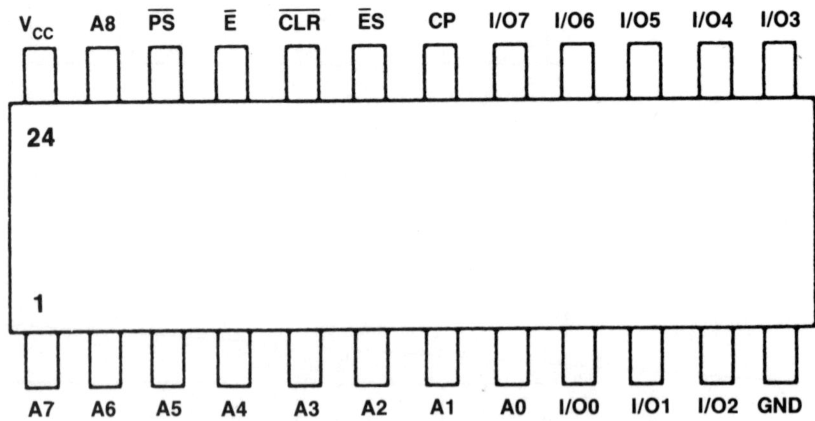

Temperature Range: Operating: 0°C to +70°C
Ambient w/Power: −55°C to +125°C
Storage: −65°C to +150°C

Power Requirements: Supply Voltage: −.5V to +7V
Input Voltage: −3V to +7V
Program Voltage: +14V

Access Time: 25 to 40 nS

Logic: Supplied with all logic high or 1

1024 × 8 BIT TTL PROM

This 8K bit PROM is constructed with bipolar TTL D-type (master-slave) registers. This memory device can hold 1024 words, each with an 8-bit width. Following programming, data is read from this PROM by placing the desired address on the address input lines and pulsing a clock signal on the CLK pin. The register's data is then placed on the data output lines where it remains stable until changed. The outputs in this PROM are typically three-state.

Device Example: Signetics 82HS187

Package: 24-pin DIP

Pin Connections:

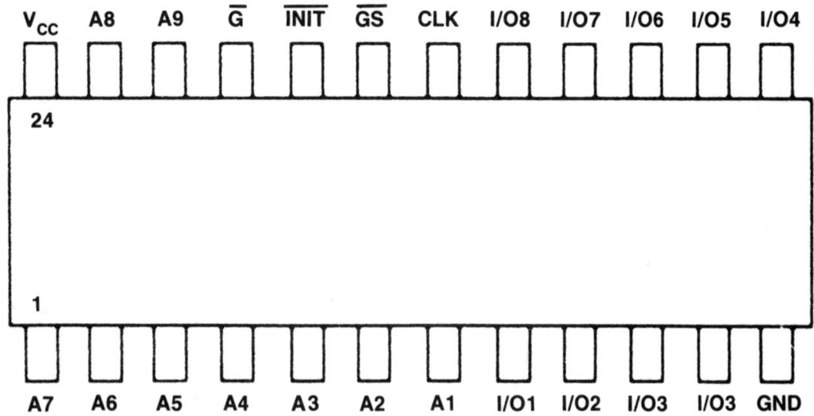

Temperature Range: Operating: 0°C to +75°C
Storage: −65°C to +150°C

Power Requirements: Supply Voltage: +.5V to +7V
Input Voltage: −1.2V to +5.5V

Access Time: 45 to 55 nS

Logic: Supplied with all logic high or 1

2048 × 8 BIT TTL PROM

Similar to the 8K PROM, this 16K-bit PROM uses bipolar TTL D-type (master-slave) register construction. The register structure can hold 2048 words, each with an 8-bit width. The increased flexibility of this memory device has necessitated the inclusion of one or more chip enable CE address pins. These chip enable pins permit the ganging of 16K-bit PROMs within a logic circuit. All of the outputs are three-state.

Device Example: Signetics 82S191C

Package: 24-pin DIP

Pin Connections:

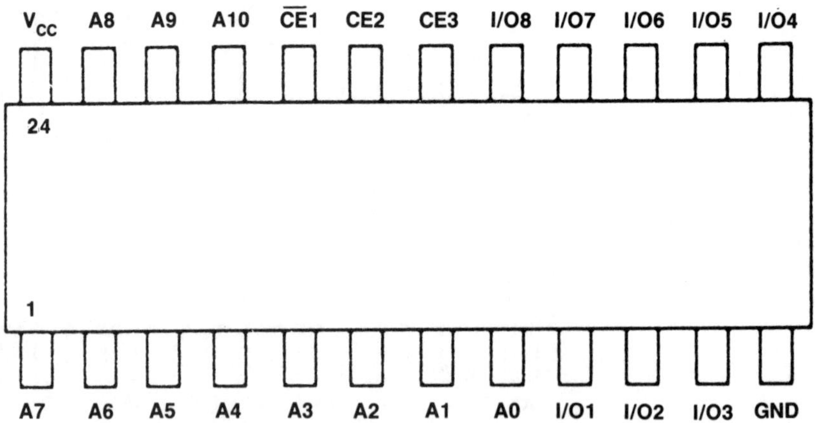

Temperature Range: Operating: 0°C to +75°C
Storage: −65°C to +150°C

Power Requirements: Supply Voltage: +.5V to +7V
Input Voltage: −1.2V to +5.5V

Access Time: 35 nS

Logic: Supplied with all logic low or 0

4096 × 8 BIT TTL PROM

This 32K-bit PROM is TTL compatible with bipolar TTL D-type (master-slave) registers. A total of 4096 words, each with an 8-bit width can be stored within this PROM's registers. Examples of this PROM have one to two chip-enable pins for connecting extra memory devices in the same circuit. All of the outputs are three-state.

Device Example: Signetics 82HS321

Package: 24-pin DIP

Pin Connections:

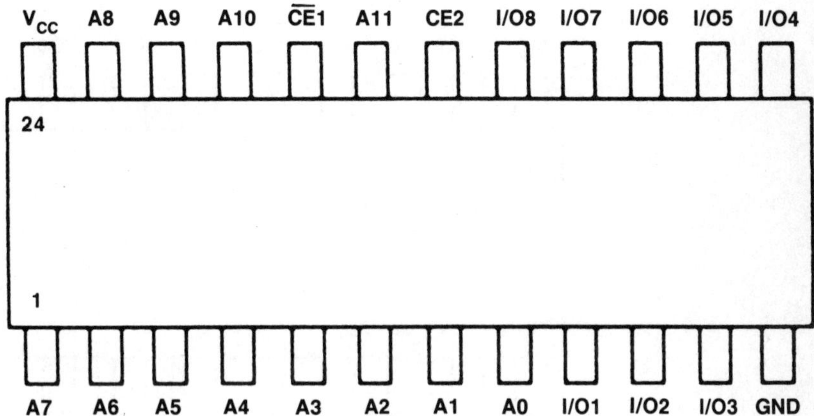

Temperature Range: Operating: 0°C to +75°C
Storage: −65°C to +150°C

Power Requirements: Supply Voltage: +.5V to +7V
Input Voltage: −1.2V to +5.5V

Access Time: 45 nS

Logic: Supplied with all logic high or 1

8192 × 8 BIT TTL PROM

A 64K-bit PROM that is TTL compatible with bipolar TTL D-type (master-slave) registers. This PROM can store a total of 8192 words, each with an 8-bit width within its internal registers. The number of chip enable pins can vary between 1 and 3. These pins (labeled CE or CS) allow for expansion of the PROM with other memory devices within a digital circuit. All of the outputs are three-state.

Device Example: Fairchild 93Z667

Package: 24-pin DIP

Pin Connections:

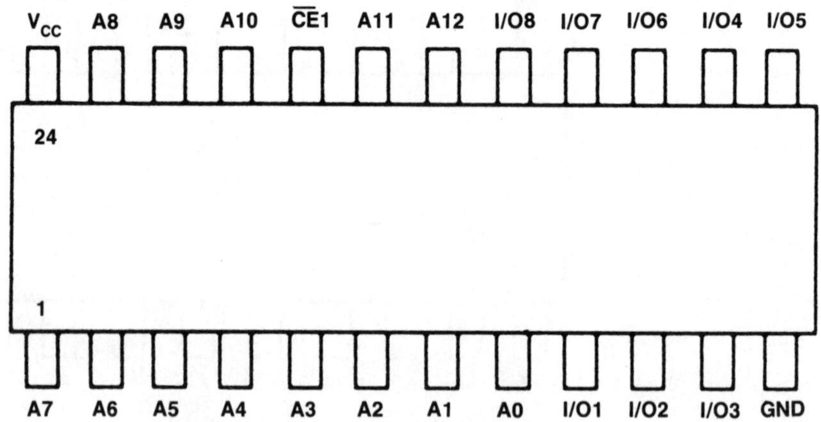

Temperature Range: Operating: 0°C to +75°C
Storage: −65°C to +150°C

Power Requirements: Supply Voltage: +.5V to +7V
Input Voltage: −1.2V to +5.5V

Access Time: 35 to 55 nS

Logic: Supplied with all logic high or 1

4

Popular EEPROMs

An EEPROM is an electrically programmable nonvolatile memory device that is constructed, for the most part, with FLOTOX technology. Typically, this device has a combined read/write life in excess of 10,000 cycles. Each of these program and erase cycles should not result in any degradation in the integrity of the EEPROMs internal registers. There is a significant reduction in the device's performance, however, after this ideal 10,000 cycle state has been reached. The prime contributing factor to this degradation is electron trapping.

Electron trapping lowers the quality of the EEPROM's tunnel oxide. This results in an increase in the volume of negatively charge particles in the tunnel. A rise in electrons in the tunnel oxide reduces the applied voltage's charged field. Therefore, a design limit of 10,000 read/write (or, program/erase) cycles should be applied to EEPROM circuits.

Both the program and erase functions of the EEPROM are related to the pulse width of the applied voltage. This pulse width not only determines the minimal amount of voltage that is required for the desired function, it also establishes the memory device's programming time. For example, in the first EEPROMs, the programming time was a lengthy 10 mS. SEEQ's 2816A 2K-byte EEPROM is an example of this IC. The current generations of these memory devices, on the other hand, have had their programming times shaved to a speedy 2 to 5 mS. Not surprisingly enough, the 2-mS EEPROMs are called "flash" EEPROMs. An example of this memory device is the Exel XL29C512 512K-bit Flash EEPROM. This rapid write time allows EEPROMs to be conveniently placed inside microcomputer designs as a nonvolatile alternative to static RAM.

One large benefit that can be derived from placing flash EEPROMs within a memory storage subsystem of a microcomputer is the total removal of power from the circuit without loss of the EEPROM's register contents. This is one performance point that separates the battery-refreshed static RAM from the truly nonvolatile EEPROM storage. Dependence on this form of memory storage can be compromised, however. The reliability of an EEPROM's memory retention can be affected by read disturb.

Read disturb is the production of spurious threshold voltage changes. These voltage disturbances occur during the EEPROM's read function. In a typical circuit, a read function is initiated through the application of a discrete applied voltage. Occasionally, this "discrete" applied voltage can deposit a tunnel oxide aberration that will gradually degrade the threshold voltage. Even with the presence of read disturb, an average EEPROM is able to retain its data in an accurate state over a finite 10-year period. Evaluating a design's amount of read disturb can significantly alter the affect that read disturb will have on an EEPROM's data retention reliability.

Another source of concern in the reliability of EEPROM data retention is in *tunnel oxide breakdown*. This extremely rare condition is the total breakdown of the tunnel oxide's ability to retain an applied voltage. This failure can result from the application of a dangerously high electrical field across the oxide. Keeping a circuit's voltage levels within the performance specifications of the EEPROM greatly reduces the probability of occurrence for this error.

Most of the commercially available EEPROMs are made from NMOS, CMOS, or QMOS technology. These products offer an in-circuit programming and erasing capability at a nominal +5V. While the advantage of this read/write convenience might look attractive in memory storage design, this plus must be weighed against the minus of a finite number of read/write cycles.

2048 × 8 BIT CMOS EEPROM

This 16K-bit EEPROM is constructed with CMOS floating gate technology. This memory device has 2048 words, each with an 8-bit width. For the most part, this package is limited to 10-mS write times with varying voltages. Along with this long write time is a long read time. A 200 nS read time is typical with this EEPROM. Both the inputs and the outputs of this device are TTL compatible.

Device Example: SEEQ 2816A

Package: 24-pin DIP

Pin Connections:

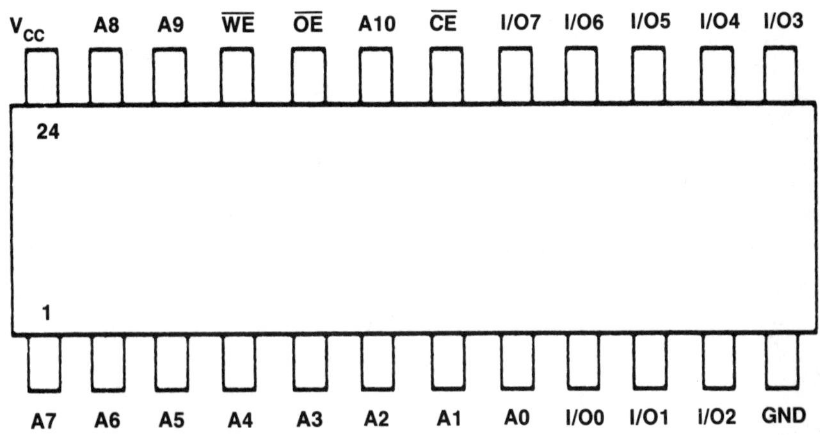

Temperature Range: Operating: 0°C to +70°C
Storage: −65°C to +150°C

Power Requirements: Supply Voltage: +.5V to +7V
Program Voltage: +4.5V to +5.5V

Access Time: 200 nS

8192 × 8 BIT CMOS EEPROM

A +5V operating voltage powers this 64K-bit EEPROM. Construction is with CMOS floating gate technology. This memory device has 8192 words, each with an 8-bit width. Write times vary for this package with many manufacturers switching to the faster 2-mS flash EEPROMs. Read times are still limited to 200 nS. In an effort to increase design flexibility, many of the examples of the EEPROM are pin compatible with several of the more popular EPROMs. Several of the leading manufacturers have added microprocessor latches to the address circuitry of their EEPROMs. The Fujitsu MBM28C64 64K-bit EEPROM is an example of this type of memory IC. All interface ports of this device are TTL compatible.

Device Example: Intel 2864A

Package: 28-pin DIP

Pin Connections:

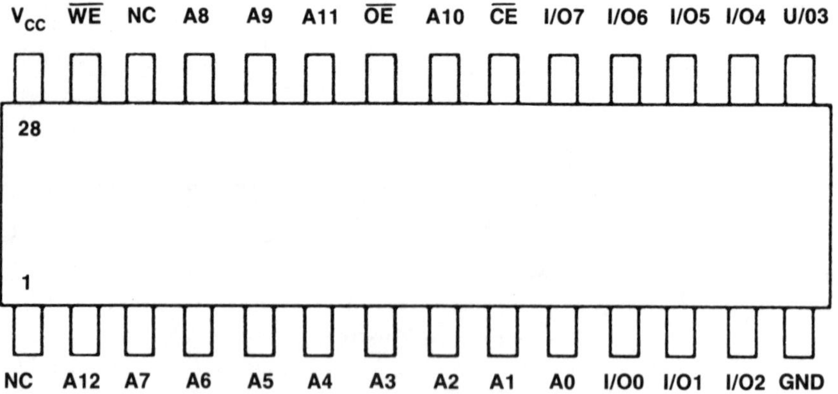

Temperature Range: Operating: 0°C to +70°C
Storage: −65°C to + 150°C

Power Requirements: Supply Voltage: +.5V to +7V
Program Voltage: +4.5V to +5.5V

Access Time: 250 to 200 nS

65536 × 8 BIT CMOS EEPROM

As the production costs of EEPROMs decreases and the problems of data retention are reduced, the size of the commercial EEPROM increases. One of the leading examples of this trend is the 512K-bit EEPROM. Construction is with CMOS floating gate technology. This memory device has 65536 words, each with an 8-bit width. This package traditionally uses flash write times. There has even been a significant reduction in the speed of this EEPROM's read times. Values in the 150 nS range are fairly common. Once again many of the 28-pin EPROMs are pin compatible with this EEPROM. Additionally, TTL compatibility has been designed into this memory devices address ports.

Device Example: EXAR XL29C512

Package: 28-pin DIP

Pin Connections:

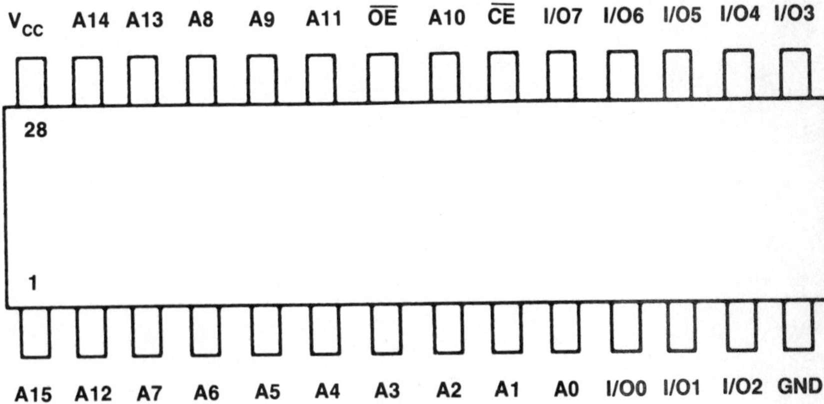

Temperature Range: Operating: 0°C to +70°C
Storage: −65°C to +150°C

Power Requirements: Supply Voltage: +.5V to +7V
Program Voltage: +4.5V to +5.5V

Access Time: 150 nS

5

Popular EPROMs

Most EPROMs are constructed with FAMOS transistor technology. Although this is a similar technology that is used in many PROMs, the presence of a quartz window in the upper surface of the EPROM's carrier represents the most dramatic difference between these two memory devices.

This clear window in the EPROM's dorsal side is used for exposing the FAMOS cell gates to UV light. Exposing the EPROM to UV light is used for bulk erasing the device's registers. A lengthy exposure to this light causes all of the gates to discharge and return them to their native state. One requirement of the UV light is the presence of a high-intensity photon strength. This is necessary for forcing the resident floating gate electrons through the insulating silicon dioxide substratum and returning the EPROM to its original logic.

EPROMs that are erased in this fashion are typically shipped with a logic 1 as their native state. Therefore, programming an EPROM requires changing the charge on a memory gate to a logic 0. Similarly, erasing an EPROM returns the logic of the memory gate to a logic 1. There are exceptions to this "rule," however. Intel's 1702A EPROM has a native state of a logic 0. This condition is changed through programming by altering a specified memory location to a logic 1. Luckily for today's EPROM programmer, the Intel 1702A is virtually obsolete. Therefore, the most frequently encountered EPROMs will be shipped with all registers holding a logic 1.

Programming an EPROM completely lacks an industry standard. Chief among these differences is the required programming voltages. The numerous commercially available EPROMs can require a +12.5V, +21V, or +25V programming voltage. Furthermore, this voltage must be applied to a specific programming pin. Adding further confusion to EPROM programming, many of the popular EPROMs use different pins for receiving this programming voltage. As a total illustration of this programming "mess," consider the following EPROM programming "standards:"

Requirements	2716	2732	2764
Program Pin Number	#21	#20	#1
Program Voltage	+25 V	+25 V	+12.5 V

There are two common methods for dealing with the large variety of different EPROM programming requirements. The most common of these solutions involves personality modules that configure an EPROM programmer to deal with the peculiarity of a specified EPROM. A personality module is a user-modified DIP carrier that tailors the programming voltage to the specified EPROM and routes this shaped voltage to the required programming pin. These voltage-oriented modifications are typically performed with diodes and resistors that are soldered between the various pins of the DIP carrier (see Fig. 5-1). Using personality modules lends the EPROM programmer a large degree of versatility, but it does entail a considerable amount of effort in their design and construction.

An easier, but more complex method of dealing with the numerous EPROM programming specifications is through a microprocessor-controlled

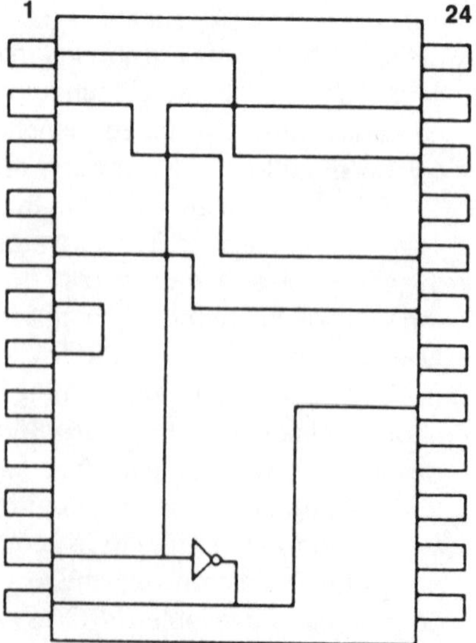

Fig. 5-1. Schematic diagram for a personality module.

EPROM programmer. This solution uses complex software for directing the programming parameters to the destination EPROM. Although the virtue of this method is the elimination of the construction of several personality modules there is a limitation in being able to accommodate future EPROM designs and programming parameters.

There are two important performance points to consider when designing with EPROMs. First, an EPROM will suffer a dramatic drop in its data retention reliability after 100 program/erase cycles. This limitation in life should be strictly adhered to, otherwise data corruption will be an unfortunate result.

The other performance point deals with the rate of charge decay in a programmed EPROM. An EPROM's charge decay is a factor of electrons exiting from the floating gate. In a typical programmed EPROM, this decay results in a loss of approximately 25 percent charge after 10 years. In terms of data retention reliability, charge decay is not as serious as the number of program/erase cycles. Both points, however, should be heeded in EPROM design.

256 × 8 BIT NMOS EPROM

The original EPROM. This 2K-bit EPROM is constructed with NMOS floating gate technology. This memory device has 256 words, each with an 8-bit width. Programming is through a − 40V voltage. No clock signal is used in this static memory during its operation.

Device Example: Intel 1702A

Package: 24-pin DIP with quartz window

Pin Connections:

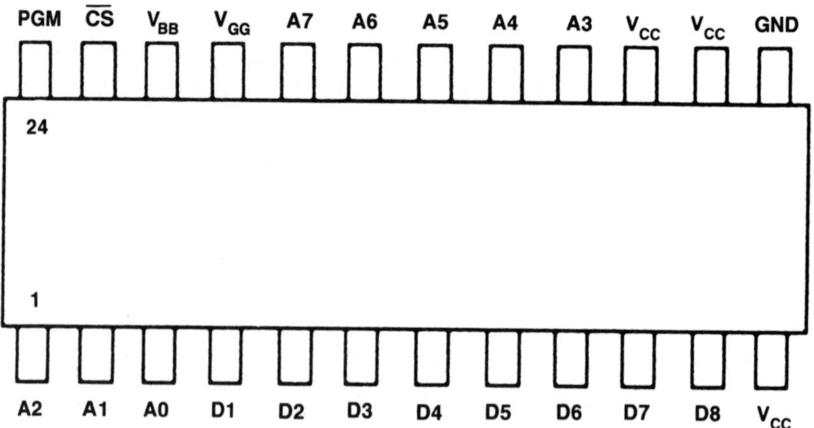

Temperature Range: Operating: 0°C to +70°C
Storage: −55°C to +85°C

Power Requirements: Supply Voltage: +4.5V to +5.5V
Program Voltage: −40V

Access Time: 1 mS

Logic: Supplied with a logic 0

Programming Pin: Pin 16

1024 × 8 BIT NMOS EPROM

This 8K-bit EPROM is constructed with NMOS floating gate technology. This memory device has 1024 words, each with an 8-bit width. Programming is through a +26V voltage with a .5 mS pulse requiring a repetition of 200 times for ensuring a successful program cycle. This static memory uses no clock signal during its operation.

Device Example: Intel 2708

Package: 24-pin DIP with quartz window

Pin Connections:

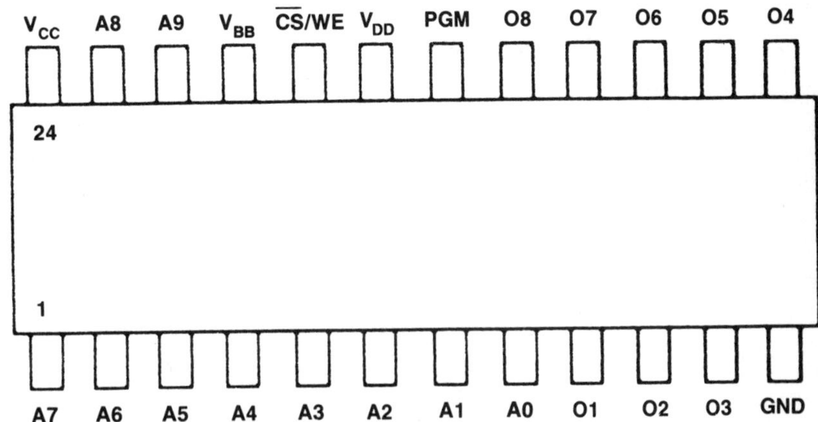

Temperature Range: Operating: 0°C to +70°C
Storage: −65°C to +125°C

Power Requirements: Supply Voltage: +4.5V to +5.5V
Program Voltage: +26V

Access Time: 450 nS

Logic: Supplied with a logic 1

Programming Pin: Pin 18

2048 × 8 BIT NMOS EPROM

True 8- and 16-bit microcomputer systems were finally able to directly interface with this memory device. A 16K-bit EPROM constructed with NMOS floating gate technology, this EPROM has 2048 words, each with an 8-bit width. There are several power supply requirements for this EPROM. The standard 16K-bit EPROM uses a +5V power supply. Other versions, however, use three separate power supplies. A +25V voltage is used as the programming pulse with a 2-mS pulse delay. No clock signal is required during operation.

Device Example: Intel 2716

Package: 24-pin DIP with quartz window

Pin Connections:

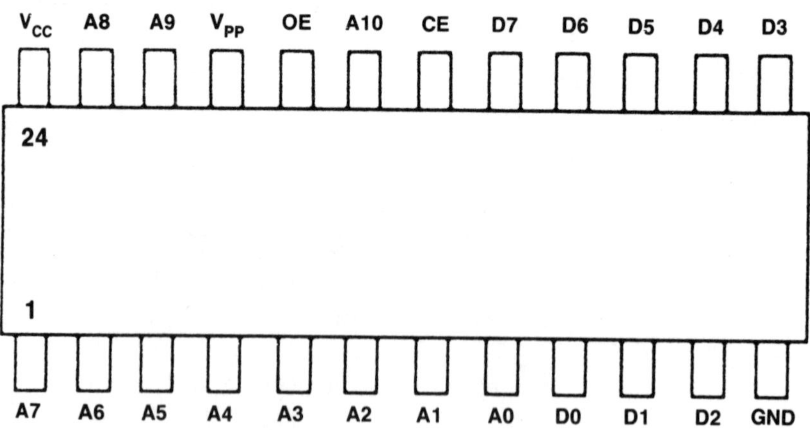

Temperature Range: Operating: 0°C to +70°C
Storage: −65°C to +125°C

Power Requirements: Supply Voltage: +4.5V to +5.5V
Program Voltage: +25V

Access Time: 350 nS

Logic: Supplied with a logic 1

Programming Pin: Pin 21

4096 × 8 BIT NMOS EPROM

The large memory space of this EPROM permits the creation of custom character generators or data look-up tables. This 32K-bit EPROM uses NMOS floating gate technology with 4096 words, each with an 8-bit width. A typical 32K-bit EPROM needs a +5V power supply and a +25V programming voltage. No clock signal is required during operation.

Device Example: Texas Instruments TMS2732A

Package: 24-pin DIP with quartz window

Pin Connections:

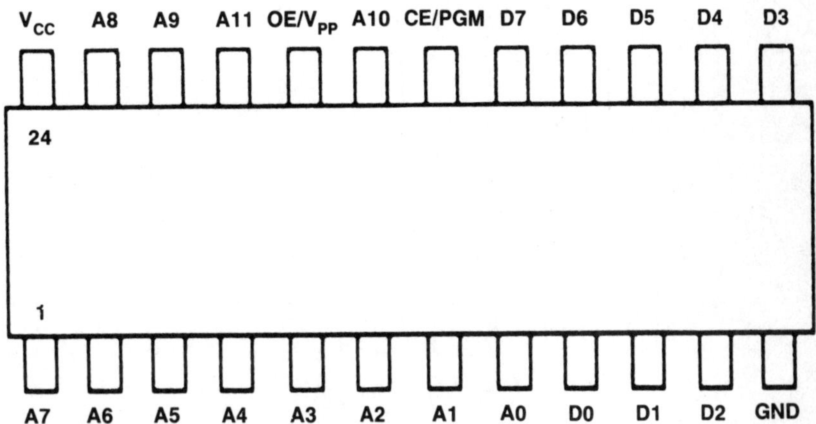

Temperature Range: Operating: 0°C to +70°C
Storage: −65°C to +125°C

Power Requirements: Supply Voltage: +4.5V to +5.5V
Program Voltage: +25V

Access Time: 170 to 450 nS

Logic: Supplied with a logic 1

Programming Pin: Pin 20

8192 × 8 BIT CMOS EPROM

Microprocessor compatibility is firmly entrenched with this EPROM. This 64K-bit EPROM uses CMOS floating gate technology arranged in 8192 words, each with an 8-bit width. A nominal +5V is needed for power with +12.5V used for programming. No clock signal is required during operation and the output is TTL compatible.

Device Example: Hyundai HY27C64

Package: 28-pin DIP with quartz window

Pin Connections:

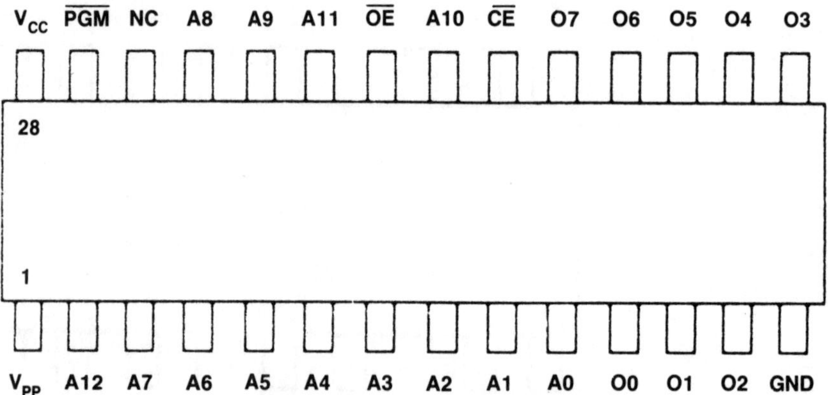

Temperature Range: Operating: 0°C to +70°C
Storage: −65°C to +125°C

Power Requirements: Supply Voltage: +4.5V to +5.5V
Program Voltage: +12.5V

Access Time: 150 to 300 nS

Logic: Supplied with a logic 1

Programming Pin: Pin 27

16384 × 8 BIT CMOS EPROM

Using low-power CMOS technology, this 128K-bit EPROM can hold 16384 words, each with an 8-bit width. Normal operation is from a single +5V power supply with a +12.5V programming voltage. No clock signal is required for operation. Three-state output buffers provide this EPROM with TTL compatibility.

Device Example: Texas Instruments TMS27C128

Package: 28-pin DIP with quartz window

Pin Connections:

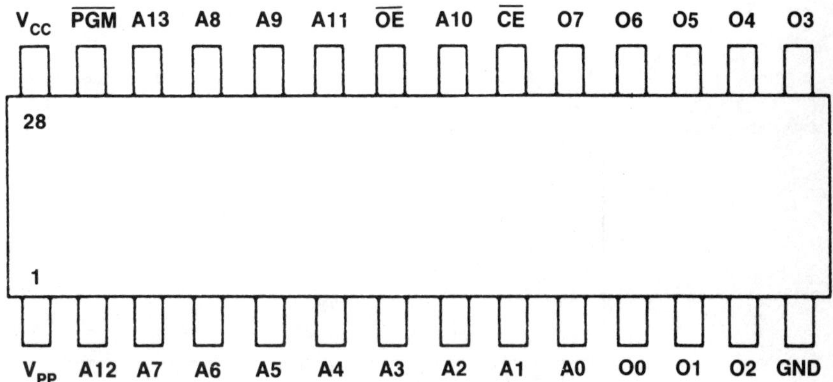

Temperature Range: Operating: 0°C to +70°C
Storage: 65°C to +125°C

Power Requirements: Supply Voltage: +4.5V to +5.5V
Program Voltage: +12.5V

Access Time: 150 to 450 nS

Logic: Supplied with a logic 1

Programming Pin: Pin 27

32768 × 8 BIT CMOS EPROM

High-speed processing and low power consumption are key features in the fabrication of this 256K-bit CMOS EPROM. A total of 32768 words, each with an 8-bit width can be stored in this EPROM. Operation is from a single +5V power supply with a +12.5V voltage required for programming. No clock signal is required for operation. Three-state output buffers provide this EPROM with TTL compatibility.

Device Example: VLSI Technology VT27C256

Package: 28-pin DIP with quartz window

Pin Connections:

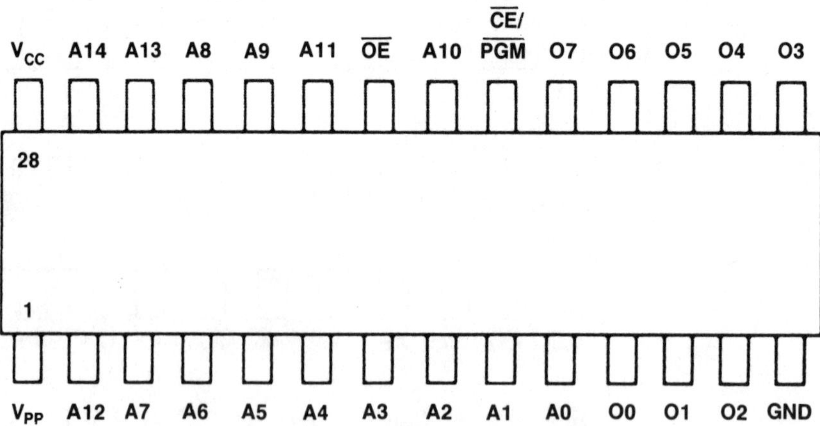

Temperature Range: Operating: 0°C to +70°C
Storage: −65°C to +125°C

Power Requirements: Supply Voltage: +4.5V to +5.5V
Program Voltage: +12.5V

Access Time: 170 to 450 nS

Logic: Supplied with a logic 1

Programming Pin: Pin 22

65536 × 8 BIT CMOS EPROM

A static memory device that is available in either NMOS or CMOS technologies. Both of these processes contribute to this 512K-bit EPROM's high-speed processing and low power consumption. There is a total programming space of 645536 words, each with an 8-bit width. Enormous programming libraries can be written into this IC. Operation is from a single +5V power supply with a +12.5V voltage required for programming. No clock signal is required for operation. Three-state output buffers provide this EPROM with TTL compatibility.

Device Example: VLSI Technology VT27C512

Package: 28-pin DIP with quartz window

Pin Connections:

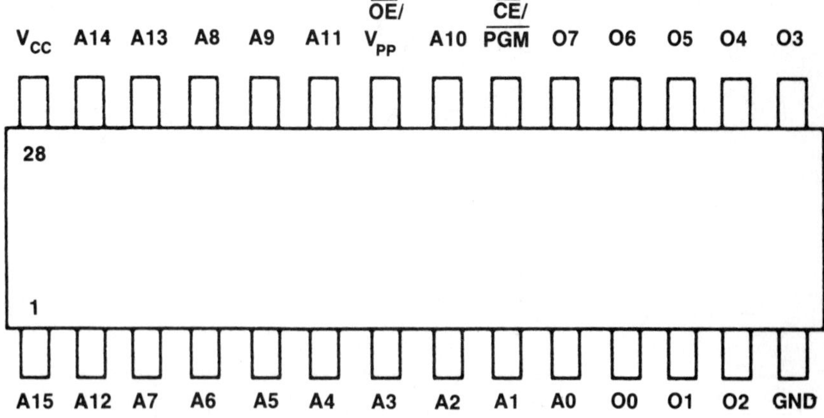

Temperature Range: Operating: 0°C to +70°C
Storage: −65°C to +125°C

Power Requirements: Supply Voltage: +4.5V to +5.5V
Program Voltage: +12.5V

Access Time: 170 to 450 nS

Logic: Supplied with a logic 1

Programming Pin: Pin 1

131072 × 8 BIT CMOS EPROM

Recent advances in the fabrication of EPROMs have lead to the 1024K-bit or 1M-bit EPROM. This static memory device is made with CMOS technology. The CMOS nature of this 1M-bit EPROM is vital in providing the highest processing speed with the lowest power consumption. The available programming space is a remarkable 131072 words, each with an 8-bit width. A programming area this large makes it possible for complete productivity software packages to be written into these EPROMs. This technology opens the door for microcomputer-based ROM drives. Operation is from a single +5V power supply with a +12.5V voltage required for programming. No clock signal is required for operation. Three-state output buffers provide this EPROM with TTL compatibility.

Device Example: Toshiba TC571000D

Package: 32-pin DIP with quartz window

Pin Connections:

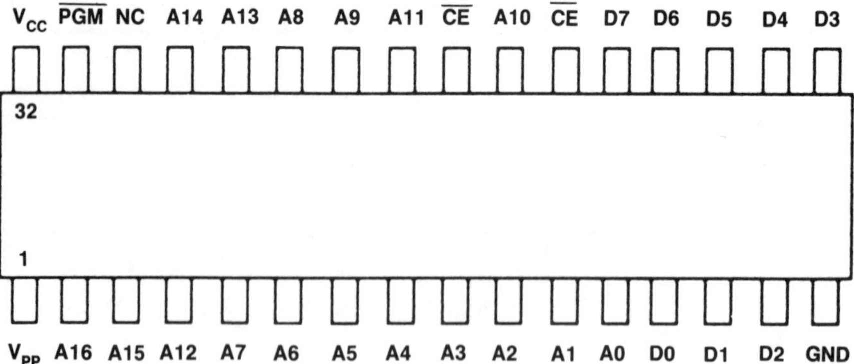

Temperature Range: Operating: 0°C to +70°C
Storage: −65°C to +125°C

Power Requirements: Supply Voltage: +4.5V to +5.5V
Program Voltage: +12.5V

Access Time: 150 to 200 nS

Logic: Supplied with a logic 1

Programming Pin: Pin 1

65536 × 16 BIT CMOS EPROM

New technologies, like Texas Instruments' HVCMOS, are making megabit EPROMs commonplace. Even the former barriers of IC lithography and mask photography are quickly being hurdled in the designs of EPROMs that are capable of dealing with the faster 32-bit microprocessors. This 1M-bit EPROM features a special internal memory arrangement with 65536 words holding 16-bit wide data. The static construction of this memory device eliminates the need for a clock signal during operation. The TTL-compatible output from this IC is 16 bits wide and provides an easy interface with a 32-bit microprocessor. Even with all of this power, this chip still operates from a single +5V power supply with a +12.5V voltage required for programming. Three-state output buffers provide this EPROM with TTL compatibility.

Device Example: Fujitsu MBM27C1024

Package: 40-pin DIP with quartz window

Pin Connections:

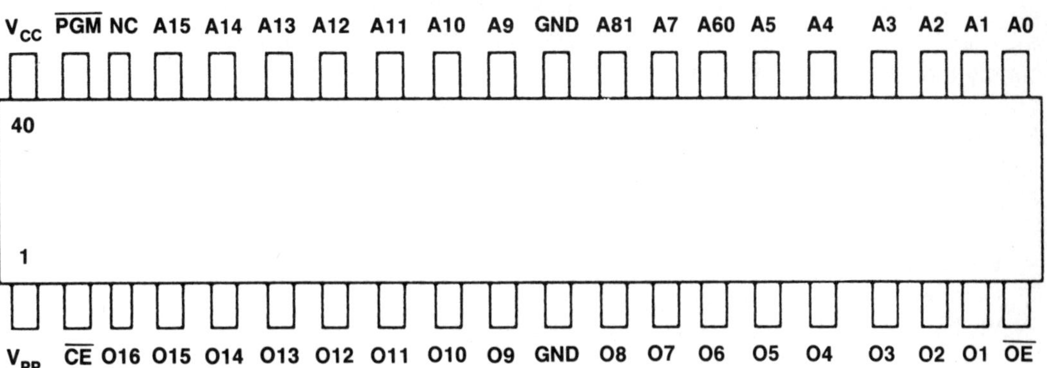

Temperature Range: Operating: 0°C to +70°C
Storage: −65°C to +125°C

Power Requirements: Supply Voltage: – +4.5V to +5.5V
Program Voltage: +12.5V

Access Time: 150 to 200 nS

Logic: Supplied with a logic 1

Programming Pin: Pin 1

6

The Bit Smasher

Integrating an EPROM into a circuit design is more than just a matter of skillful schematic diagramming. An important consideration must also be given to the actual programming of the EPROM. Programming an EPROM can be most simply thought of as the writing or "burning in" of a predetermined set of binary data at a specified address location. Once this data/address combination has been established it will eventually become the fixed inner workings of an EPROM. Before any programming can take place, however, three important EPROM selection criteria must be fulfilled:

- Write and debug the program.
- Determine the final size of the program.
- Match an EPROM to the required program space.

Granted, these first two selection factors are obvious in their merit. Creating an EPROM-based program "on-the-fly" would be a ridiculous, if not impossible, proposition. Therefore, careful planning and evaluation of the final program must be made prior to committing this data to the floating gates of an EPROM. There are two courses of action for writing, debugging, and sizing an eventual EPROM program.

The first method is the most laborious. In this case, all of the program's data must be entered physically into the intended circuit. Analog switches, RAM, ROM, and/or microcomputer-based terminal control could be used for evaluating the validity of the programming (see Fig. 6-1). No matter which of these techniques is used, however, only careful record keeping can hope to minimize the occurrence of error. Remember all of these test actions will

Fig. 6-1. Quartz erasure window of a 27128 EPROM.

need to be repeated during the programming of the target EPROM. As such, flicking analog switches can become extremely taxing even after testing only a 64-byte program.

Another far more practical evaluation method utilizes the storage and processing abilities of a microcomputer. This method also offers an answer to the need for accurate and thorough record keeping. By using a microcomputer, the intended program can be repeatedly tested, altered, and corrected with the results saved onto a floppy disk medium. Later when the EPROM is ready for receiving the programming, the microcomputer can serve as the host for transmitting the data and address locations to the EPROM for their subsequent writing. This processing, storage, and transmission ability of the microcomputer can be an important ally when programming a 512K-bit EPROM.

Following the solution to these first two steps in EPROM selection, the appropriate memory device must be chosen for receiving the programming. Faced with over 20 different EPROMs to choose from (this value is exclusive of the number of different EPROM manufacturers), the selection process can become cloudy. For the most part, however, the smaller memory organization size EPROMs can be eliminated. In other words, the 1702s, 2708s, 2716s, and 2732s offer such a limited amount of programming space that their use is impractical. A better solution would be found in the 2764s, 27128s, 27256s, and 27512s. These EPROMs contain the amount of data storage space that is capable of dealing with today's larger programming. For example,

- The 2764 is organized in an 8K × 8 or 64K-bit memory structure.
- The 27128 is organized in a 16K × 8 or 128K-bit memory structure.
- The 27256 is able to hold 32K × 8 or 256K bits of data.
- The 27512 can store up to 64K × 8 or 512K bits of data.

Another fringe benefit to using these larger capacity EPROMs is that many of them require a lower programming voltage. While this virtue isn't important when using pre-programmed EPROMs, its value does become readily apparent to the EPROM programmer.

EPROM PROGRAMMING CONSIDERATIONS

No matter which EPROM you select, there are a series of five simple programming steps that must be performed:

- Load the address on the EPROM's address pins.
- Load the program data on the EPROM's data pins.
- Disable the output enable.
- Apply the programming voltage.
- Pulse the program pin for approximately 50 mS.

Figure 6-2 is a representation of a typical EPROM. This figurative EPROM is pictured in its operational state. In other words, the power for this memory device is being drawn from the circuit with address and data control under the direction of an outside microprocessor.

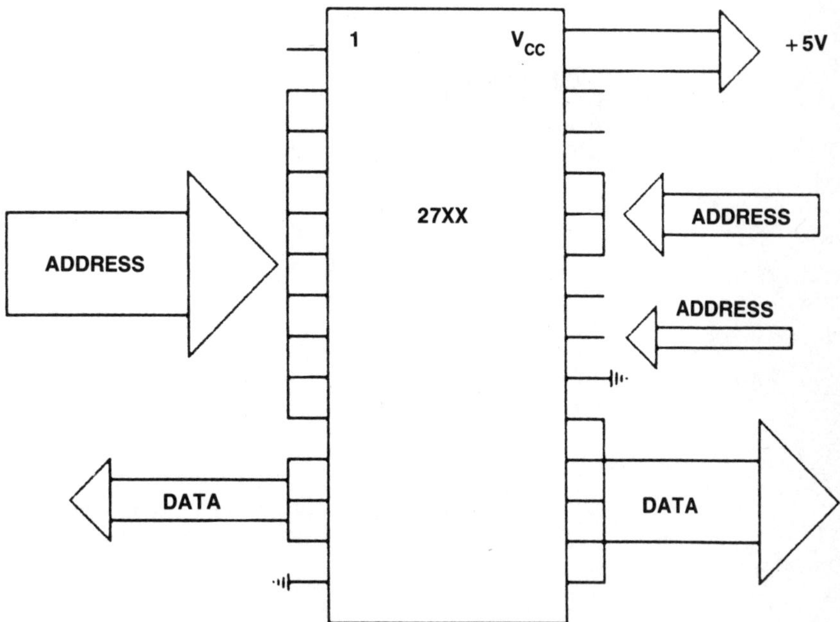

Fig. 6-2. A figurative operational 2764 EPROM.

During programming, the nature of the EPROM's pins changes. Figure 6-3 shows the loading of the IC's address lines (A0 to A12). In its operational state, this EPROM's address lines are used for specifying a memory location for reading its stored data. In its programming state, however, these same address lines are used for specifying the memory location for *writing* the programmed data. A typical 2764 EPROM is capable of programming 8192 memory locations; locations 00h (0 0000 0000 0000) through 1FFFh (1 1111 1111 1111).

Once the address lines have been loaded with the correct memory location, the location's data must be placed on the data input lines (O0 to O7). In Figure 6-4, the data output lines in the EPROM's operational state become the data input lines during programming. Within this illustration, O0 is the least significant bit (LSB) and O7 is the most significant bit (MSB).

The final three steps in EPROM programming involve pin-level voltage changes. The first of these changes deals with both the output enable and chip enable pins. Figure 6-5 shows that these pins are connected to the system power supply and ground, respectively, during programming. This connection

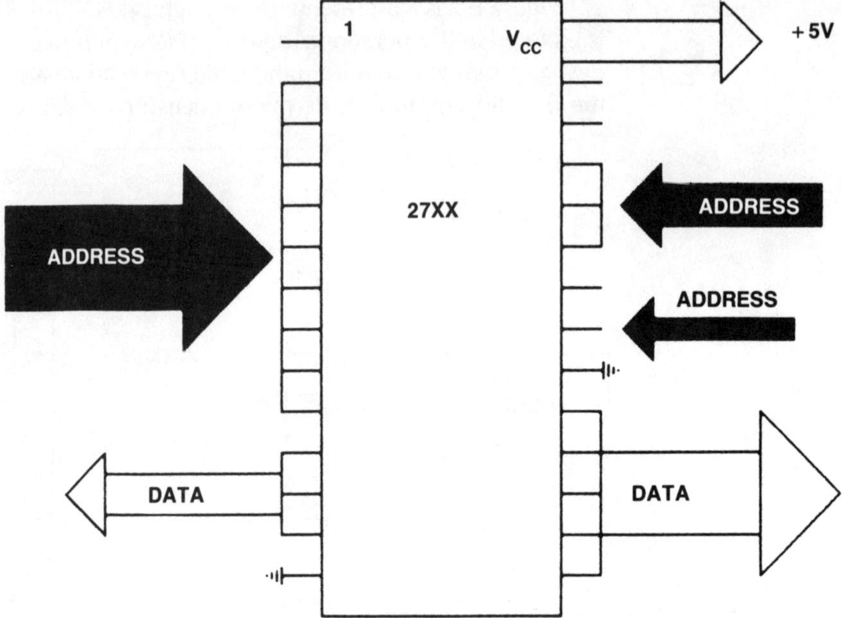

Fig. 6-3. In step 1 of programming a 2764 EPROM, the address is loaded onto pins A0-A12.

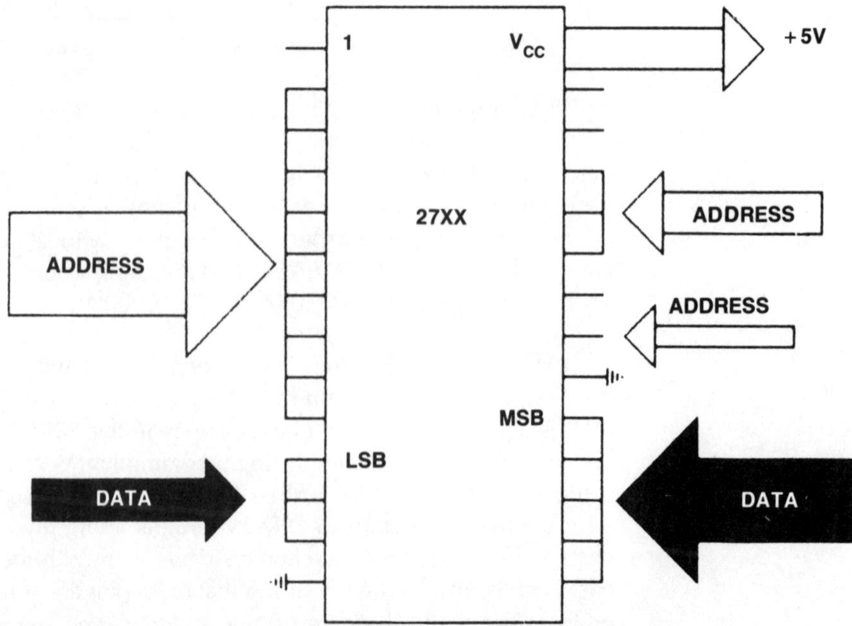

Fig. 6-4. Step 2, load the data onto pins D0-D7.

places the output enable in a TTL high and the chip enable in a TTL low condition. In its operational state, the EPROM's output enable and chip enable are both low. Therefore, making the output enable pin high disables this function and allows data to be written to the EPROM.

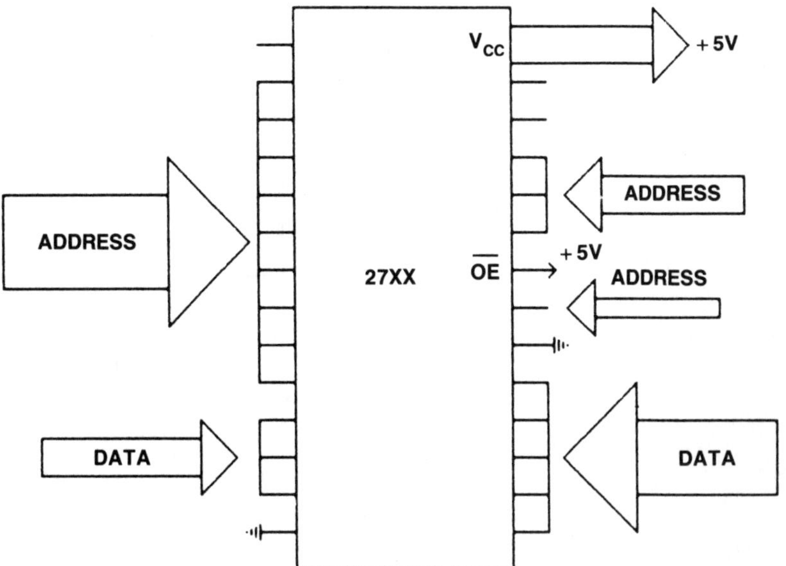

Fig. 6-5. Step 3, disable the output enable pin.

After bringing the output enable pin high and chip enable pin low, the programming voltage is applied to programming voltage supply pin (see Fig. 6-6). For the most part, there are three different programming voltages that must be met for today's EPROMs: +25V, +21V, and +12.5V. Of these three power levels, only the +21V and +12.5V are the most frequently used. These voltages cover the popular 2764, 2764A, 27128, and 27128A. Both of the "A" designated EPROMs (i.e., 2764A and 27128A) use the more convenient +12.5V programming voltage. Combining this modest programming voltage requirement with its large memory capacity, the 27128A should become your EPROM of choice.

The final step in the programming of an EPROM deals with a close tolerance pulse applied to the programming pin (see Fig. 6-7). This pulse, a high-to-low-to-high fluctuation, is the programming circuit's +5V TTL power supply that is channeled through the EPROM's programming pin. The duration of this pulse is critical to the successful programming of the EPROM. A standard of 50 mS (with a minimum of 45 mS and 55 mS being an absolute maximum) pulse duration is found on 2764, 2764A, 27128, and 27128A EPROMs. The accurate application of this pulse results in the latching and burning in of the set data at the specified address location.

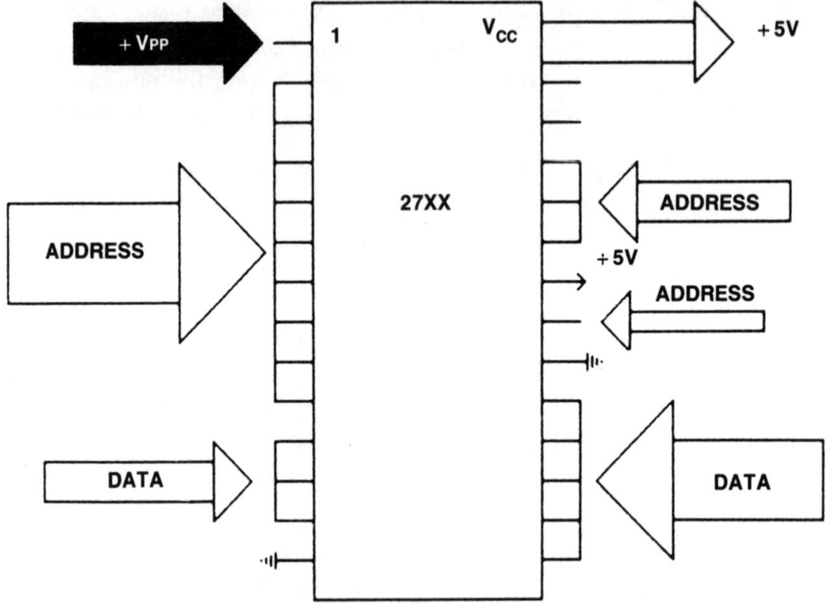

Fig. 6-6. Step 4, apply the programming voltage.

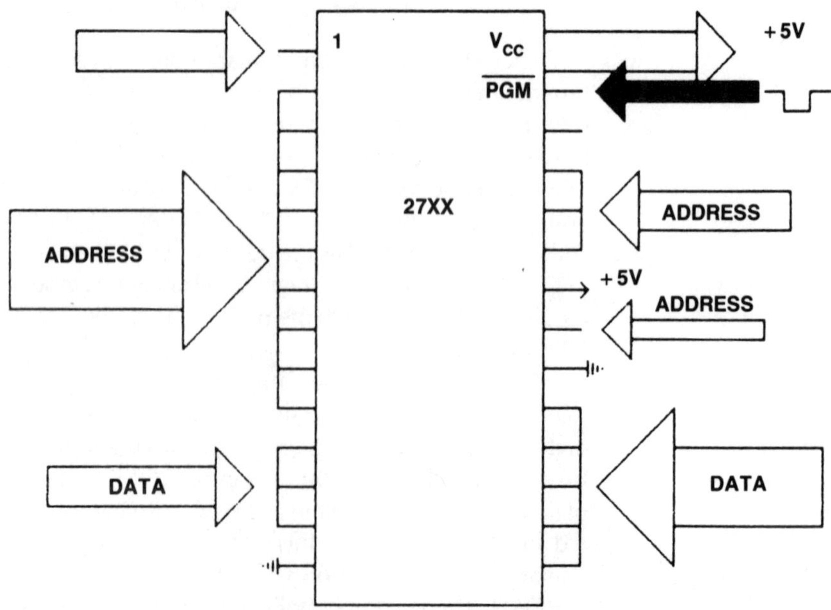

Fig. 6-7. Step 5, send the programming 50 mS pulse to the EPROM.

One problem with this pulse programming method is the length of time that is required to program the EPROM. For example, based on the 50 mS pulse duration, a 27128 EPROM requires approximately 13.7 minutes for complete programming (this time value is exclusive of the time that is needed for setting up the address and data lines). A solution to this time factor is available from several manufacturers. By using a fast programming algorithm based on a closed-loop verification cycle, EPROM programming times can be reduced dramatically. In operation, this fast algorithm uses an initial 1 mS pulse which is followed by a verification check. This initial pulse is repeated until the verification is positive. Once the check is correct, an over-program pulse of 3 to 4 times the initial pulse number is applied. In other words, if eight 1 mS initial pulses were required for proper testing, then a 24-to-32 mS over-program pulse would be applied. Therefore, a complete programming cycle with an average number of tests would take approximately 9.3 minutes on a 27128 EPROM.

A final requirement for fast-programming EPROMs is the manditory change in the IC's supply voltage. In normal programming and operation, this voltage is +5V. During fast programming, however, this voltage must be increased to +6V. Following the entire fast programming sequence of initial and over-program pulsing, the supply voltage must be returned to the native +5V state.

PROJECT 3: CONSTRUCTION OF THE BIT SMASHER

An extremely simple EPROM programmer can be constructed from a limited number of parts. The Bit Smasher (see Fig. 6-8) is a low-cost

Fig. 6-8. A prototype version of the Bit Smasher.

programmer that is able to write, verify, and read 2764 and 27128 EPROMs. As a cost-cutting measure, each of these operations is performed by hand through analog switches and LEDs. While this method does greatly reduce programming speed, the Bit Smasher is more than adequate enough for building all of the projects that are discussed in this book.

Only six ICs are necessary for building the Bit Smasher (see Fig. 6-9). Central among these chips is the 555 Timer. This IC, when coupled with two capacitors and a resistor, generates the 50 mS program pulse. This generated pulse is an inverse low-high-low pulse, therefore the signal is routed through a 7406 Hex Inverter Buffer/Driver with open-collector high-voltage output. This IC converts the pulse into the needed high-low-high pulse.

The Bit Smasher can be either constructed from point-to-point wiring or by using the supplied PCB (printed circuit board) template (see Fig. 6-10). If you are unfamiliar with using a PCB template, refer to Appendix A for complete instructions on preparing a solderable PCB. If you prepare a PCB, Fig. 6-11 shows the parts layout for soldering the components onto the finished board.

No matter which construction method you decide to use, begin by soldering five IC sockets to the selected board. Next the ZIF (zero insertion force) socket should be added. Follow the attachment of these sockets with the remaining resistor packs, capacitors, switches, LEDs, and potentiometer. Before you press the ICs into their sockets, make all of the power connections to the Bit Smasher.

TESTING THE BIT SMASHER

There are two levels of testing before the completed Bit Smasher can become a bona fide EPROM programmer. First, all of the power connections should be verified for their indicated voltages. Use the following procedure for testing the Bit Smasher voltages:

1. Make the power connections that are illustrated in Fig. 6-12.
2. Switch the power switch on. NOTE: Immediately turn switch off if you notice any excessive heat or smoke.
3. Obtain a multimeter.
4. Refer to Figure 6-13 for all voltage test locations.
5. Compare each indicated voltage with the correct results in the following table:

Bit Smasher Voltages

Test 1	+21 VDC
Test 2	+5 VDC
Test 3	< +2.0 VDC

C1 - 1mf electrolytic capacitor
C2 - .01mf capacitor
IC1 - 555
IC2 - 7406
IC3 - 317T
LED 1 - LED Light Bar
Q1 - MPS2222A
R1 - 10K-ohm resistor
R2 - 1K-ohm resistor DIP
R3 - 220-ohm resistor
R4-R5 - 4.7K-ohm resistor
R6 - 33K-ohm resistor
S1 - SPST NO switch
S2-S4 - SPST switch
SW1 - SPDT switch bank
ZIF 1 - 28-pin Zero insertion Force Socket

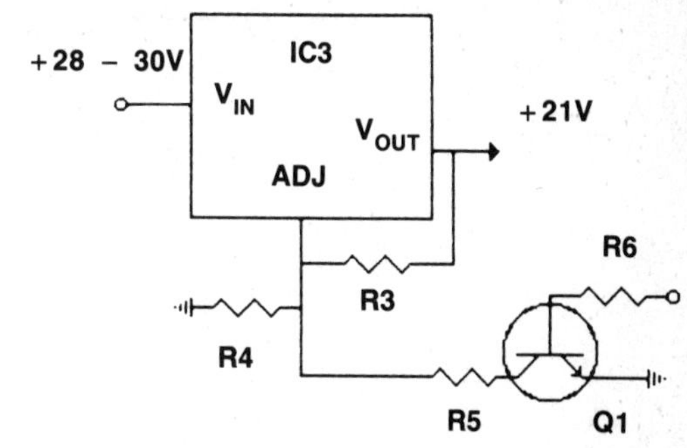

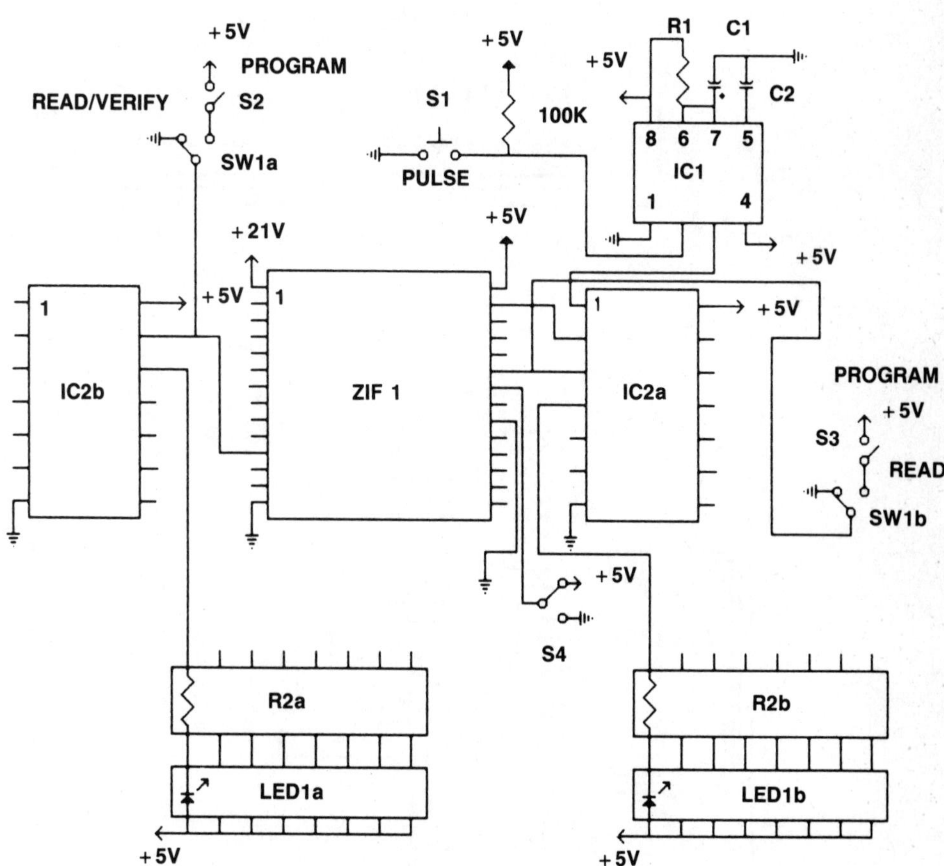

Fig. 6-9. Schematic diagram for the Bit Smasher.

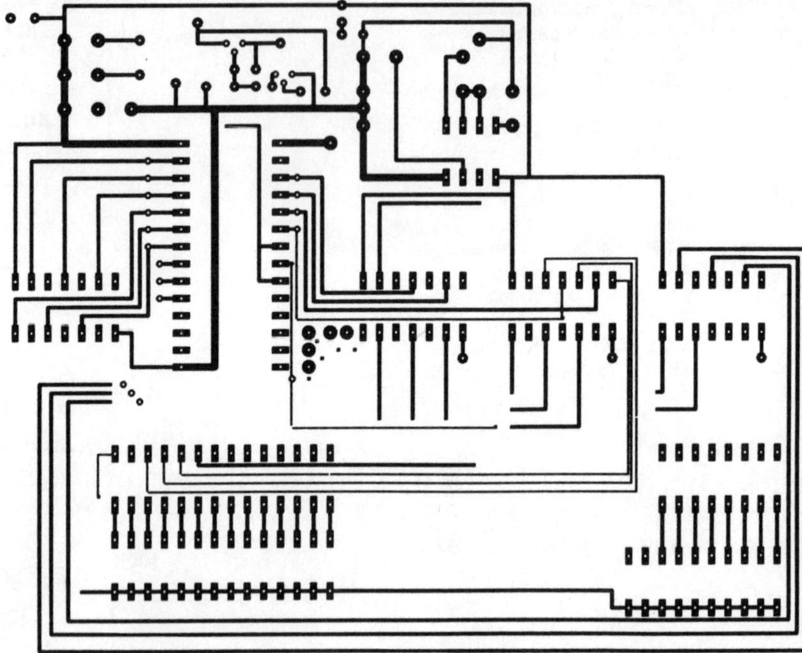

Fig. 6-10A. Component side of the Bit Smasher PCB template.

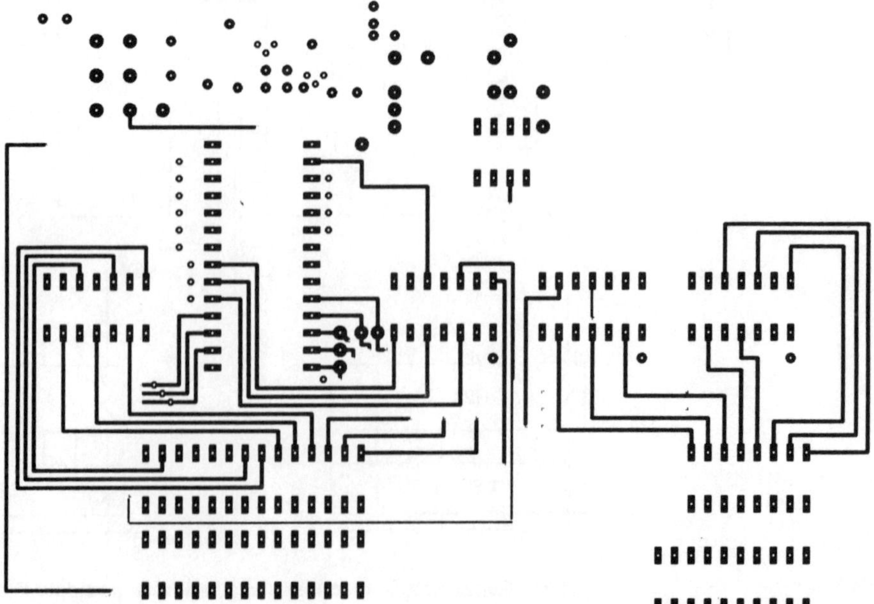

Fig. 6-10B. Solder side of the Bit Smasher PCB template.

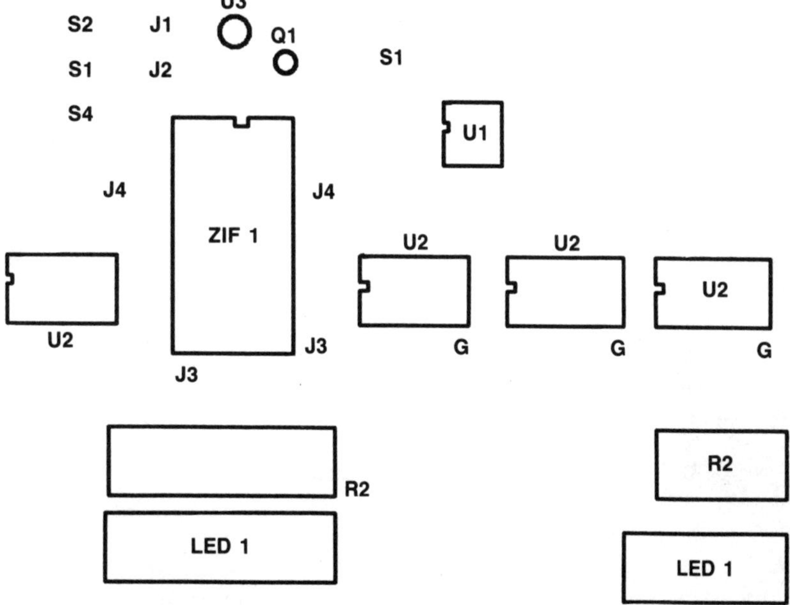

Fig. 6-11. Parts layout for the Bit Smasher PCB.

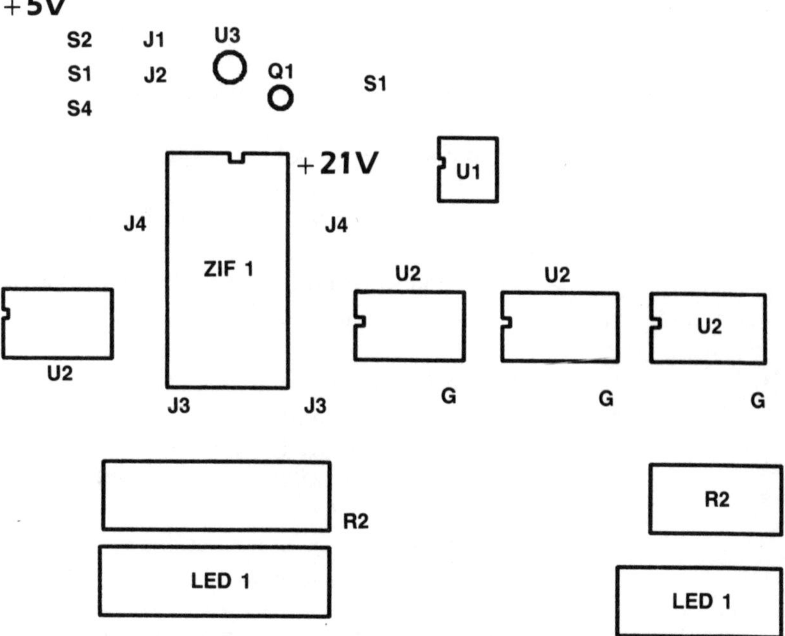

Fig. 6-12. Power connections for the Bit Smasher.

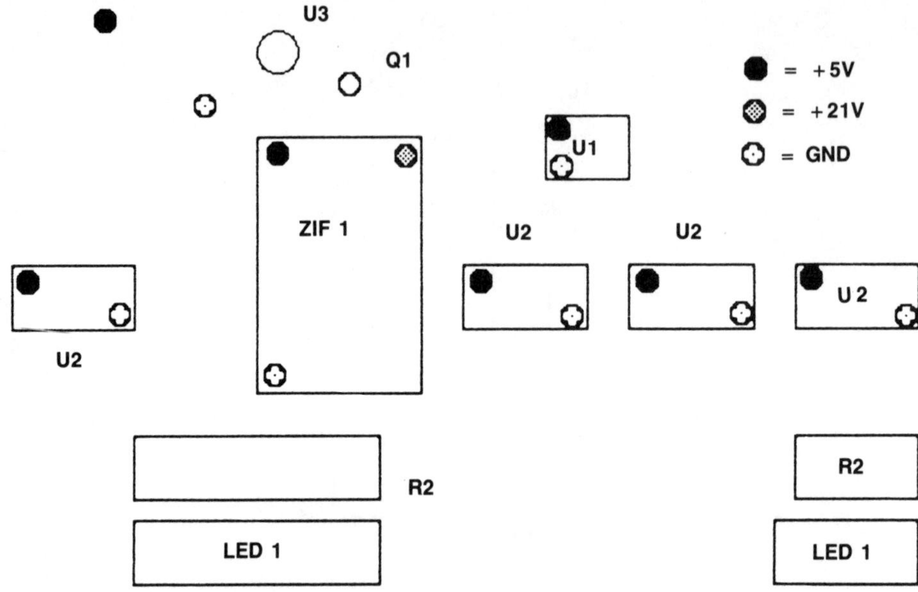

Fig. 6-13. Voltage test locations for the Bit Smasher.

If each of these voltage tests has been performed correctly, then all of the Bit Smasher ICs can now be inserted into their respective sockets. Figure 6-14 shows the socket for each IC. Now, with all of the ICs in their sockets, each of the voltage tests from steps 1 through 5 should be repeated. This time, however, use a logic probe for verifying the low and high status of each test location.

The final test for the completed Bit Smasher is an operational test. This test can be performed with either a 2764 or a 27128 EPROM inserted in the ZIF. If you are testing the 14-address-line 27128, remember to make an amendment to your test procedure that will accommodate the extra address line. Use the following procedure for testing the programming, verifying, and reading states of the Bit Smasher:

1. Use the switch settings and LED readings in Fig. 6-15 for conducting this battery of tests.
2. Read the address locations listed in Table 6-1.
3. Program each address location with its associated data as listed in Table 6-2.
4. Verify each programmed address location by reading the data from each memory location.

A careful construction technique will yield a 100 percent operational EPROM programmer. Should any of the above tests fail to execute properly,

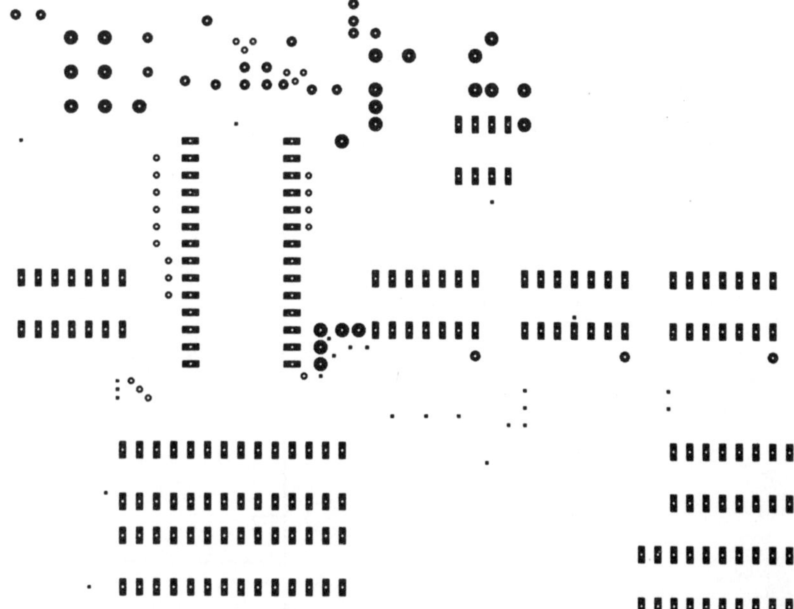

Fig. 6-14. IC socket locations for the Bit Smasher.

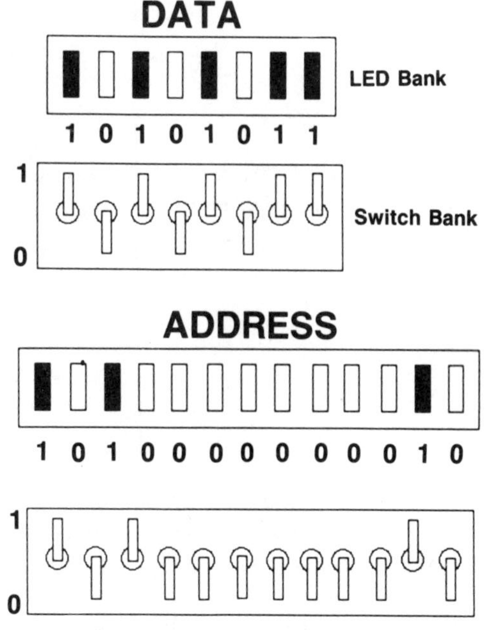

Fig. 6-15. LED readings for testing the Bit Smasher.

Table 6-1. Bit Smasher Read Address Locations

Address	Data
00000000	
00001111	
11110000	
10101010	
01010101	
11111111	
1000000000000	
1000000000001	
1111111111111	
*For the 27128:	
10000000000000	
10000000000001	
11111111111111	

Table 6-2. Bit Smasher Program Address Locations

Address	Data
00000000	00000000
00001111	00110011
11110000	11001100
10101010	00110011
01010101	11001100
11111111	00000000
1000000000000	11001100
1000000000001	00110011
1111111111111	00000000
*For the 27128:	
10000000000000	11001100
10000000000001	00110011
11111111111111	00000000

however, the culprit might be either the programming voltage or the programming pulse. A quick test from a multimeter can answer the programming voltage question. Unfortunately, two problems can plague the programming pulse. The first is the pulse shape and the second fault might be the pulse duration. In either case, an oscilloscope test is the only method for accurately determining the true shape and duration of this pulse.

USING THE BIT SMASHER

There are three operations that can be performed with the Bit Smasher: read, program, and verify. In this application, the read and verify operations are performed in the same manner.

Read

1. Place the Bit Smasher in the read mode (READ/VERIFY).
2. Neutralize the data switches.
3. Load the desired address location on the address switches.
4. Read the LED for the binary representation of the data at the loaded address location.

Program

1. Place the Bit Smasher in the program mode (PROGRAM).
2. Set the data switches to the correct binary representation.
3. Load the desired address location on the address switches.
4. Press the program button (PULSE).

Verify

1. Place the Bit Smasher in the verify mode (READ/VERIFY).
2. Neutralize the data switches.
3. Load the desired address location on the address switches.
4. Read the LED for the binary representation of the data at the loaded address location.

PROJECT 4: THE BIT SMASHER II

Whereas Bit Smasher was only able to run from household line current and program 2764 and 27128 EPROMs, Bit Smasher II is able to operate with battery power and program 2764A and 27128A EPROMs. The major advantage of using these suffix "A" EPROMs is the reduced programming voltage. A modest +12.5V on pin #1 is enough voltage for programming these memory devices. Furthermore, a nice power supply that is able to provide both the circuit voltage, as well as the +12.5V programming voltage can be constructed from a battery source.

All of the operational specifications for the Bit Smasher II are identical to those found on the original Bit Smasher. Only a minor modification to the power section of this EPROM programmer circuit is required (see Fig. 6-16). Figure 6-17 and Figure 6-18 show a revised PCB template and component layout diagram reflecting these changes, respectively.

A new set of test figures and tables stressing the new voltages of the Bit Smasher II are found in Figures 6-19 through 6-21 and Tables 6-7 and 6-8. During the testing of the Bit Smasher II, simply use these new illustrations and test values with the same test procedure that was outlined previously for the Bit Smasher.

Operationally, the Bit Smasher II follows the same read, program, and verify procedures as described for the Bit Smasher. There are only two

C3 - .1 mF electrolytic capacitor
C4 - 1 mF electrolytic capacitor
IC3 - 317T
R3 - 220-ohm resistor
R4 - 10K-ohm potentiometer

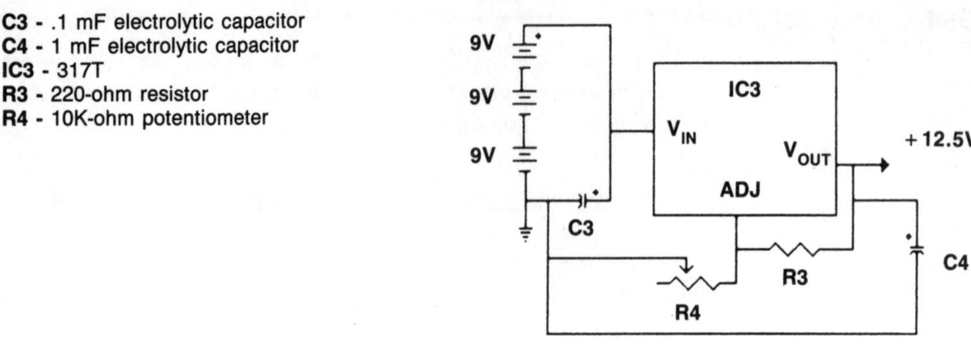

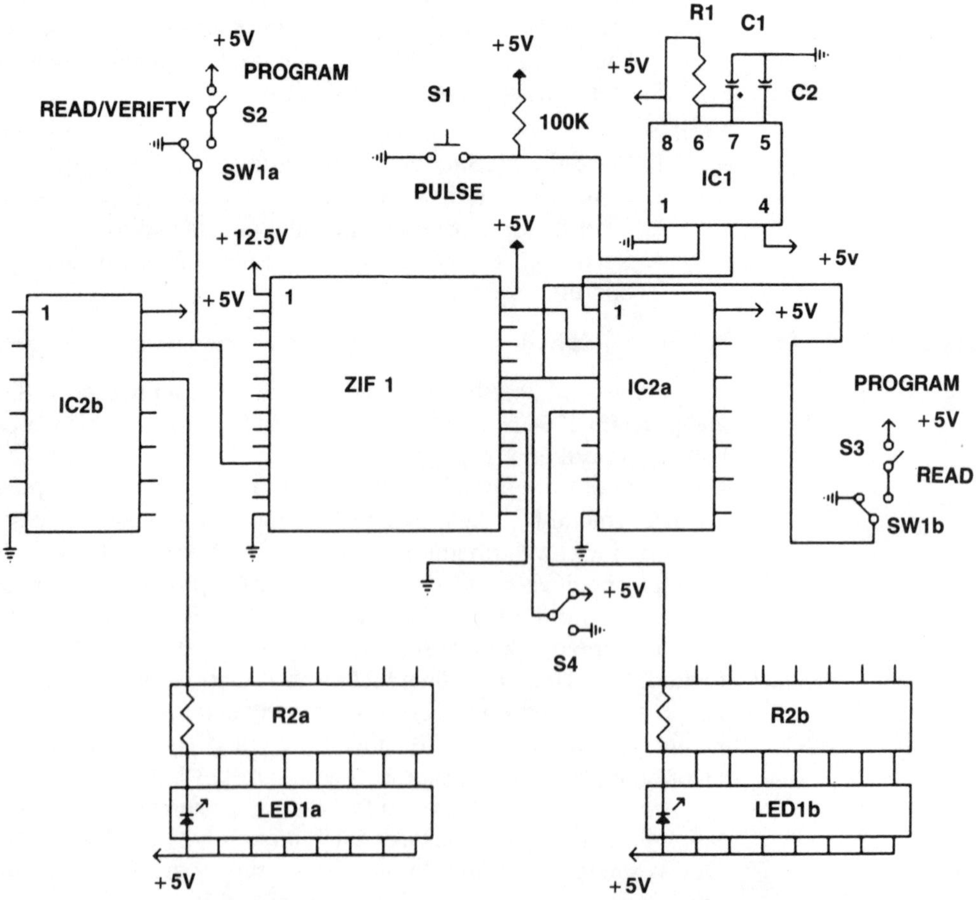

NOTE: Repeat I/O connections for all address and data lines.

Fig. 6-16. Schematic diagram for the Bit Smasher II power supply.

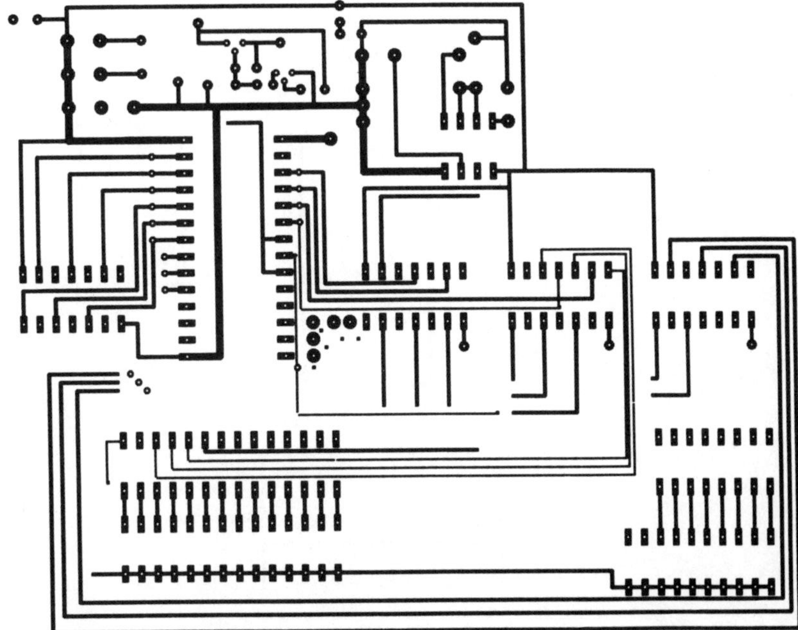

Fig. 6-17a. Component side of the Bit Smasher II PCB template.

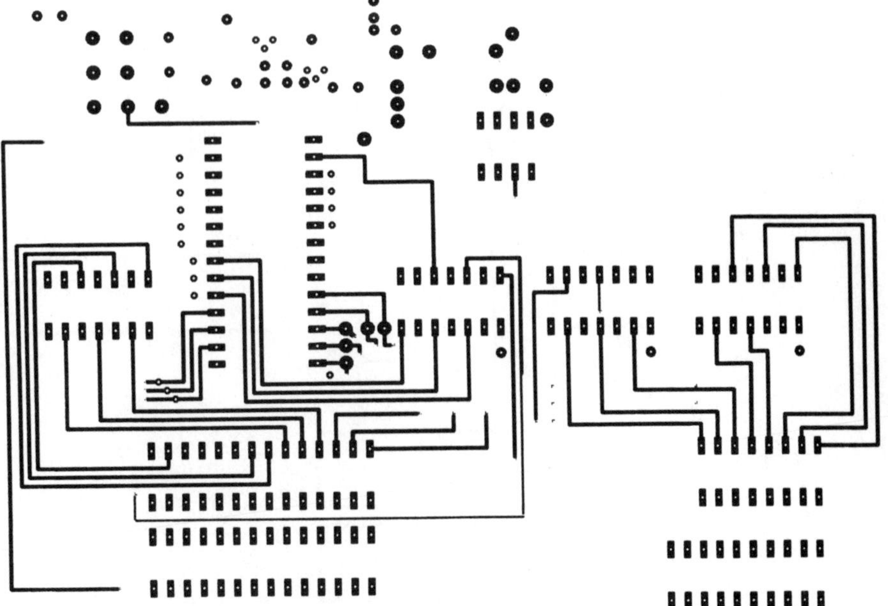

Fig. 6-17b. Solder side of the Bit Smasher II PCB template.

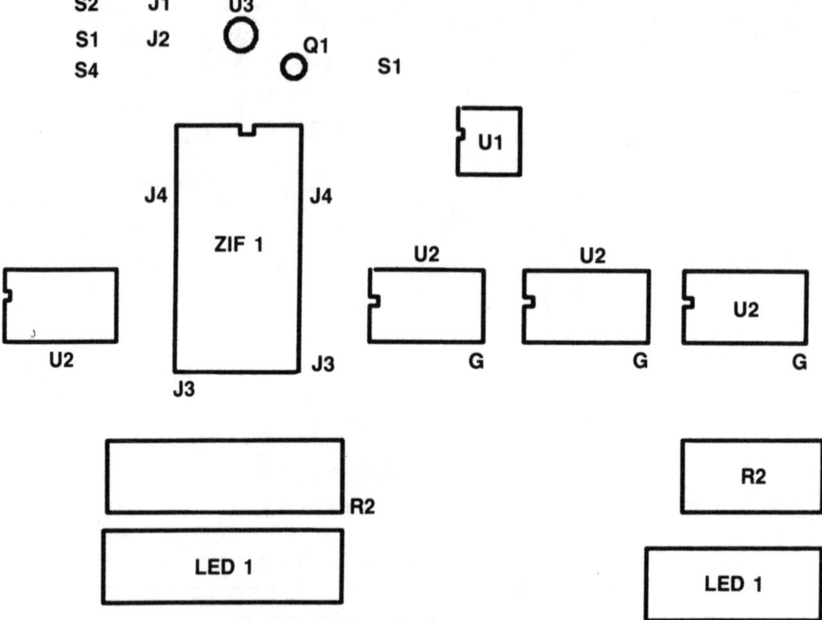

Fig. 6-18. Parts layout for the Bit Smasher II PCB.

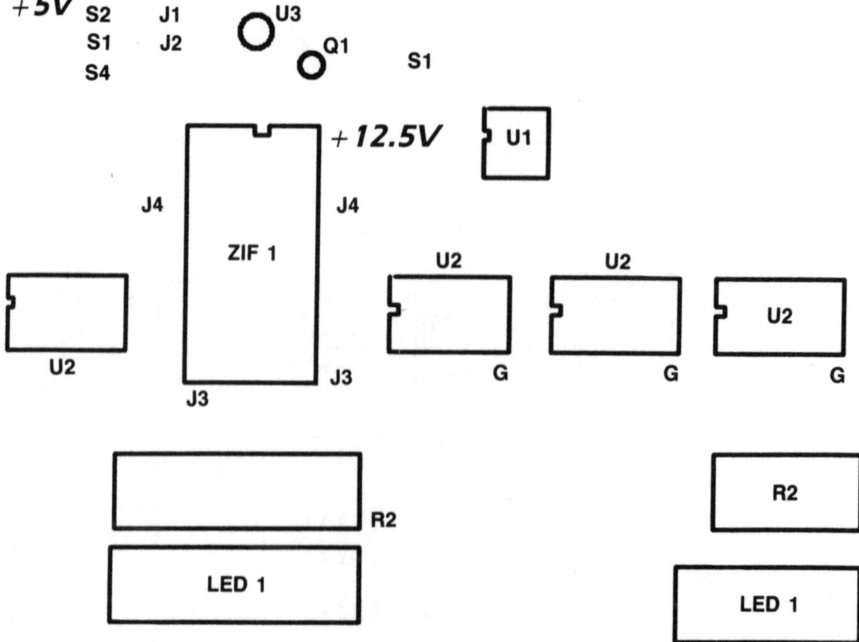

Fig. 6-19. Power connections for the Bit Smasher II.

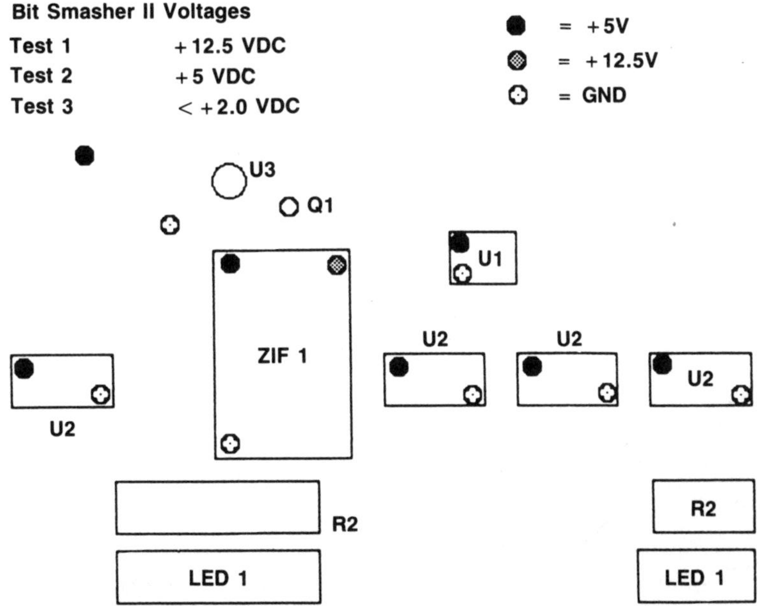

Fig. 6-20. Voltage test locations for the Bit Smasher II.

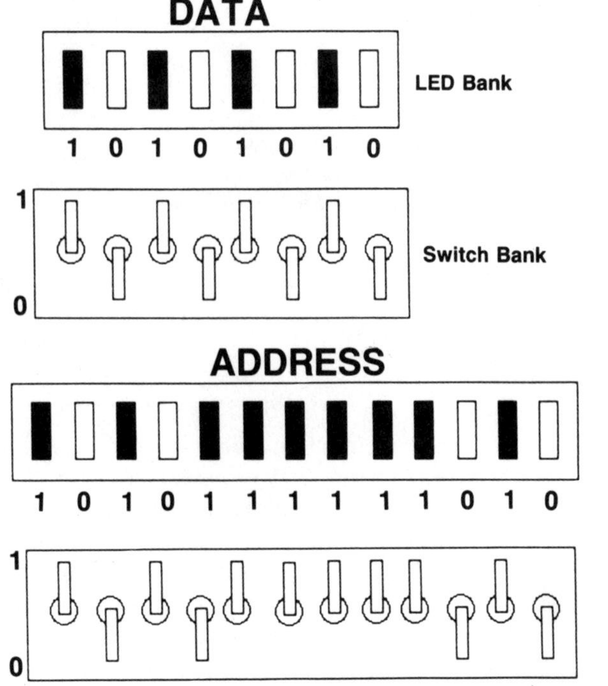

Fig. 6-21. LED readings for testing the Bit Smasher II.

Table 6-3. READ Address Locations for Testing the Bit Smasher.

Address	Data
00000000	
00001111	
11110000	
10101010	
01010101	
11111111	
1000000000000	
1000000000001	
1111111111111	
*For the 27128A:	
10000000000000	
10000000000001	
11111111111111	

Table 6-4. PROGRAM Address/Data Locations for Testing the Bit Smasher.

Address	Data
00000000	00000000
00001111	00110011
11110000	11001100
10101010	00110011
01010101	11001100
11111111	00000000
1000000000000	11001100
1000000000001	00110011
1111111111111	00000000
*For the 27128A:	
10000000000000	11001100
10000000000001	00110011
11111111111111	00000000

important functional differences that are inherent to the Bit Smasher II, however. First, the battery power supply must be kept fresh and within a 1 to 2 volt tolerance level. Failure to maintain the stated supply and programming voltage levels will lead to EPROM writing errors. Testing the voltages with a multimeter prior to use is an important safeguard against this problem.

The second point to consider during the operation of the Bit Smasher II is that this programmer has been designed for reading and writing 2764A and 27128A EPROMs only. Trying to program any other EPROM type can result in damage to both the EPROM and the Bit Smasher II.

7

EPROgraMmer

Programming an EPROM with the Bit Smasher of Chapter 6 can involve several hours worth of switch throwing and LED reading. When used for writing small programs that contain approximately 100 to 500 bytes of data, the inconvenience of the Bit Smasher's user interface is only a minor nuisance. But when attempting to fill the total 8K byte memory of a 2764, flicking these switches proves to be a debilitating limitation.

A superior solution to major EPROM programming efforts is *remote, redundant supervision*. Recognizing the need for some form of an external control source, this *new* EPROM programmer should feature the following aids:

- Write large 8K byte-plus programs into EPROMs
- Verify the address and data information during each write
- Read a specified EPROM memory location and display its data
- Provide automatic programming functions
- Work with numerous EPROM types
- Operate in varied environments
- Use a modest power supply
- Be expandable for accommodating future EPROM programming needs
- Offer intelligent EPROM programming options and control

Based on this lengthy list of requirements, the only means for satisfying all of these features is through a microcomputer-controlled EPROM programmer. Actually, these features are the specifications for the EPROgraMmer; a Centronics parallel-port-equipped EPROM programming peripheral. But how can an EPROM programmer connected to a computer's parallel port provide such elaborate writing and reading functions?

The operation of the EPROgraMmer is fully detailed in Fig. 7-1. Translation of this operational flowchart into strict digital circuit terms can prove to be confusing, however. Basically, the EPROgraMmer is initially set in either a program (WRITE) or read (READ) mode. Selection of the correct mode activates the proper chip enable pins on the EPROM and supplies the necessary operation voltages (i.e., +21V for WRITE and +5V for READ).

With this manual mode selection process completed, the actual EPROM programming or reading can begin. Both of these actions involves a different set of procedures. In programming a 2764 with the EPROgraMmer, for example, the host computer sends the required memory address location for programming through its parallel port. A Quad D-Type Flip-Flop with complementary outputs and common direct clear the 74LS175 clocks this byte into an Octal D Flip-Flop 74LS374 for latching and subsequent loading into the EPROM's upper address lines (A12 to A8). During this transmission, the computer is directed to wait until the EPROgraMmer is able to receive additional bytes.

When these upper five address lines have been latched, the computer is able to send the lower eight address lines (A7 to A0) in a second parallel byte through another 74LS374 via a clocked signal from the 74LS175.

On the command of the EPROgraMmer, a third byte, is sent from the controlling computer. As with the previous two bytes, this byte is latched by a third 74LS374 under the selection of the 74LS175. This third byte, which contains the 8 bits of programming data, is latched into the EPROM's data lines.

Now that both the address lines and the data lines have been loaded with the specified information, a fourth and final byte is sent from the computer for triggering the 50 mS programming pulse. As with the Bit Smasher, this programming pulse is provided by a resistor-capacitor configured 555 Timer.

Following the wave of this programming pulse, the 74LS175 is reset and the computer is requested to send another address for programming. This writing procedure is repeated for each address until the EPROM has been programmed. A set of LEDs provides a visual programming verification during the entire writing process. Using the EPROgraMmer, memory address locations do not have to be written in a sequential fashion. In other words, any address can be written to at anytime during programming.

Reading the memory contents of a 2764 address location is an even simpler operation with the EPROgraMmer. First, the programmer must be placed in the READ mode. This is performed through a manual switch flipping. Then using a similar address latching procedure the first five bits of the address's upper address location are sent from the computer to the EPROgraMmer via the parallel port.

Once a 74LS374 has latched this information, the byte indicating the lower address location is sent from the computer. At this point, the contents of the

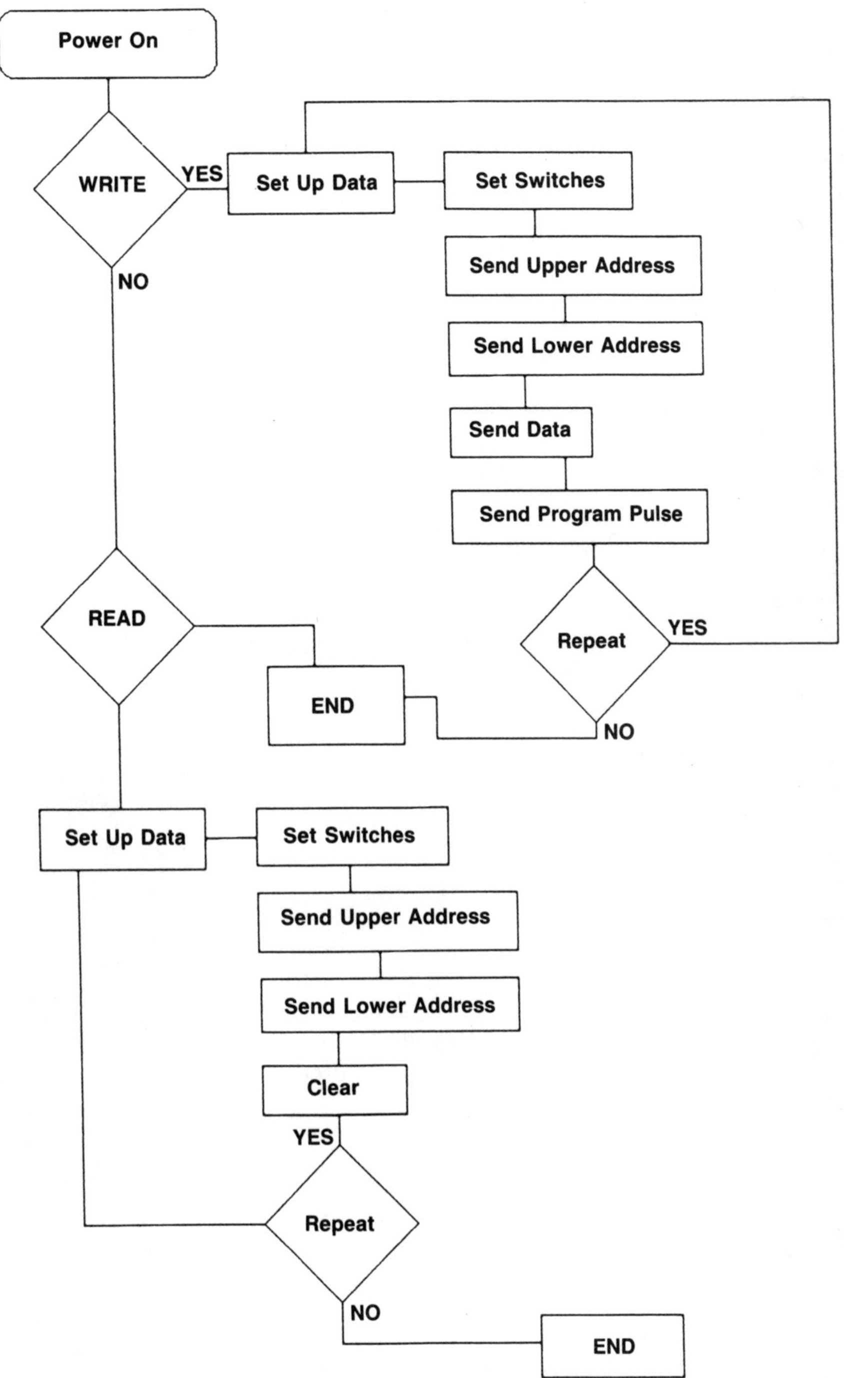

Fig. 7-1. Operational flowchart for the EPROgraMmer.

specified memory location can be read from the attached LEDs. This data display will be held until a precise software control signal is transmitted by the computer. Following this signal, another address location can be examined.

PROJECT 5: CONSTRUCTION OF THE EPROGRAMMER

The EPROgraMmer is a sophisticated EPROM programmer that is constructed from a handful of digital ICs. This low-cost circuit (see Fig. 7-2) is able to write, verify, and read 2764 and 27128 EPROMs. Any computer with a Centronics-type parallel port should be able to interact with the EPROgraMmer. At the very least only a few connections might need rerouting for meeting the port needs of other computers.

A total of 11 ICs are necessary for building the EPROgraMmer (see Fig. 7-3). The 74LS175 and three 74LS374s are the prime movers and carriers of the address and data information that is sent to the programmer from the computer. Signal differences in various computer's parallel ports might demand that additional buffers, inverters, and/or drivers be added to this basic circuit before any EPROMs can be burned.

Either point-to-point wiring or a homebrew PCB should be used for building the EPROgraMmer. Unlike the Bit Smasher, a PCB template has not been provided with this project. As a possible aid to the designing of your

Fig. 7-2. A 27128 EPROM inserted into the ZIF socket of a prototype version of the EPROgraMmer.

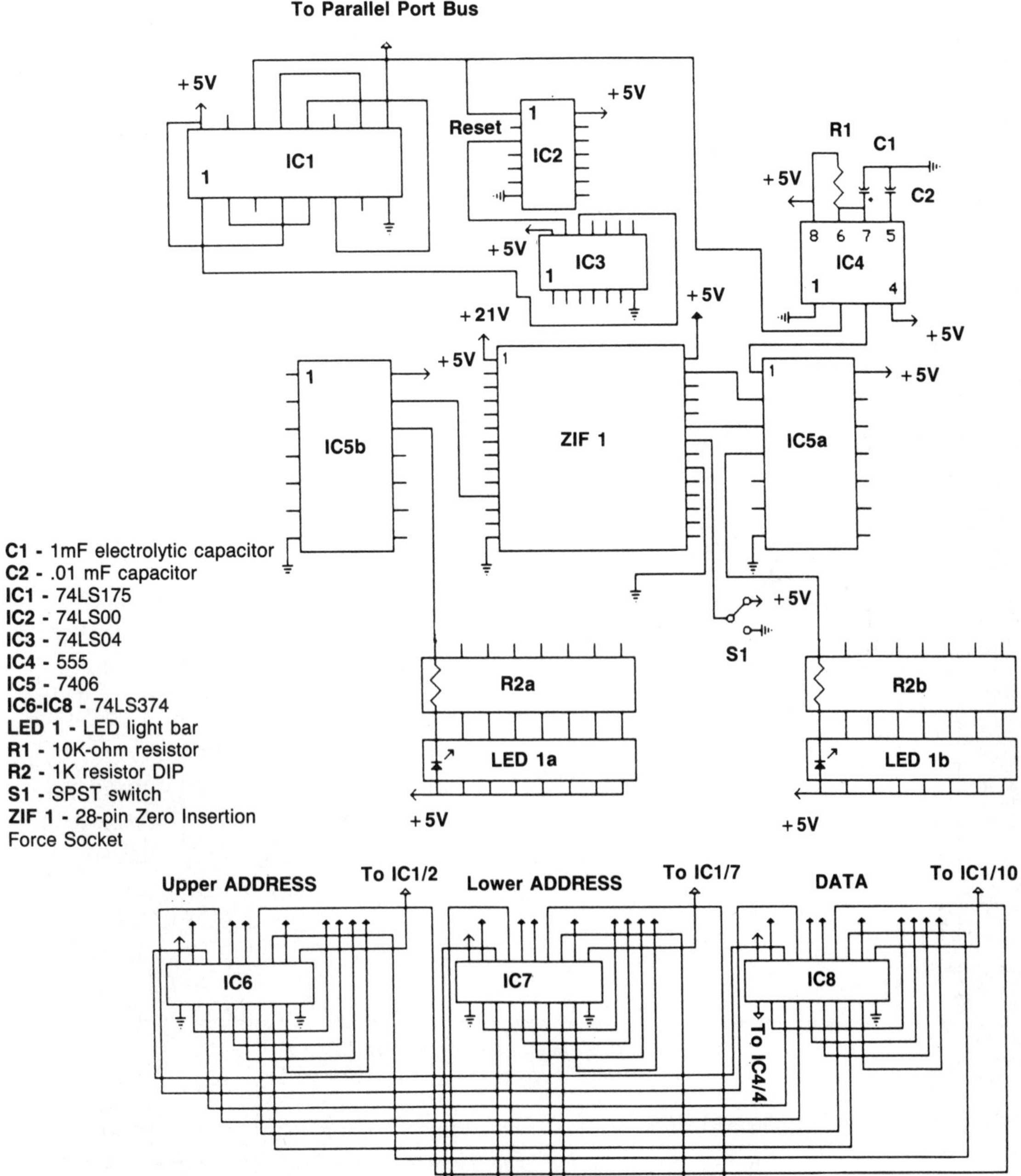

Fig. 7-3. Schematic diagram of the EPROgraMmer.

own PCB template, a suggested parts layout for the needed components is shown in Fig. 7-4.

Construction follows the same path as used with the Bit Smasher. The first step is to solder all of the IC sockets into their respective locations on the board. After these sockets have been positioned, a ZIF socket, for holding the target EPROMs during programming, should be soldered into place. With all of the sockets attached, the remaining support components (resistors, capacitors, LEDs, diodes) can be soldered onto the board. Before the ICs are pressed into their sockets, all of the power supply connections should be made to the circuit board. The completed EPROgraMmer is now ready for testing.

U1 = 74LS175
U2 = 74LS00
U3 = 74LS04
U4 = 555
U5 = 7406
U6 = 74LS374
U7 = 74LS374
U8 = 74LS374
P1 = Parallel Port Connector
ZIF 1 = Zero Insertion Force Socket
R2 = Resistor DIP
LED = LED Light Bar

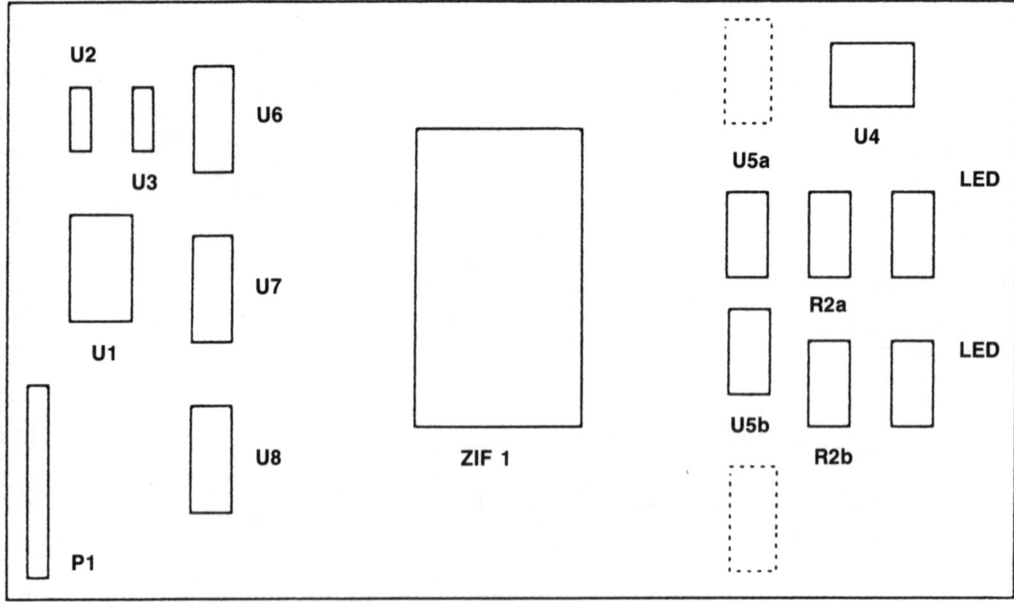

Fig. 7-4. Parts layout for the EPROgraMmer.

TESTING THE EPROGRAMMER

Before any of the ICs have been added to the EPROgraMmer, all of the power supply voltage levels should be tested. These connections can be verified by following this outlined procedure:

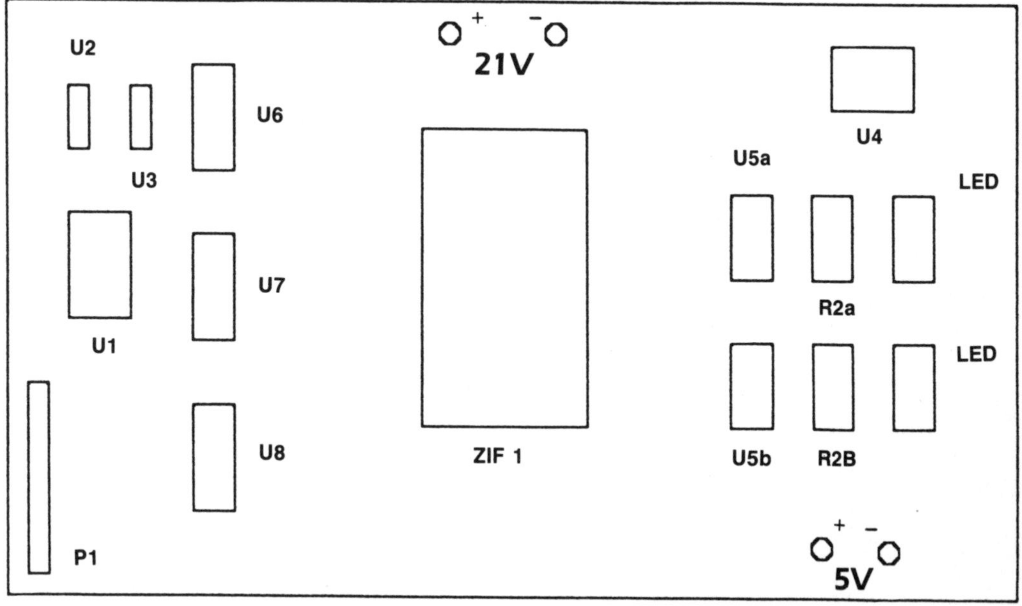

Fig. 7-5. Power connections for the EPROgraMmer.

1. Make the power connections that are illustrated in Fig. 7-5.
2. Switch the power switch on. NOTE: Immediately turn this switch off if you notice any excessive heat or smoke.
3. Obtain a multimeter.
4. Refer to Fig. 7-6 for all voltage test locations.
5. Compare each indicated voltage with the correct results in the following table.

Test 1	+21 VDC
Test 2	+5 VDC
Test 3	< +2.0 VDC

If each of these voltage tests yielded good results, then all of the EPROgraMmer's ICs can now be inserted into their respective sockets. Figure 7-7 shows the correct socket for each IC. Now, with all of the ICs in their sockets, each of the voltage tests from steps 1-5 should be repeated. This time, however, use a logic probe for verifying the low and high status of each test location.

There is one last test for the assembled EPROgraMmer. This is an operational test. A 2764 should be inserted into the ZIF socket during this

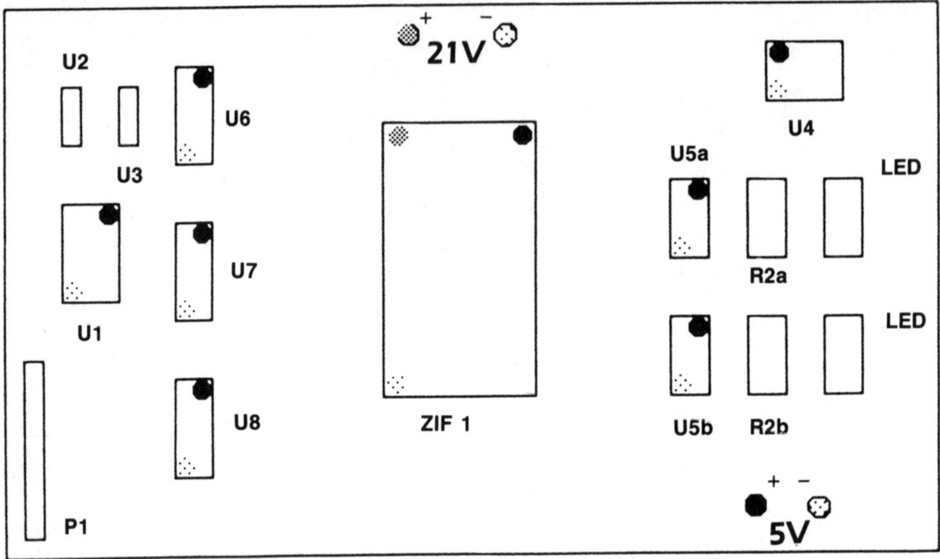

Fig. 7-6. Voltage test locations for the EPROgraMmer.

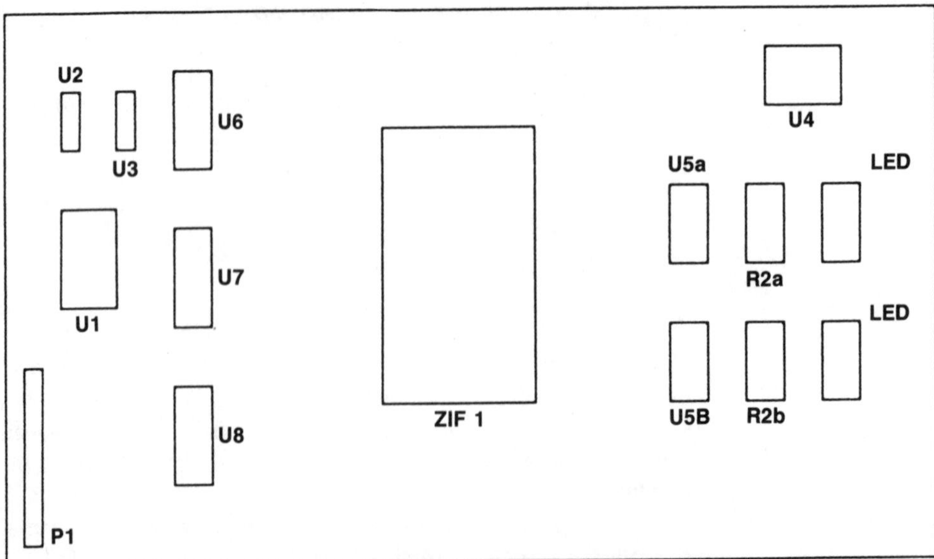

Fig. 7-7. IC socket locations for the EPROgraMmer.

test. The following test procedure will check the programming, verifying, and reading states of the EPROgraMmer:

1. Use the LED readings in Fig. 7-8 and the following program for conducting this battery of tests.
2. Read the target EPROM's address locations.
3. Program each address location with its associated data.
4. Verify each programmed address location by reading the data from each memory location LED bank.

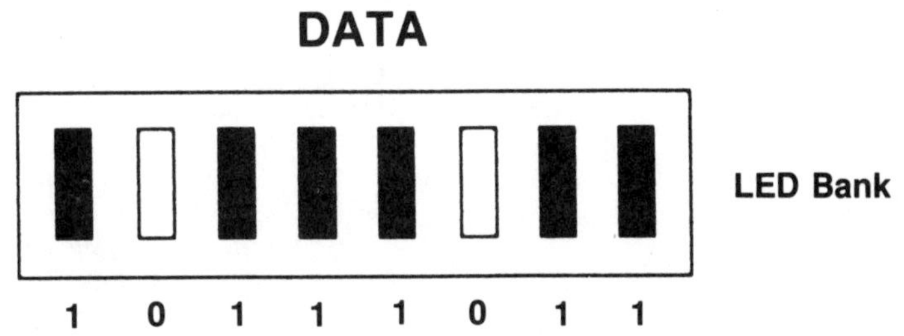

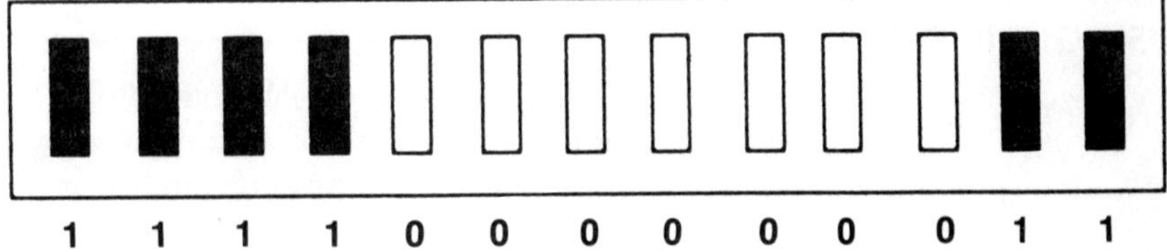


```
100 ON ERROR GOTO 160
110 REM INSERT THE PRINTER PORT VALUES FOR PORT ADDRESSES
120 READ X
130 OUT Y,X
140 WAIT Z, 128, 128
150 GOTO 120
160 END
170 REM THIS IS THE PROGRAM DATA
180 REM EXAMPLE [DATA 128, 0, 204, 255]
190 REM THIS EXAMPLE SETS THE UPPER ADDRESS AT 10000000
200 REM SETS THE LOWER ADDRESS AT 00000000
210 REM SETS THE DATA AT 11001100
220 REM PROGRAMS THE EPROM WITH 11111111
```

Fig. 7-8. LED readings for testing the EPROgraMmer.

If you followed all of the above construction and testing procedures, then the EPROgraMmer is now ready for operational use. Problems at this point, however, might be attributable to the parallel port interface. Figure 7-9 is a pin connection diagram for the EPROgraMmer's designed parallel port. This specification follows the pin assignments used in the IBM PC parallel port (e.g., IBM Monochrome Display and Printer Adapter). Other parallel ports can be easily modified to this specification through a converter cable.

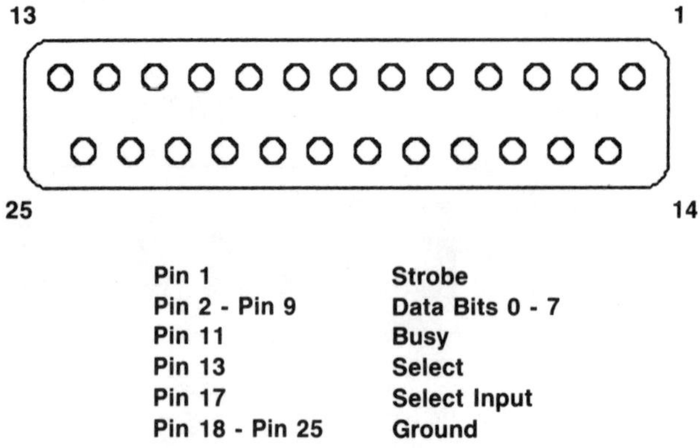

Fig. 7-9. Pin assignments for the IBM PC Monochrome Adapter parallel port.

USING THE EPROGRAMMER

Three EPROM operations can be performed with the EPROgraMmer: read, program, and verify. Each operation is controlled by a host computer. Both 2764 and 27128 EPROMs can be programmed in this manner.

Read

1. Set the EPROgraMmer mode switch in the read position (READ).
2. Send the upper five address bits via the host computer's parallel port (the 27128 will need six address bits).
3. Send the lower eight address bits to the EPROgraMmer.
4. Read the LED bank for the binary representation of the data at the loaded address location.
5. Clear the address lines for the next read.

Program

1. Set the EPROgraMmer switch in the program mode (WRITE).
2. Transmit the upper five (2764) or six (27128) address bits.
3. Transmit the lower eight address bits.
4. Send the data byte over the computer's parallel port.
5. Send the program pulse command.

Verify

1. This is an interactive operation that occurs during programming.
2. Following the transmission of the data byte, the data line LED bank will show the information that is being programmed.
3. Read the LED for the binary representation of the data at this time.
4. An incorrect data byte can only be corrected by erasing the entire EPROM. (NOTE: In extremely rare cases, an incorrect data byte can be corrected by rewriting the address location. This correction method is only possible where a programmed logic 1 is to be reprogrammed as a logic 0.)

PROJECT 6: THE EPROGRAMMER II

The virtues of computer programming can also be applied to the low-voltage 2764A and 27128A EPROMs. This alteration also simplifies the original EPROgraMmer design and enables this computer-based programmer to operate with battery power. Basically, the reduced programming voltage of the 2764A and 27128A, a modest +12.5V, can be supplied with a battery pack. Furthermore, this same power source can also be made to drive the EPROgraMmer circuitry. This results in a truly portable, computer-based EPROM programmer.

Most of the operational specifications for the EPROgraMmer II remain the same as those of the original EPROgraMmer. By changing the power section of this EPROM programmer, a battery-powered circuit can be interfaced to even small portable notebook-style computers (see Fig. 7-10). Figure 7-11

Parts List

C1 - .1mF electrolytic capacitor
C2 - 1mF electrolytic capacitor
IC1 - 317T
R2 - 22-ohm resistor
R1- 10K-ohm potentiometer

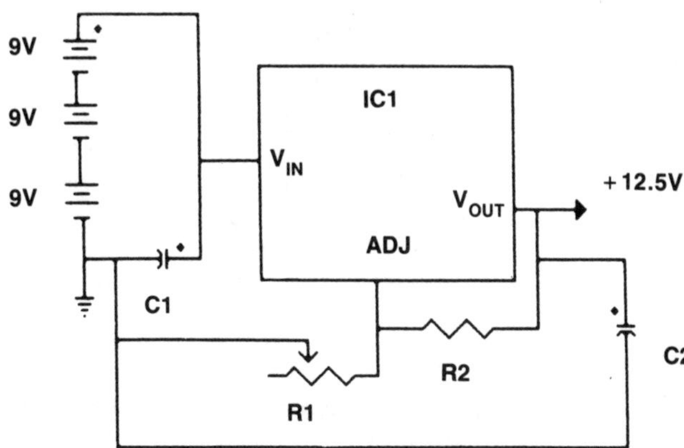

Fig. 7-10. Schematic diagram for the EPROgraMmer II power supply.

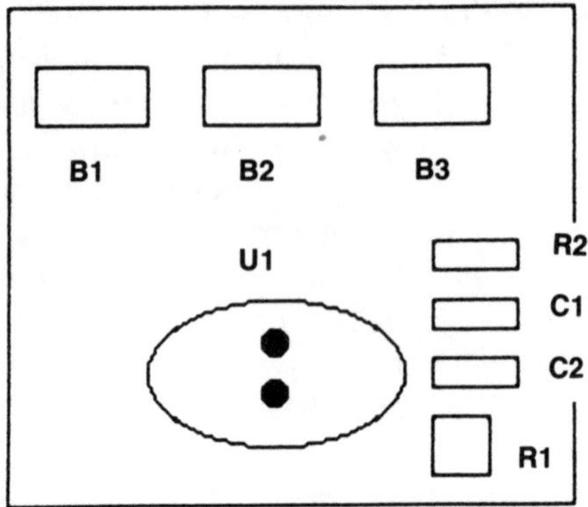

Fig. 7-11. Parts layout for the EPROgraMmer II power supply.

shows a suggested component layout for designing a PCB template.

New test figures and tables stressing the reduced voltages of the EPROgraMmer II are found in Figs. 7-12 through 7-14. Use these new illustrations and test values for the EPROgraMmer II with the test procedures that were previously discussed for the EPROgraMmer.

The EPROgraMmer II uses the same read, program, and verify procedures as described for the EPROgraMmer. For the best results, however, remember

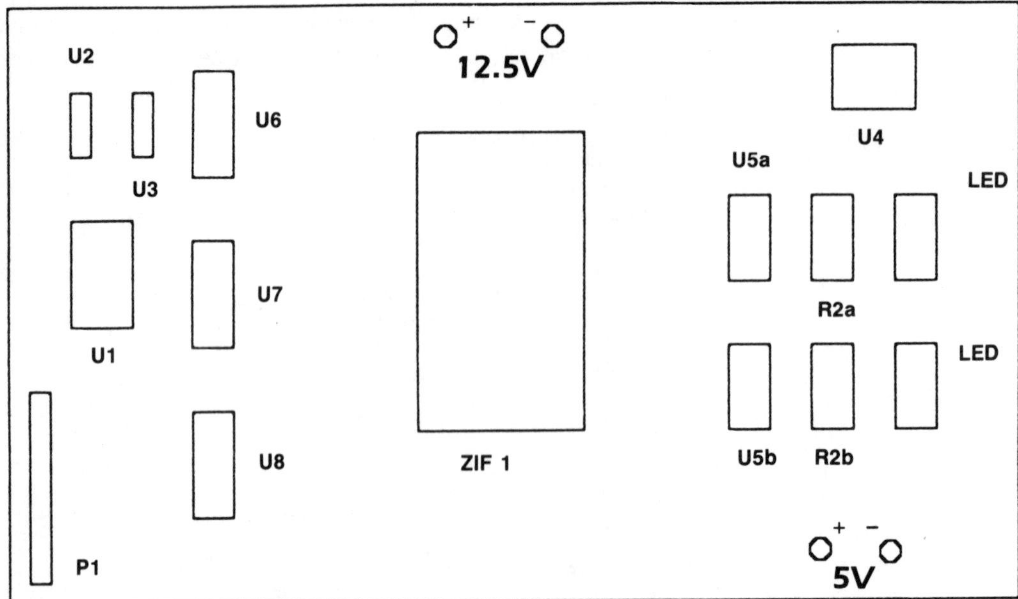

Fig. 7-12. Power connections for the EPROgraMmer II.

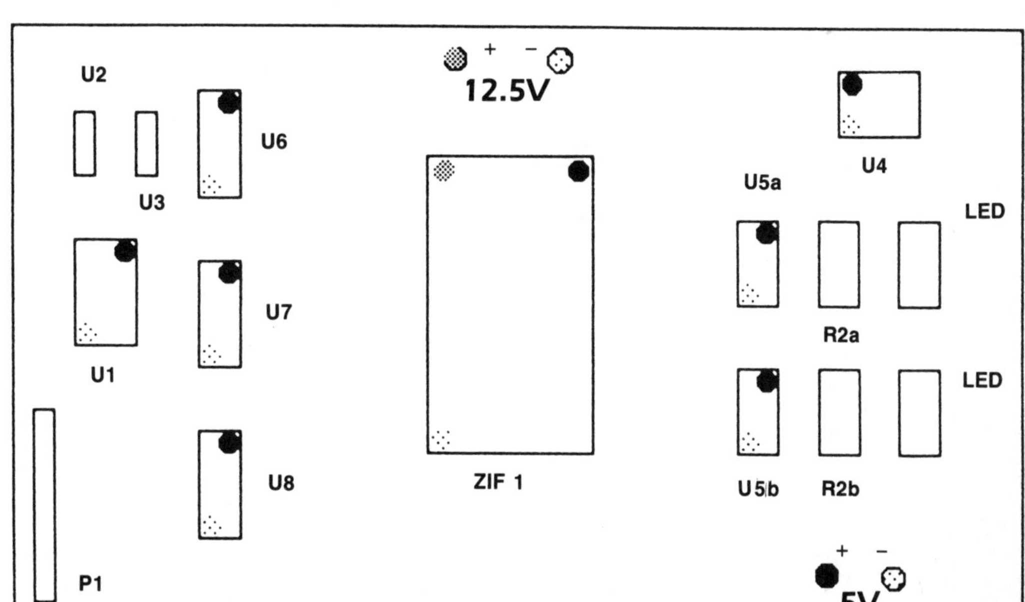

● = +5V

▒ = +12.5V

∴ = GND

EPROgraMmer II Voltages

Test 1	**+12.5 VDC**
Test 2	**+5 VDC**
Test 3	**< +2.0 VDC**

Fig. 7-13. Voltage test locations for the EPROgraMmer II.

these two points inherent to the EPROgraMmer II, however. First, keep the battery power supply fresh and within a 1 to 2 volt tolerance level. Straying outside this voltage can lead to EPROM writing errors. The current voltages can easily be monitored with a multimeter.

The second operational point to remember is that this programmer has been designed for reading and writing 2764A and 27128A EPROMs, only. Trying to program any other EPROM type can result in damage to both the EPROM, the EPROgraMmer II, and, possibly, the host computer's parallel port.

U1 = 74LS175
U2 = 74LS00
U3 = 74LS04
U4 = 555
U5 = 7406
U6 = 74LS374
U7 = 74LS374
U8 = 74LS374
P1 = Parallel Port Connector
ZIF 1 = Zero Insertion Force Socket
R2 = Resistor DIP
LED = LED Light Bar

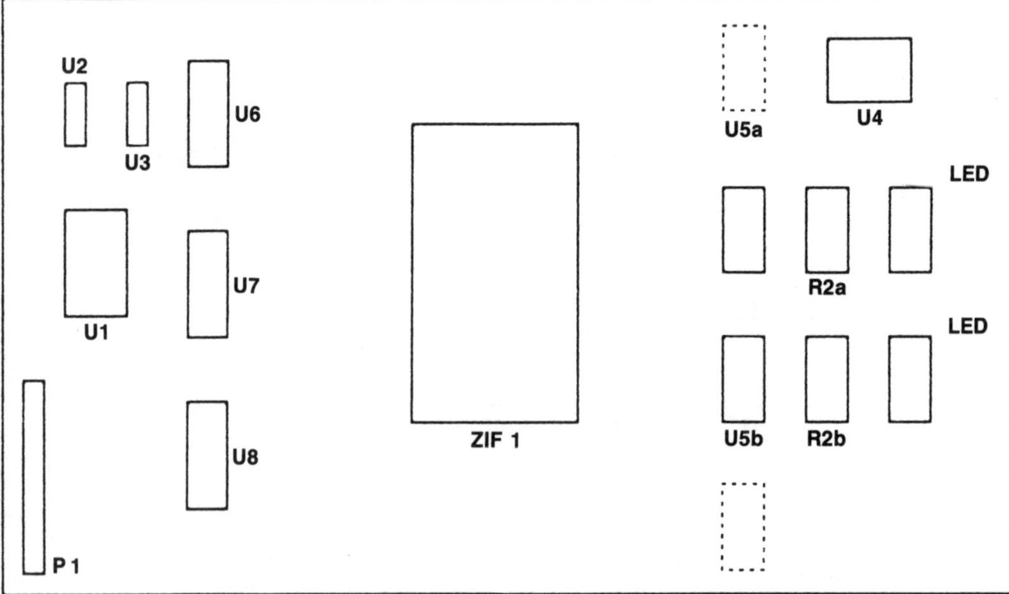

Fig. 7-14. IC socket locations for the EPROgraMmer II.

PROJECT 7: THE THREE-LINE BURNER

One drawback to using a parallel port interface for programming EPROMs is that true, intelligent interaction with the computer is lost. In other words, there is no way for the EPROM programmer to directly communicate with the computer. Granted, both EPROgraMmer and EPROgraMmer II are able to halt the sending of data, but neither programmer is able to send a memory location's data back to the host, for example. This limitation can be a serious negative point in a completely computer-directed EPROM programming, verifying, and reading session.

The most direct solution to this problem is a serial EPROM programmer. By using a host computer's RS-232C serial port, the programmer could not only receive address and data information, but it could also send this information back to the computer. This is the basis for the Three-Line Burner.

By adding three new ICs to the original EPROgraMmer, the Three-Line Burner is born. Foremost among this new triad of chips is the universal asynchronous receiver/transmitter (UART). This is a serial-to-parallel conversion chip that takes all of the address and data bits that are received in serial fashion from the computer and transfers them in a parallel fashion to the EPROM. As an alternative to the Intersil ICL232, two ICs can be substituted for driving the UART: Quad Line Driver MC1488 and Quad Line Receiver MC1489.

Figure 7-15 shows the completed Three-Line Burner along with its associated parts list. A suggested parts layout for a PCB design is illustrated in Fig. 7-16.

The testing of the Three-Line Burner follows the same procedures used for evaluating the EPROgraMmer II.

Even though the Three-Line Burner is a serial device, it follows the same read, program, and verify procedures as described for the EPROgraMmer and the EPROgraMmer II. You will require new software, however. The following program demonstrates the modifications that will be necessary for driving the Three-Line Burner with an RS-232C port.

```
100 ON ERROR GOTO 160
110 OPEN ''COM1:300,N,8,1'' AS #1
120 READ X
130 IF X=1001 THEN GOTO 160
140 PRINT#1,X
150 GOTO 120
160 CLOSE#1:END
170 REM THIS IS THE PROGRAM DATA
180 REM EXAMPLE (DATA 128, 0, 204, 255, 1001)
190 REM THIS EXAMPLE SETS THE UPPER ADDRESS AT
    10000000
200 REM SETS THE LOWER ADDRESS AT 00000000
210 REM SETS THE DATA AT 11001100
220 REM PROGRAMS THE EPROM WITH 11111111
230 REM PROGRAMMING ENDS WITH 1001
```

An optional construction procedure would be to make the Three-Line Burner work with 2764A and 27128A EPROMs. This option would also permit battery operation of the Three-Line Burner. Figure 7-17 offers one possible solution to converting the Three-Line Burner from a 2764 and 27128 EPROM programmer into a 2764A and 27128A EPROM programmer.

PROJECT 8: THE ABeEP I

With only a minor interface modification, a bus-specific EPROM programmer can be built from the original EPROgraMmer circuit design. In this case, an Apple IIe will provide the bus; the ABeEP I (Apple Bus IIe EPROM Programmer) has been born.

Parts List

C1-C2 - 56pF capacitor
C3-C5 - 22mF electrolytic capacitor
IC1 - IM4702
IC2- IM6402
IC3 - 74LS04
IC4 - ICL232
R1- 10M-ohm resistor
S1- SPST switch
X1- 2.4576 MHz crystal

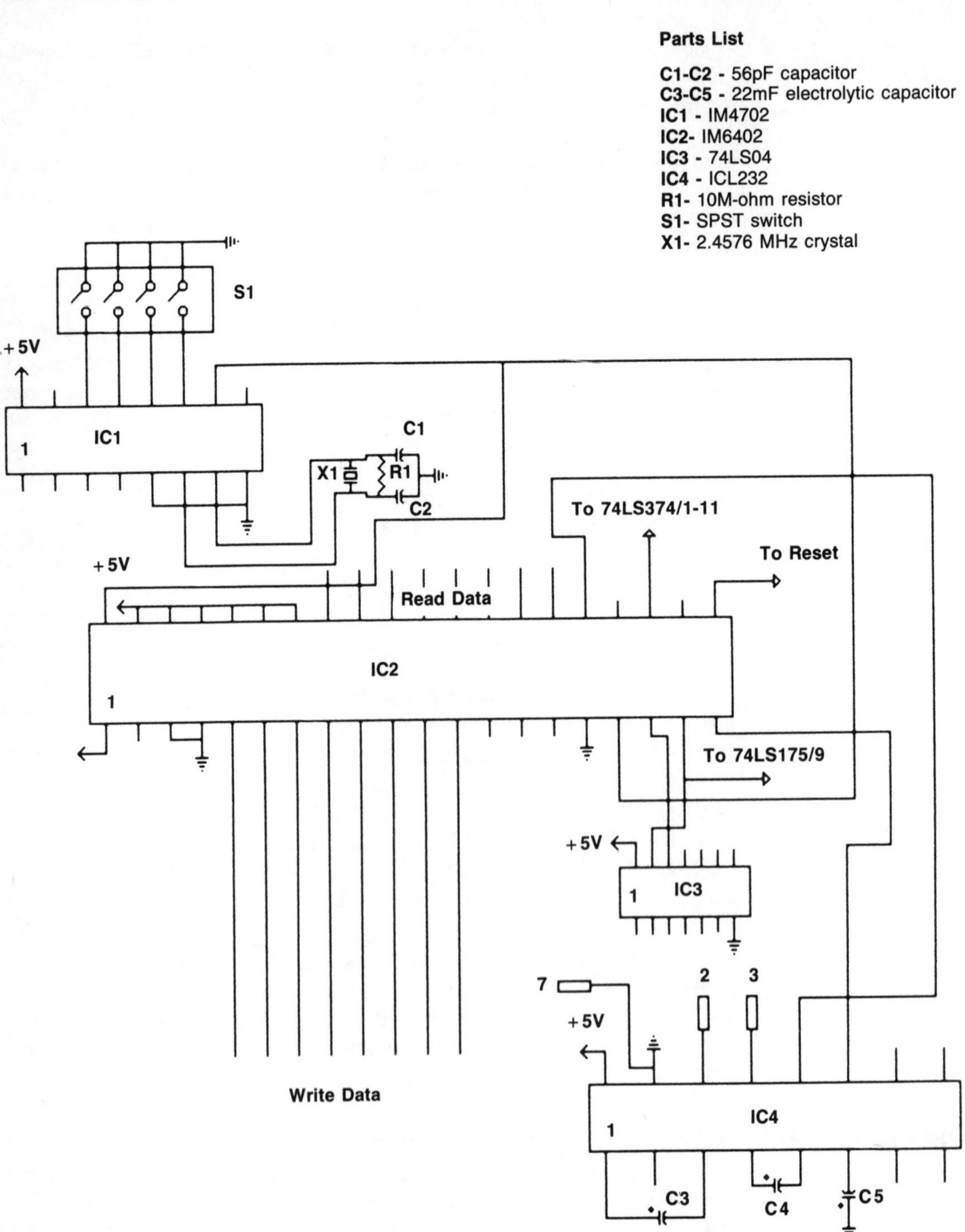

Fig. 7-15. Schematic diagram for the Three-Line Burner.

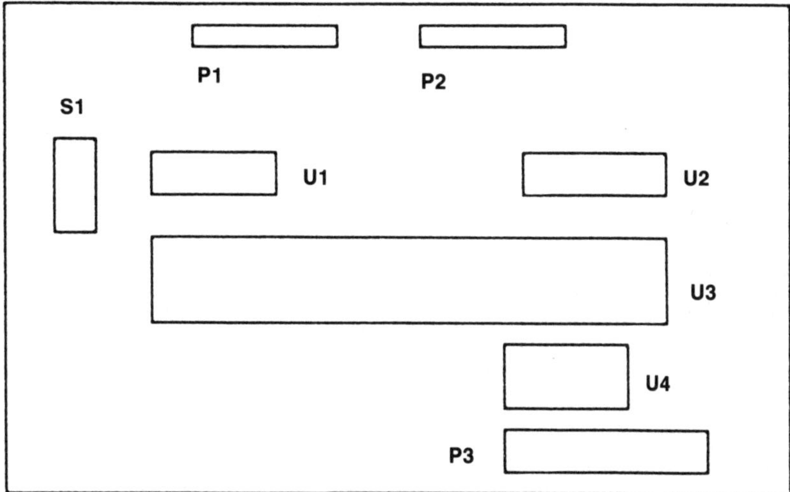

Fig. 7-16. Parts layout for the Three-Line Burner.

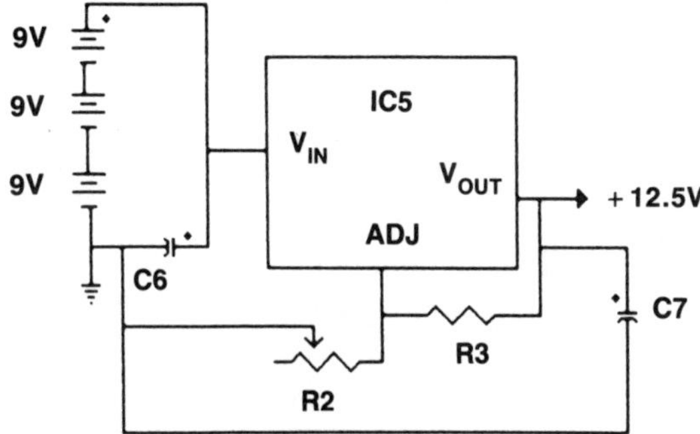

Fig. 7-17. Schematic diagram for the Three-Line Burner battery power supply.

One point that is worth considering when designing a bus-specific EPROM programmer is the limitation of positioning the EPROM's ZIF socket under the host computer's protective cover. In other words, every time an EPROM is to be programmed, the computer's main hatch must be opened for gaining access to the programmer. If your EPROM burning needs are limited to infrequent programming sessions, however, then this additional step can be easily overlooked when measured against the convenience of working with the ABeEP I.

Essentially, the ABeEP I is the basic EPROgraMmer design adapted to the Apple IIe internal expansion slot bus. This adaptation requires the addition of only some minor interface components for completion. These interface components consist primarily of five buffer/driver ICs.

In its present configuration, the ABeEP I is able to program 2764A or 27128A EPROMs. This restriction is dictated by the design of the Apple bus. An extra touch with the Apple IIe expansion slot is the presence of a +12V pin. This supply voltage makes the programming of +12.5V 2764A and 27128A EPROMs extremely easy and, therefore, serves as a design guideline in this EPROM programmer's construction.

Figure 7-18 shows the ABeEP I design. A suggested parts layout for a PCB design is illustrated in Fig. 7-19.

The installation of the ABeEP I inside an Apple IIe restricts access to the circuit's test points. Use extreme care when following the test procedures that were previously discussed for the EPROgraMmer II.

An entirely new set of programming for the read, program, and verify functions is necessary with the ABeEP I. This software should be written in Applesoft BASIC. The same format that was used in the previous programming examples has been followed with the example presented in the following listing. Virtually all of this EPROM programmer's functions can be controlled through software. The single action that is required of the operator is the adjustment of the DIP switches prior to EPROM programming and/or reading/verifying.

```
100 READ X, Y
110 REM INSERT THE POKE VALUES FOR PORT ADDRESSES Y
120 REM FOR EXAMPLE SLOT #4 USES 50176-50431 (DEC)
    VALUES
130 POKE Y, X
140 FOR P=1 TO 100:NEXT P
150 GOTO 120
160 END
170 REM THIS IS THE PROGRAM DATA
180 REM EXAMPLE (DATA Y, 128, Y, 0, Y, 204, Y, 255)
190 REM THIS EXAMPLE SETS THE UPPER ADDRESS AT
    10000000
200 REM SETS THE LOWER ADDRESS AT 00000000
210 REM SETS THE DATA AT 11001100
220 REM PROGRAMS THE EPROM WITH 11111111
230 REM EACH NEW POKE ADDRESS/DATA VALUE IS
    SPECIFIED WITH Y
240 REM THE DATA Y FOR SLOT #4 IS 50240
```

PROJECT 9: THE EPROM PROGRAM TESTER

If an error is made during the programming of an EPROM, you have only two available options. First, you could correct the erroneous program by changing the errant 1's to 0's. This method is valid only when the programming error can be traced to this exact faulty 1 and 0 logic transposition. If,

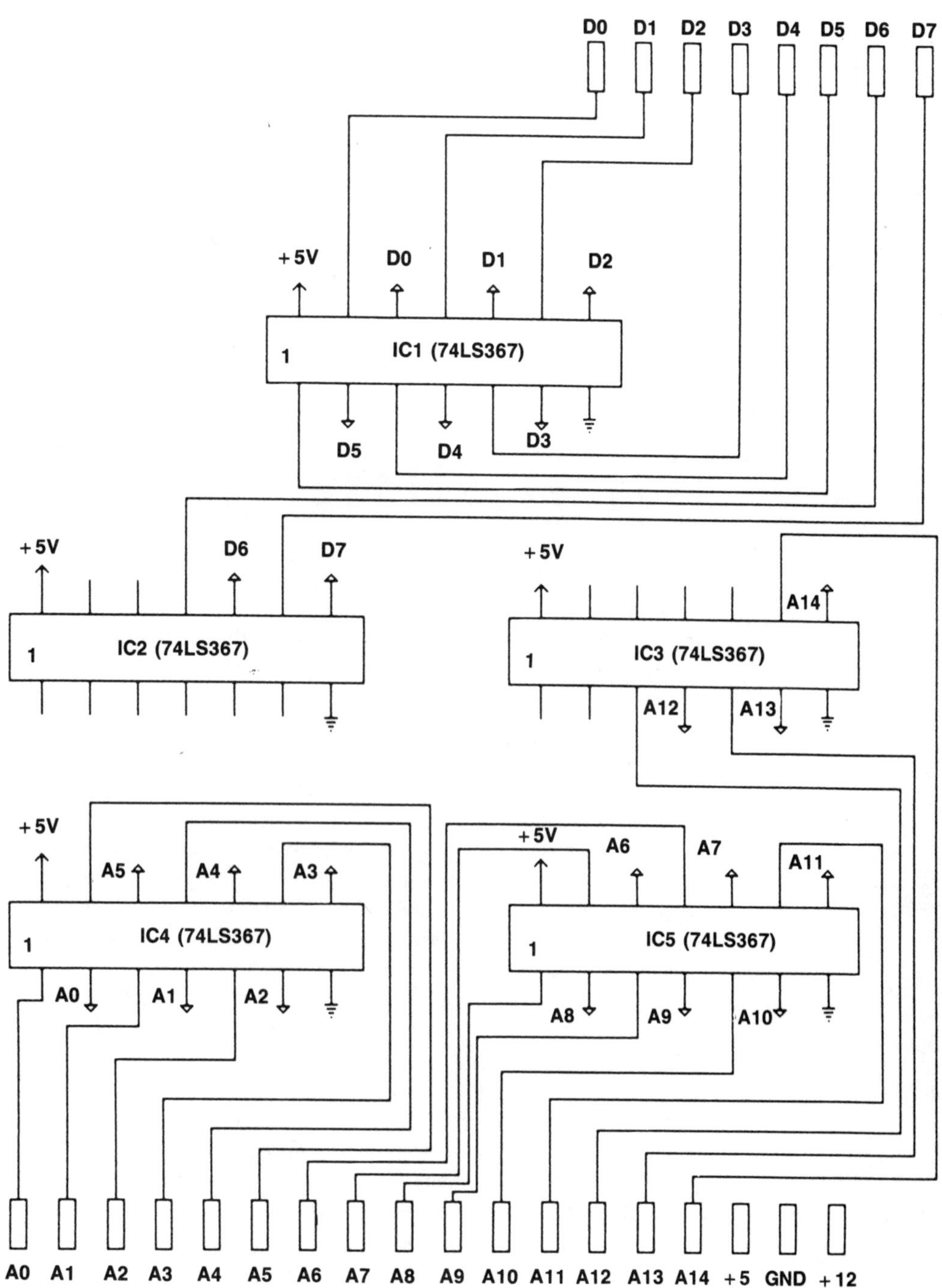

Fig. 7-18. Schematic diagram for the ABeEP I.

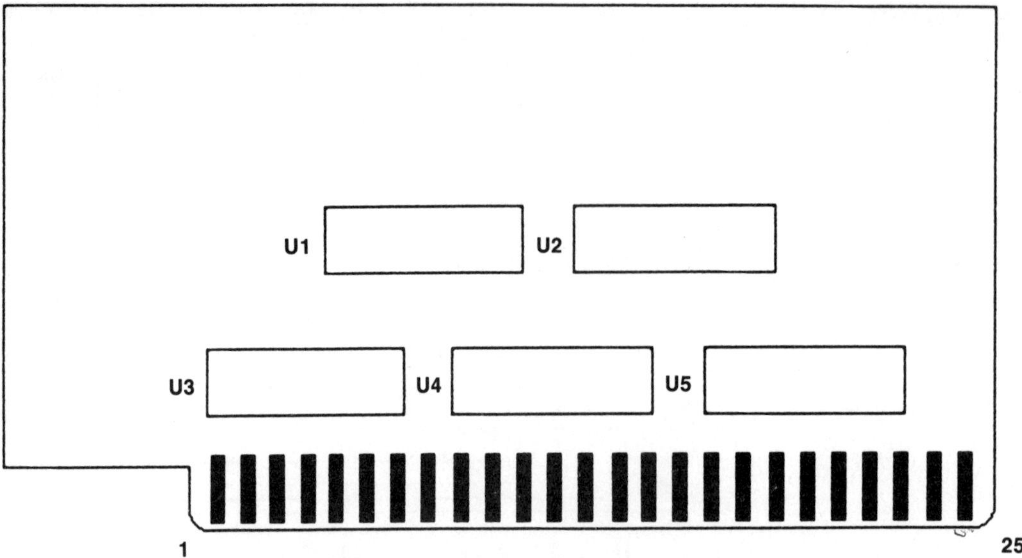

Fig. 7-19. Parts layout for the ABeEP I.

for example, your program solution requires that a programmed 0 be changed into a logic 1, then you must face the second correction option; erase the entire EPROM and start over. Actually, this option is not a viable option to the EPROM programmer. This option is the least acceptable due to an EPROM's total bank erasure requirement. In other words, when an EPROM is erased, *all* of its memory registers are cleared. Therefore, a programming error would mandate a new EPROM programming session.

One method for dealing with this laborious bank erasure correction option is to debug an EPROM's programming in a controlled test environment prior to writing this data to the EPROM. The most common means for testing and debugging an EPROM's programming is with a microcomputer-based EPROM simulation program. Unfortunately, a separate simulation program would have to be written for all of the major microcomputers. This would then limit the resultant EPROM program simulator to a specific microcomputer. A better solution to this software simulator is the flexible low-cost hardware EPROM Program Tester (or EPT).

The EPROM Program Tester consists of a pin-compatible 8192-word-by-8-bit 6264 Static RAM that is configured to resemble a 2764 and 2764A EPROM. The RAM-based EPROM Program Tester is able to write, read, and verify in the same manner as the 2764 and 2764A. Several differences between the 6264 Static RAM and the 2764 EPROM make the EPT a significant evaluation environment:

✤ No +21V or +12.5V programming voltage is needed with the EPT

- No complex 50 mS programming pulse hardware is required on the EPT
- No parallel or serial interface is used in the EPT design
- Virtually any microcomputer can use the EPT without a hardware modification
- All of the EPT's control is via a simple software link
- A battery pack provides the EPT with a pseudo-non-volatile memory life

The EPROM Program Tester is plug-compatible with any 2764, 2764A, or 6264 microcomputer socket. Therefore, during operation the host computer's EPROM (2764 or 2764A) IC or defined static RAM (6264) IC is removed from its socket. The EPT is then inserted into this vacant location. In order to facilitate this replacement, the EPT can interface with this empty socket through a jumper cable equipped with a 28-pin header. Alternatively, a 28-pin header can be soldered directly to the board housing the EPT. No matter which connection method is used, keep the distance between the EPT and the microcomputer EPROM/RAM socket less than six inches.

Figure 7-20 shows the design of the EPT along with its associated parts list. A suggested parts layout for a PCB design is illustrated in Fig. 7-21.

The EPT should be tested with the same procedures that have been used on all of the previous projects. Be sure to eliminate the programmer voltage test, however. The EPT does not require any voltages other than its +5V supply voltage.

Operation of the EPT is performed through a machine-specific software link. This software is able to simulate the program, read, and verify functions of an EPROM with the 6264 Static RAM. Ideally, the programming that is to be tested with the EPT should be loaded into the 6264 prior to operation within the microcomputer (see following program listing). This precaution is especially true with ROM-based routines. Any of the other EPROM programmer projects in this chapter can be quickly modified to meet the programming requirements of the EPT. Once this code has been loaded into the static RAM, it can be evaluated with test programming. This software is a bare bones approach to evaluating EPROM programs with the EPT. Specific memory locations, addresses, and command protocols should be extensively evaluated for each particular code.

```
100 REM COPY ROM DATA INTO THE EPT
110 FOR X=0 TO 511
120 POKE (Y+X), PEEK (Z+X)
130 NEXT X
140 REM THIS EXAMPLE WILL COPY 64 8-BIT ASCII
    CHARACTERS INTO THE EPT
150 REM Y=THE STARTING ADDRESS FOR THE EPT
160 REM Z=THE STARTING ADDRESS FOR THE ROM
    CHARACTER DATA
```

Parts List

B1- 5 volt Nicad battery
C1 -2.2mF capacitor
IC1-IC2, IC4-IC5 - 74LS367
IC6 - 7805
R1- 100-ohm resistor

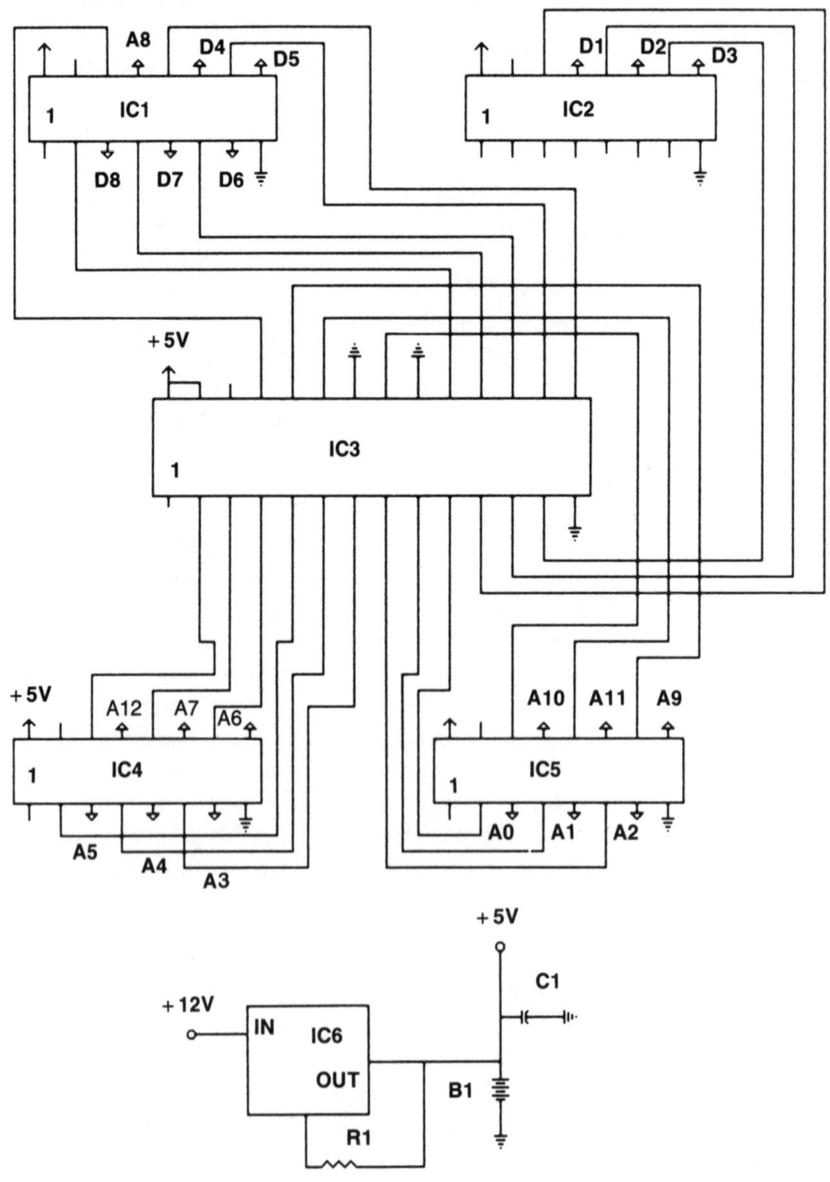

Fig. 7-20. Schematic diagram for the EPT.

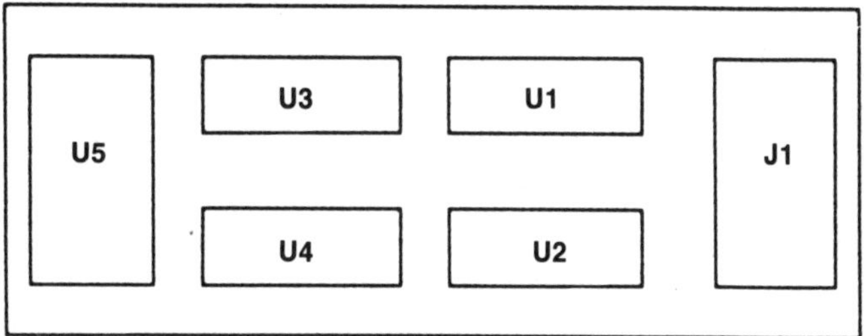

Fig. 7-21. Parts layout for the EPT.

PROJECT 10: BUILDING A ROM DRIVE

An important design element of the EPT is the ZIF socket that holds the 6264 Static RAM. By removing this IC and inserting a pre-programmed 2764 (A) EPROM into the ZIF socket, a ROM drive can be created. Basically, this ROM drive enables the test microcomputer to access the EPROM's code through the removed EPROM IC or RAM IC. In practice, specific program-

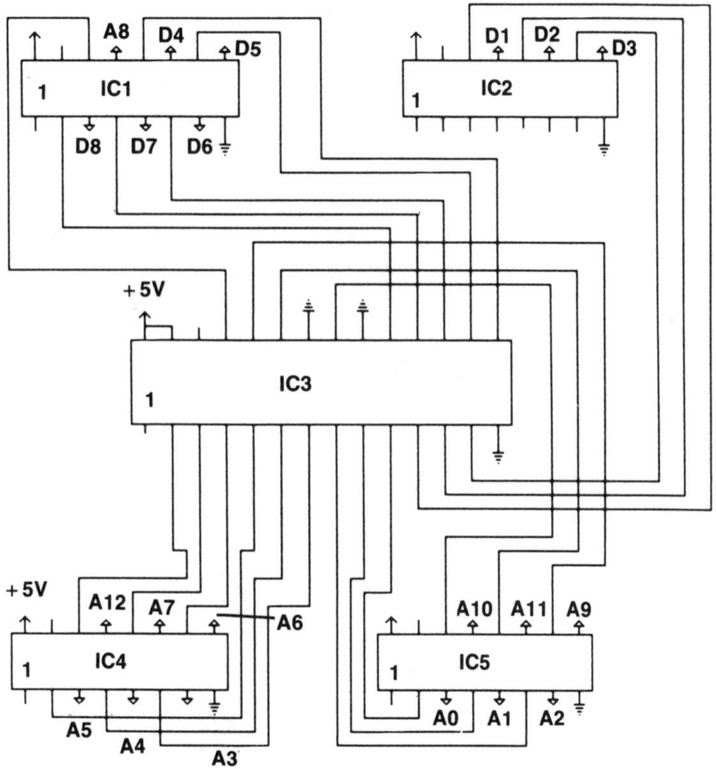

Fig. 7-22. Schematic diagram for a ROM drive.

ming applications could be written to an EPROM and then accessed through the EPT interface. As an operational example, this point can be most fully utilized in the restrictive memory of a portable computer. Portables like the Tandy 102, Tandy 200, and NEC 8201A use static RAM along with a modest set of ROM-based software. The EPT ROM Drive when connected to an empty static RAM socket would be able to build on this ROM-housed software concept. Figure 7-22 presents a schematic diagram for modifying the EPT into a ROM Drive. If the 8192-×-8 bit size of the 2764 is restrictive, an even greater memory map can be organized by substituting a 27128 (A) EPROM for the 2764.

8

Programming an EPROM

Aside from the physical hardware (and support software) that is necessary for programming an EPROM, a determination must also be made with regards to the programming format. The format that is used for programming an EPROM is usually established by the capabilities of the EPROM programmer. This format alignment is a design-level selection. In other words, the programmer must be built with an eye on its intended programming format. For example, the Bit Smasher (see Chapter 6) is only capable of programming EPROMs in a binary format. This limitation is the result of this programmer's design and not a function of the EPROM. A typical EPROM can be programmed in a variety of different formats. Therefore, an EPROM's programming format can be as diverse as the design of the programmer.

A recent count of the number of different EPROM programming formats totals 15 varieties. These include the more popular: binary, ASCII, hex, and Intel Hex formats. In the previous two chapters, the binary, ASCII, and hex programming formats were used with the described EPROM programmers. With the bulk of the commercial EPROM programmers, however, Intel Hex is the more frequently used programming format.

INTEL HEX

Intel Hex is an EPROM programming format that was developed by Intel Corporation (the founding manufacturer of EPROM technology) for writing EPROMs through microcomputer-controlled RS-232C serial interfaces. The employment of the RS-232C interface permits data to be both transmitted and received by the host computer. The presence of this two-way communication line provides this programming format with a distinct performance edge over the other commonly used formats.

Essentially, Intel Hex is a byte-checking format that reduces the chance for a costly EPROM programming error. Even though Intel Hex makes extensive use of hexadecimal addresses, data, and checksums, several EPROM programmers that use this format offer an ASCII translation of the hexadecimal code. Table 8-1 is a listing of typical ASCII translations for Intel Hex hexadecimal codes.

Table 8-1. Intel Hex-ASCII Conversion Table.

ASCII	Hexadecimal
NUL	00
LF	0A
CR	0D
^Z	1A
0	30
1	31
2	32
3	33
4	34
5	35
6	36
7	37
8	38
9	39
:	3A
A	41
B	42
C	43
D	44
E	45
F	46

Two record formats are used in Intel Hex: Data Record Format and End of File Record Format. Both of these record formats accommodate a byte total and checksum.

Data Record Format

This record format is used for holding the target EPROM's address and data information. The Data Record Format consists of:

:TA00DC

In this example,

: = record format delimiter
T = total number of bytes in this record format
A = starting address for this record format
00 = a Data Record Format
D = one data byte; additional bytes may be added for representing a given address (A)
C = checksum

Each EPROM address location is repeated with a similar record format. The checksum (C) is the two's complement of the sum of all of the bytes that are contained within the specified Data Record Format. In other words, C contains the negative binary value for T + A + D represented as a hexadecimal number.

Following the entry of this Data Record Format, a carriage return or linefeed is specified. The ASCII use of these codes transmit (or receive) as a 0D and 0A in Intel Hex, respectively. These codes are placed directly after the checksum (C).

End of File Record Format

The end of an Intel Hex program is represented with this record format. The End of File Record Format is represented as:

:TA01C

In this example,

: = end of file record format delimiter
T = total number of bytes in this record format
A = starting address for this record format
01 = an End of File Record Format
C = checksum

Several different combinations of these values can be used for indicating an End of File Record Format.

:00A01C

Where

: = delimiter
00 = end of file indicator byte total
A = address

01 = (optional); End of File Record Format
C = checksum

:20A01C

Where

: = delimiter
20 = a full Data Record Format
A = address
01 = End of File Record Format
C = checksum

And,

:T(<20)A01C

Where

: = delimiter
T(<20) = a partial Data Record Format
A = address
01 = End of File Record Format
C = checksum

During an Intel Hex programming session, the use of these different End of File Record Formats is governed by the direction of travel for the program data. In other words, the transmit and receive modes of the host computer determine which of these end-of-file indicators is most suitable. Numerous examples of "intelligent" commercial EPROM programmers are able to "understand" any of these end of file variations, regardless of the data's path. This advanced degree of format sophistication is enabled through an on-board program housed in the programmer's ROM.

The conclusion of RS-232C communication between the host computer and the EPROM programmer is commonly signaled with a string of Control-Z characters (1Ah). This string should be placed on its own line, following the End of File Record Format.

An Intel Hex program can be written with any word processing program that doesn't insert control codes into the text. Alternatively, an assembly language monitor program can be used for directly writing the hexadecimal form of an Intel Hex program. As an illustration of working with Intel Hex, the following example outlines each of the steps required in writing a program with this format:

```
:10000000434F4E47524154554C4154494F4E532E45
} INSERT THE PROGRAM'S
} ROUTINES HERE
:00000001FF
```

SIMPLE EPROM PROGRAMMING

One of the largest complaints against EPROM programming is the difficulty that is inherent in writing such a program. For the most part, some form of hexadecimal programming is required for writing data into the address locations of an EPROM. Unfortunately, this is a foreign tongue to most computer programmers. High-level languages, such as FORTRAN, C, and BASIC, have replaced the need for programmers to learn the complexities of machine-level languages.

There are two solutions to beating this potential EPROM programming limitation. First, write the program with a high-level language *compiler*. Excellent compilers, like Borland International's Turbo BASIC, are available for a wide range of microcomputers. These compilers afford the programmer the luxury of writing a program in a familiar language with the subsequent, and more painful, translation into a machine-level form executed by the compiler. An even larger benefit of Borland International's Turbo BASIC is that the compiler-created machine-level form will function independently of the compiler environment. Another interpretation of this benefit is that the resultant code can be used without paying an additional royalty or licensing fee. This freedom from payment makes Turbo BASIC programs ideal for EPROM programming.

Before leaping to Turbo BASIC and other compilers for satisfying all of your EPROM programming needs, remember that the resultant machine-level code is written in the host microcomputer MPU's command set. In other words, an EPROM programmed in Turbo BASIC for the IBM PC's 8088 MPU will not function correctly in a circuit based on the Motorola 6808 MPU. Granted, the 8088-based Turbo BASIC program will function correctly in a NEC V-20 circuit, an 8086 circuit, and a stand-alone MPU-less circuit (this circuit is dependent on the exact nature of the circuit and the function that is provided by the EPROM). But any other circuit holding an 8088 coded EPROM which is controlled by an MPU that is not 8088 compatible will experience operational problems.

The best means for circumventing these MPU-induced limitations is through data table EPROM programming. *Data table programming* is the second solution for avoiding the rigors of complex machine-level programming. While data table programming is a form of machine-level language, it is far simpler in its creation. As with using compilers for writing EPROM code, there is a limitation with this programming method.

Data tables are simple "look-up" charts for digital circuits. A data table consists of specific address locations holding bytes of data. This data is accessed through a decoder circuit which loads a needed address into the EPROM and then reads the data output. Because of this simplicity, detailed operational or functional programming is difficult to write in a data table form. Therefore, data tables are usually used for holding display character patterns, speech synthesizer phonemes, or keyboard encoded data. Another benefit of writing data tables is that they can be easily created with all of the EPROM programmers in this book.

In the following pages, three different projects document the programming of an EPROM data table. Each of these projects is complete with circuit construction information, program listings, and operation notes. Each of these projects is a stand-alone unit with all of its required coding being drawn from the on-board EPROM. Concluding this chapter is an examination of advanced EPROM programming in machine-level languages.

SYNTHESIZED SPEECH DATA TABLE (PROJECT II: SPEECH SYNTHESIZER)

In 1976, the Naval Research Laboratories developed a small and compact algorithm that could handle all of the analyzing and translation duties that are normally associated with converting a written word into a speech-synthesized word. The elegant nature of this text-to-speech algorithm has made it the most popular method for converting ASCII text into synthesized speech.

The General Instrument CTS256A-AL2 is an NMOS IC that contains an on-board text-to-speech algorithm that translates ASCII text into allophonic code strings. These allophonic code strings are specifically matched to the data input signals that are used by the General Instrument SPO256-AL2 speech synthesizer IC. Therefore, tying the CTS256A-AL2 together with the SPO256-AL2 creates an inexpensive text-to-speech processing system.

Figure 8-1 is a serial interface text-to-speech ASCII translation speech synthesizer circuit. One problem that is associated with this type of speech synthesizer is that it is incapable of correctly pronouncing certain words (e.g., "joking"). In an effort to hurdle this pronunciation difficulty, special ROM programming can be used as a "look-up" data table for holding the correct pronunciation for a given ASCII text spelling. In other words, this look-up table would contain the required phonemes for correctly uttering the above example word, "joking." Later when the ASCII text for "joking" is encountered by the CTS256A-AL2, the data table will provide the correct pronunciation.

In this circuit, an EPROM is used for holding the look-up data table pronunciations. A programmed 2732 EPROM (IC8 in this diagram) serves as the site for this look-up phoneme data table. Inside this EPROM, the data starts at an address of 3000h. As an example of programming this EPROM, here is the procedure that would be used for coding the pronunciation of "joking:"

```
<(JOKING)< = (JH OW KK1 IH NG)
13 6F 2B 29 2E A7 4A 35 2A 0C AC
```

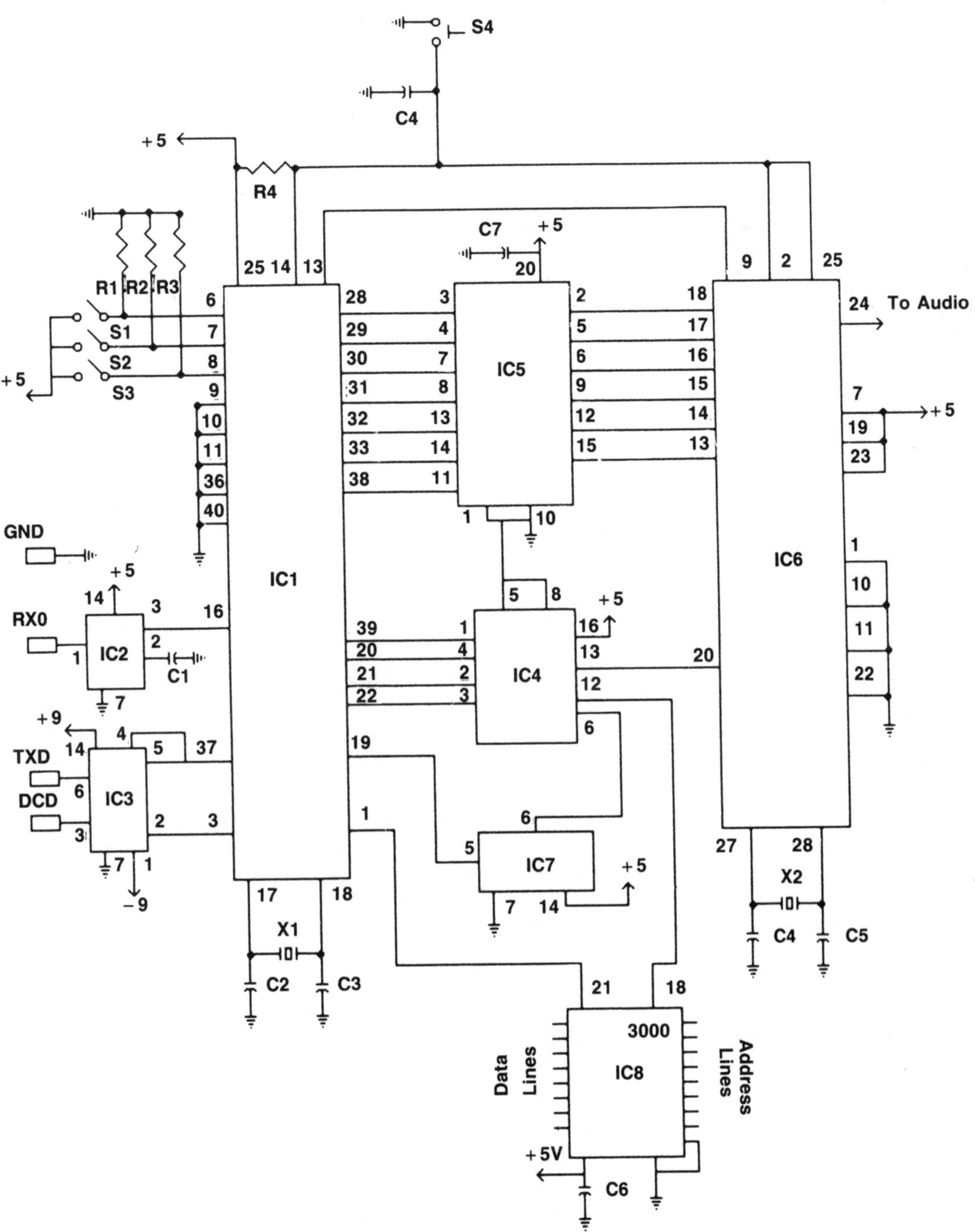

Fig. 8-1. Schematic diagram for a speech synthesizer equipped with an EPROM data table.

Programming the EPROM with "joking:"

```
3000 80 48 28 58 85 E0 35 E0 31 FF FF FF FF FF FF FF
3010 FF FF FF FF FF FF FF FF FF FF FF FF FF FF FF FF
3020 FF FF FF 1E 1F 20 21 28 29 24 25 22 23 2A 2B 26
   ;INSERT MAIN CONTROL PROGRAM
30A0 00 E0 36 31 93 31 AB 31 A9 31 B1 31 B2 31 B3 31
30B0 B4 31 E1 31 E2 32 0D 32 0E 32 0F 32 1B 32 1C 32
30C0 1D 32 1E 32 2D 32 2E 32 2F 32 30 32 3D 32 5A 32
30D0 5B 32 64 32 65 32 6F 32 70 ;EXCEPTION ROUTINE
3190 F3 EE FF 32 0D 13 6F 2B 29 2E A7 4A 35 2A 0C AC
```

MUSIC DATA TABLE (PROJECT 12: MUSIC SYNTHESIZER)

Like the speech synthesizer IC, music synthesizer ICs can be controlled via an MPU. These music synthesizers are also known as PSGs or Programmable Sound Generators. An example PSG interfaced with an MPU is illustrated in Figure 8-2. The General Instrument AY-3-8910A 40-pin IC is used in this diagram.

The generation of music with the PSG is accomplished through two 8-bit I/O ports. These ports control 16 registers. Sound duration, amplitude, envelope, and noise are functions of these 16 PSG registers. Sending over the data address bus of the PSG (DA0-DA7) determines the programming for each of these registers. Meanwhile, the read and write operation of the PSG is governed by pins 27 and 29 of the AY-3-8910A. Two logic ICs (IC2 and IC3) control the application of each operation.

By connecting an EPROM to the PSG's data lines, a programmed sound synthesizer can be created. In the above diagram, all of the register and address settings will have to be carried out through an MPU. The data for the actual sounds can be held in a 2732 EPROM, however. These data would be programmed as:

```
0001 8C 05 AA 05 91 B1 92 B2 93 B3 94 B4 95 B5 96 B6
0002 97 B7 98 B8 99 B9 9A BA 9B BB 9C BC 9D BD 9E BE
0003 9F BF ;END OF MUSIC ROUTINE
0004 9F BF DF FF ;SILENCE
```

CHARACTER DATA TABLE (PROJECT 13: MESSAGE CENTER)

Most computer systems have their display character codes stored in ROM. This storage method prevents the erasure of the pixel patterns that are used to represent each keyboard keystroke. In Chapter 1, a keyboard encoder proj-

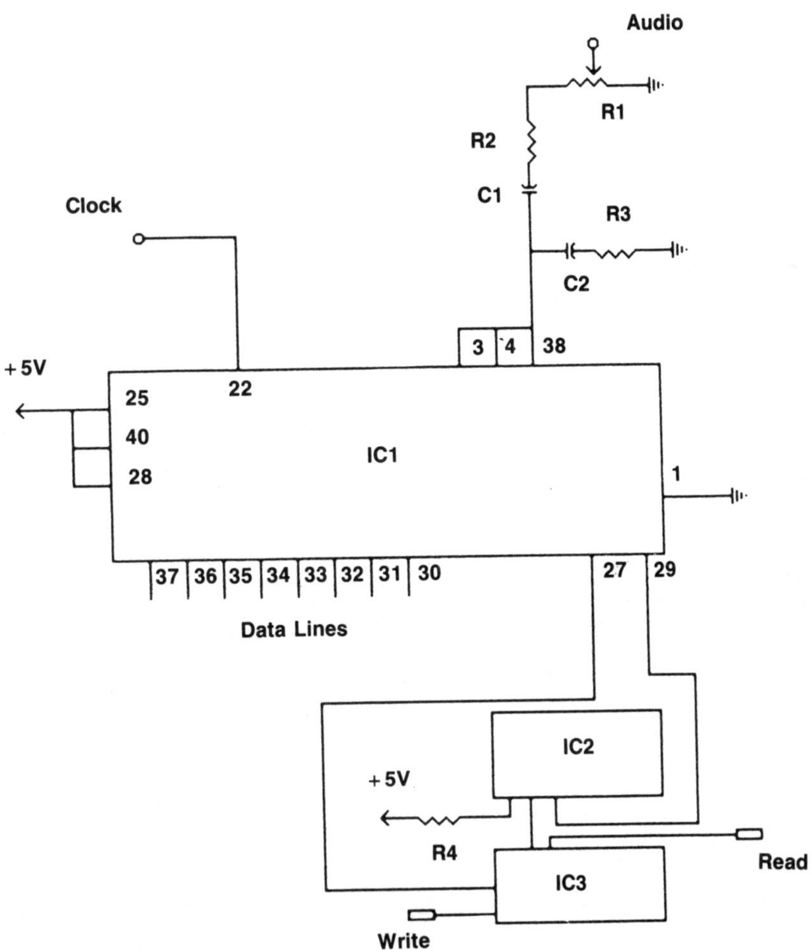

Fig. 8-2. Schematic diagram for a music synthesizer equipped with an EPROM data table.

ect was discussed for displaying the keystroke number on a common anode 7-segment display. This same project has been modified in Figure 8-3 for incorporating a ROM-based character generation data table.

In this case, a 2716 EPROM is used for IC1. This EPROM holds a custom character pattern for displaying a different image for each key press. A 7447 was used in the original keyboard encoder circuit. In this design, the data for each key press is:

key 0 01h
key 1 4Fh

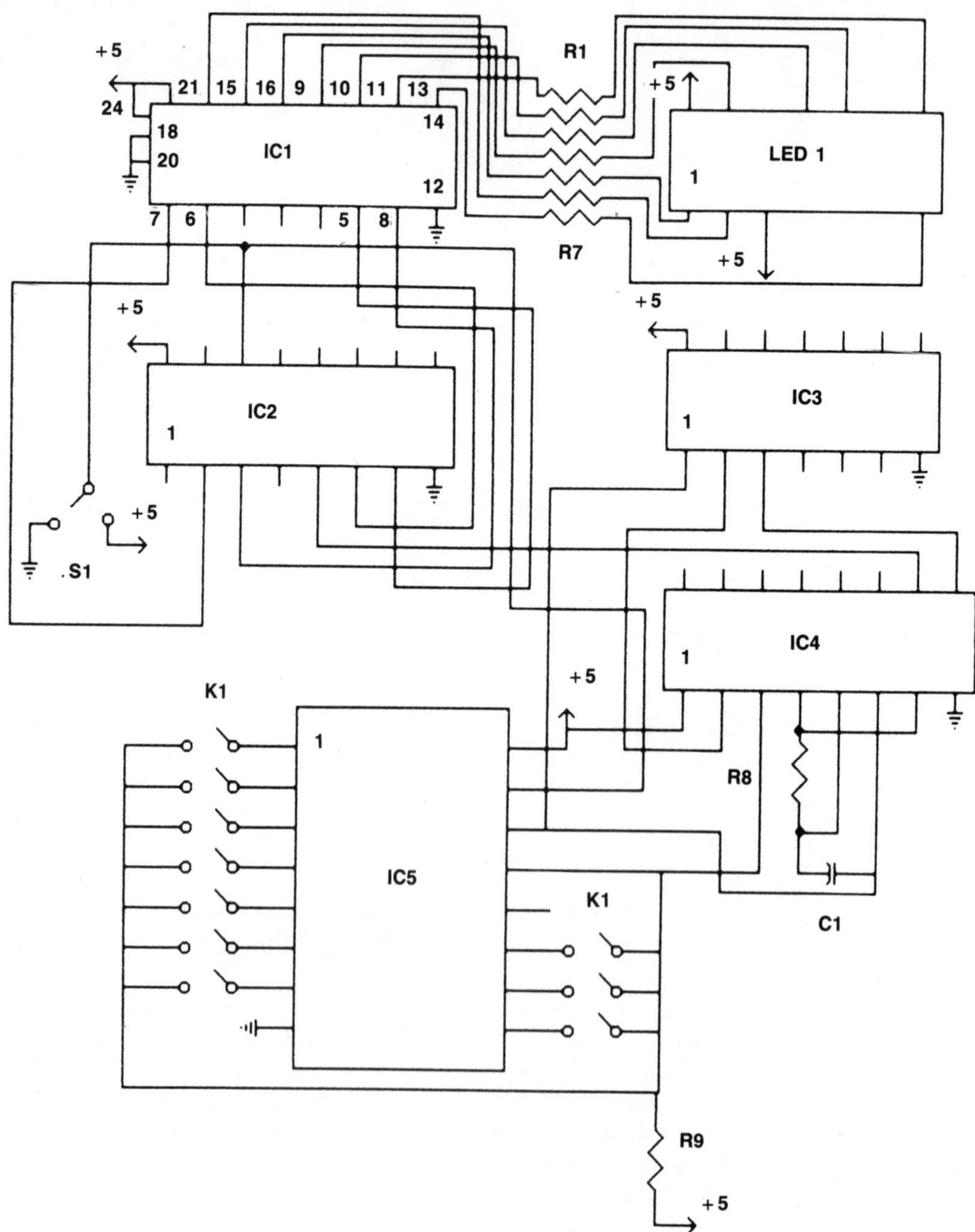

Fig. 8-3. Schematic diagram for a EPROM coded message center.

key 2 12h
key 3 06h
key 4 4Ch
key 5 24h
key 6 60h
key 7 0Fh
key 8 0h
key 9 0Ch

By using this same technique, the first 10 letters of the upper case alphabet can be applied to these 10 keys. A 2716 EPROM would be programmed in the following manner. (Remember this is a common anode display, therefore a logic 1 extinguishes a stated segment.)

0000 8 ;A
0001 0 ;B
0002 31 ;C
0003 1 ;D
0004 30 ;E
0005 38 ;F
0006 21 ;G
0007 48 ;H
0008 79 ;I
0009 47 ;J

Another form of character generator uses displays that are capable of producing the entire upper and lower case alphanumeric ASCII code list. These displays use pixel dot matrices for forming each character. A 5 × 7 pixel matrix is one of the more common display formations. In this case, an uppercase ''A'' would look like:

```
 • • •
•     •
•     •
• • • • •
•     •
•     •
•     •
```

Programming this character as columns:

3F 09 09 09 3F

ADVANCED EPROM PROGRAMMING

Other than the data table, another application feature of the EPROM is its ability to hold major system-oriented programming for ready access. This access can be either a start-up hardware initialization routine or operational software that is callable from within the microcomputer's operating system. Each of these uses requires a different interpretation of the microcomputer's memory (see Fig. 8-4 and Fig. 8-5).

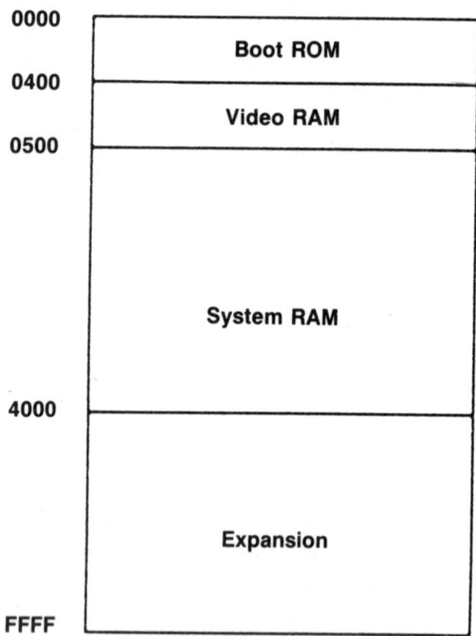

Fig. 8-4. A typical memory map for a microcomputer during the initial system boot.

A drawback to burning this form of programming into an EPROM is the restrictive nature of testing and debugging the code. Therefore, a device like the EPT (see Chapter 7) should be used for evaluating *every* piece of major EPROM code prior to inserting it permanently into the microcomputer's memory map.

Before any extensive EPROM programming project can begin, several questions need to be answered.

- What size of EPROM is required for holding the program?
- What, if any, is the program's memory overhead?
- Which MPU command set should be used?
- How will the EPROM's data be accessed?

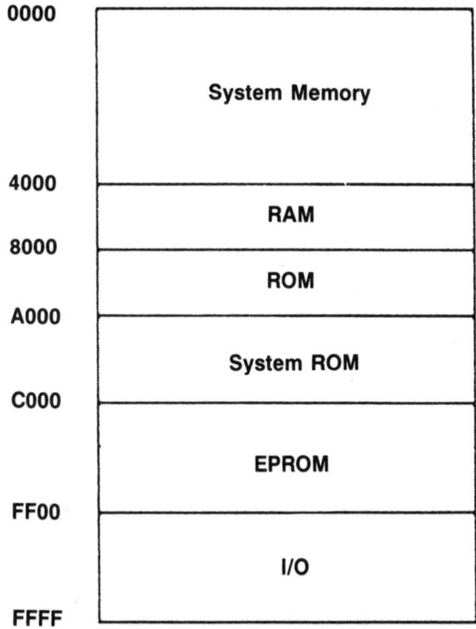

Fig. 8-5. A typical memory map for an operational microcomputer system modified by support software.

The following two examples are demonstrations of answering these questions for advanced EPROM programming.

Binary Calculator Program

Virtually any type of programming can be placed inside an EPROM. The only requirement for the successful operation of this programming is its compatibility with the host MPU. In other words, only a Z80 can execute Z80 code. Likewise, a 6809 is only able to read an EPROM that has been programmed with 6809 code. As an illustration of this point, the decimal-to-binary conversion program from Chapter 1 has been rewritten in 8088 code. These first 58h address locations are ready for programming in a target EPROM:

```
01AA 2E
01AB 8C1EB200
01AF 2E
01B0 C706AE000000
01B6 E85405
0189 E88800
01BC E81717
01BF E8AE17
01C2 E81100
```

```
01C5 2E
01C6 8E1E6401
01CA FF360200
01CE E89F17
01D1 58
01D2 B44C
01D6 E8A700
01D9 E8D600
01DC 7253
01DE E8C401
01E1 E84802
01E4 E86C02
01E7 E8C61F
01EA E8252F
01ED E85201
01F0 0F
01F1 1F
01F2 A15601
01F5 B104
01F7 D3E0
01F9 A3CE00
01FC B88000
01FF A3D200
0202 8E1E6401
```

This code was obtained with Borland International's BASIC compiler: Turbo BASIC. As such, this program will run on any system that is supported with an 8088 MPU.

Another 8088-coded example of a complete stand-alone program:

```
0100 BB 20 01
0103 B9 05 00
0106 8A 17
0108 B4 06
010A CD 21
010C 43
010D E2 F7
010F 90
0120 45 50 52 4F 4D
```

Or,

```
0100 B4 06
0102 B2 FF
```

```
0104 CD 21
0106 74 FC
0108 88 C2
010A CD 21
010C EB F4
```

Boot ROM

For the most, expansion boards that are inserted into microcomputers contain their code for performing a number of different duties. For example, these chores might include: booting the host system, partitioning the system's RAM, altering the location of a memory pointer, or loading a special program. No matter what the purpose of this code, it must be recognized by the host computer prior to execution. Therefore, microcomputer boot routines perform a regular inspection of the available expansion boards. This housekeeping duty can be detected and branched to the EPROM code according to the parameters of the microcomputer's boot code.

The best method for accessing this branching is through the system's BIOS (Basic I/O System). These BIOS "hooks" or interfaces transfer control of the microcomputer ROM over to the expansion board's on-board EPROM. Depending on the nature of the peripheral expansion board, the EPROM code that is necessary for hooking into the system BIOS can range from simplistic to extensive. The following is a simple 8088 example of interfacing with the IBM PC BIOS:

```
0000 55
0001 AA
0002 08
0003 50
0004 53
0005 51
0006 52
0007 1E
0008 68
0009 00
000A 00
000B 8E
000C D8
000D E9
000E 70
000F 03
0010 49
0011 4D
0012 50
0013 55
```

```
0014 4C
0015 53
0016 45
0017 20
0018 31
0019 30
001A 30
001B 2E
001C 32
001D 30
001E 20
001F 4D
0020 45
0021 4D
0022 4F
0023 52
0024 59
0025 20
0026 45
0027 58
0028 50
0029 41
002A 4E
002B 53
002C 49
002D 4F
002E 4E
002F 24
0030 50
```

Once the techniques for writing major EPROM programs have been mastered, then dedicated microprocessor projects can be constructed using sophisticated performance programming. Figure 8-6 is an example of this type of project.

In this project, a dedicated word processing machine has been built around the programming that is contained within a bank of EPROMs. This programming could be either written by the user or downloaded from a known word processing software package into an EPROM programmer for burning into the required memory devices. (NOTE: This practice could be a violation of the copyright laws. Please check with the software manufacturer before attempting this form of program copying.) In this case, only non-copy-protected software could be used in this manner.

The applications for dedicated hardware devices sporting extensive on-board memories are limitless. For example, handheld talking keyboards could

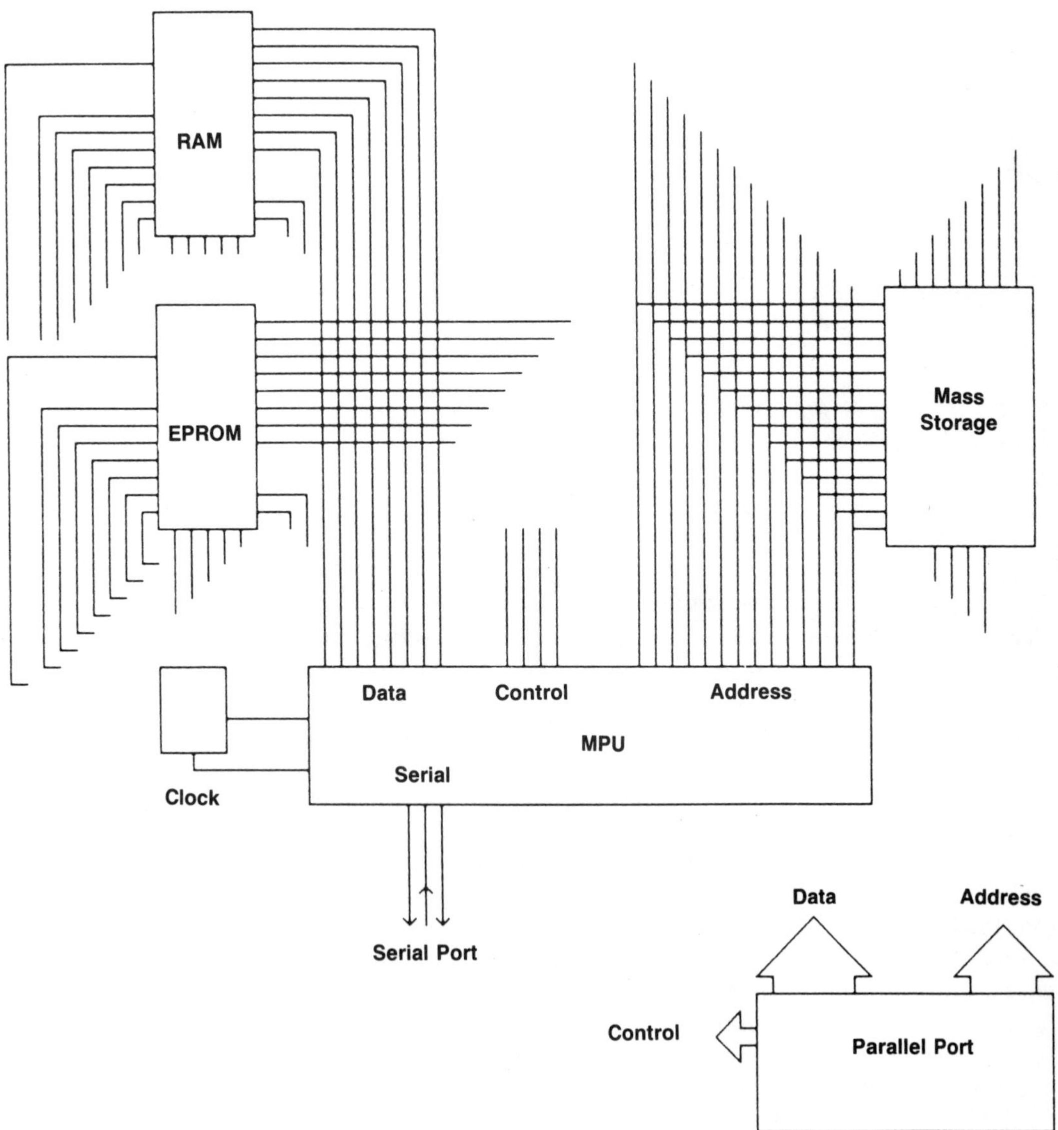

Fig. 8-6. Schematic block diagram for a dedicated word processor computer system.

give the physically handicapped a powerful communication link with the "talking" world. In this example, a speech synthesizer coupled with an EPROM-based text-to-speech algorithm would provide this link. Alternatively, an elaborate language translator could be constructed around an EPROM holding a translating program and lengthy language conversion data tables. In either application, the key to the success of the project depends on the mastery of EPROM programming.

9

Erasing an EPROM

Any error in programming an EPROM can be corrected in one of two ways. First, a programming error, where a programmed 1 was intended to be written as a 0, can be easily altered by burning this new logic 0 at the required address. This form of EPROM error correction is readily performed with an EPROM programmer. On the other hand, programming errors where programmed 0s need to be changed into 1s demands that the second error correction method be used. The second means of fixing an erroneous EPROM bit, however, is far more drastic. This method requires an EPROM eraser.

An EPROM eraser is a bulk fix to programming errors. In other words, single bits, words, and/or blocks of data cannot be individually altered with the EPROM eraser. Only the *entire* EPROM can be changed into its original unprogrammed state of all 1s. Furthermore, this is the only method for correcting *any* erroneously programmed logic 0. Therefore, if you make a logic 0 error, even if this error is limited to a single bit, then the only available option for correcting this faulty data is by erasing the entire EPROM and starting over.

EPROMs are erased through a concentrated bath of ultraviolet (UV) light. In order to execute this erasing, the UV light must fall on the delicate internal gates of the EPROM. EPROM manufacturers incorporate small quartz windows into the dorsal side of their EPROM chip carriers for providing UV light exposure to these gates.

When the UV light is exposed to the silicon dioxide insulating material, there is a rise in this layer's conductivity. This increased conductivity draws the charge away from the floating gate and initiates an electron "leak." The UV light also increases the charge of the floating gate electrons, thereby forcing them through the weakened insulation barrier. These energized electrons increase the flow of energy through the electron leak and hasten the erasure of the EPROM.

Once the electron charge has been completely removed from the floating gate, the EPROM is returned to its quiescent logic 1 state. As proof of this erasure, an examination of an EPROM's registers at this point would display binary 11111111 or hexadecimal FF for each data byte. Each of the EPROM's memory locations could be examined as verification of this condition. In fact, many EPROM programmer's perform this verification prior to writing new data into the memory devices registers.

ERASING MATHEMATICS

Each EPROM manufacturer states a required amount of time for erasing their product. This value is given as an erase energy. An EPROM's erase energy is usually expressed in terms of watt-seconds per cm^2.

To determine the proper time for erasure, you need a multiplication factor. This multiplication factor is based on the wattage of the UV light source. For example,

2-watt UV lamp = 12X
4-watt UV lamp = 6X
8-watt UV lamp = 3X

With a known multiplication factor and erase energy, the erasure time for an EPROM can be established with this equation:

$$T = F \times E$$

Where:

T = the total erase time for the EPROM
F = the UV lamp multiplication factor
E = the EPROM's erase energy

In actual examples, this equation provides an erase time value in minutes. Study these erase time equation examples:

- A 2-watt UV lamp erasing a 10-watts-second erase energy EPROM.
  $T = 12 \times 10$ watt-S/cm^2 = 120 minutes = 2 hours
- This same EPROM with an 8-watt lamp.
  $T = 3 \times 10$ watt-S/cm^2 = 30 minutes
- A 4-watt lamp erasing a 15-watts-second EPROM.
  $T = 6 \times 15$ watt-S/cm^2 = 90 minutes = 1.5 hours

Two other agents that generate UV light are the sun and conventional household/office fluorescent lamps. The multiplication factors for these sources range between 3000X and 6000X. Using these values with the previous erase time equation examples provides the following results:

- An optimal sunlight source erasing a 10-watts-second EPROM.
  3000 × 10 watt-S/cm^2 = 30,000 minutes = 500 hours = 20.8 days
- An overhead fluorescent lamp erasing the same EPROM.
  6000 × 10 watt-S/cm^2 = 60,000 minutes = 1000 hours = 41.7 days

While these erase times indicate that short exposures will be minor in their effect, the resultant damage could be significant for prolonged exposures. Therefore, to prevent accidental erasure, the quartz window on programmed EPROMs should be covered with an opaque tape. An ideal source for this tape is the write-protect tabs that are used with programmed floppy disks (see Fig. 9-1). One of these tabs should be placed over the quartz window before the programmed EPROM is removed from the programmer. Later when the EPROM is ready to be erased, this protective tab will have to be removed.

Fig. 9-1. A 2732A EPROM protected against accidental erasure.

PROJECT 14: A 4-WATT EPROM ERASER

A simple EPROM eraser can be built with a low-cost 4-watt UV lamp. This eraser will be able to erase up to three EPROMs (28-pin; e.g., 2732, 2764, 27128, 27256, 27512) in a single operation. Both the schematic diagram and parts list are modest in their content (see Fig. 9-2). The greatest amount of attention in the construction of this project is directed to the design of the eraser's housing.

Parts List

BL1 - 4-watt ballast
L1 - 4-watt UV lamp
P1 - grounded three-wire plug
S1-S2 - SPST switch

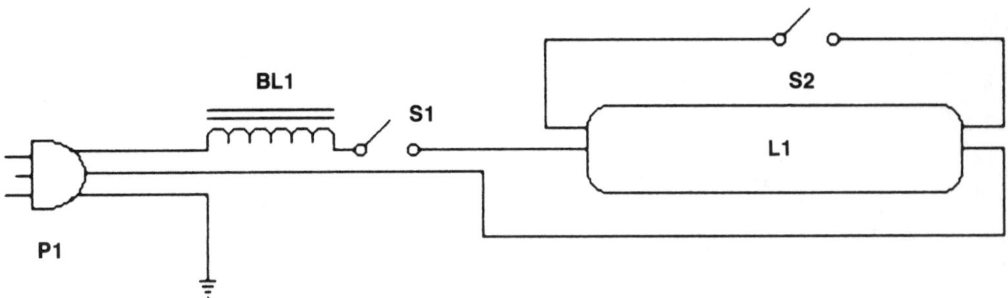

Fig. 9-2. Schematic diagram for the 4-watt EPROM eraser.

This EPROM eraser should be built inside a high-quality, sealed metal enclosure. Any of the easily obtainable metal enclosures (e.g., Radio Shack metal cabinets Part #270-25X) will hold this project. When selecting and building this enclosure remember that the final eraser *must* be totally light tight. This requirement prevents the optically dangerous UV light from escaping from the eraser into the surrounding room. The best material for preventing this contamination is a cushioning foam material. This foam should be applied to all surfaces that might lack a tight fit. Preferably, this foam should have an adhesive backing that will permit its easy placement around the enclosure's leaking openings.

In order for this 4-watt UV lamp to quickly erase an EPROM, the enclosure's floor holding the EPROMs must be less then two inches from the bulb. This distance should place the quartz window of the EPROM approximately one inch away from the UV light source. An easy technique for adjusting the height of the eraser's floor is through successive layers of conductive foam. This special material is used in the storage of static-sensitive ICs and is an ideal material for elevating, as well as insulating the target EPROMs.

When the construction has been completed, the EPROM eraser should be tested. Figure 9-3 and Table 9-2 contain the necessary test points and results for verifying that the eraser has been properly assembled. If all of these tests produce good results, then the EPROM eraser is ready for operation.

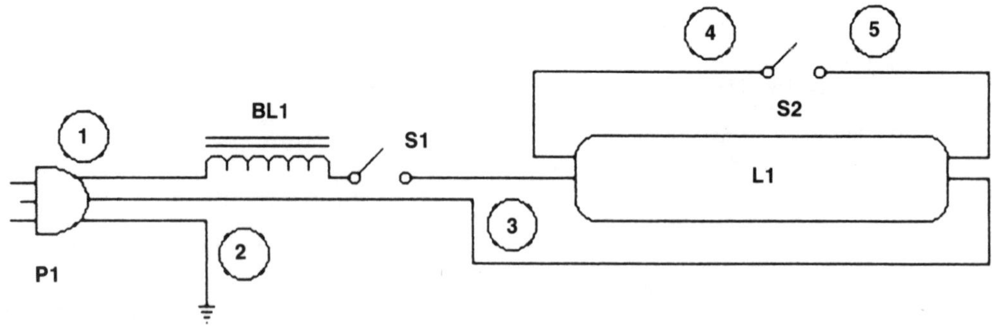

Test 1 Infinity ohms
Test 2 0 ohms
Test 3 Infinity ohms
Test 4 Infinity ohms
Test 5 >50 ohms

Fig. 9-3. Voltage test locations for the 4-watt EPROM eraser.

Five steps are required for the proper operation of this EPROM eraser:

- Unplug the eraser from its voltage source and turn both switches off.
- Place the target EPROMs on the enclosure's floor.
- Close the eraser's cover.
- Plug the eraser into its voltage source and turn both switches on.
- Turn off, unplug, and remove the erased EPROMs after the correct erase time has expired.

CAUTION: UV light from this eraser is harmful to *all* human eyes and optic centers. Avoid any visual contact with this light source.

Under normal operating conditions, this eraser should be able to provide approximately 2500 hours of erase time. In order to maintain a high degree of erasure, this UV lamp should be replaced when near this life expectancy ceiling.

PROJECT 15: AN 8-WATT EPROM ERASER

A much more powerful EPROM eraser can be built with an 8-watt UV lamp. Unlike the lower wattage eraser, this eraser will erase up to four EPROMs (28-pin and 40-pin) in a single operation. Once again, the schematic diagram and parts list offer little complexity in their content (see Fig. 9-4 and Table 9-3). The selection of the eraser's chassis, however, is far more crucial.

Parts List

BL1 - 8-watt ballast
L1 -8-watt UV lamp
P1 - grounded three-wire plug
S1-S2 - SPST switch

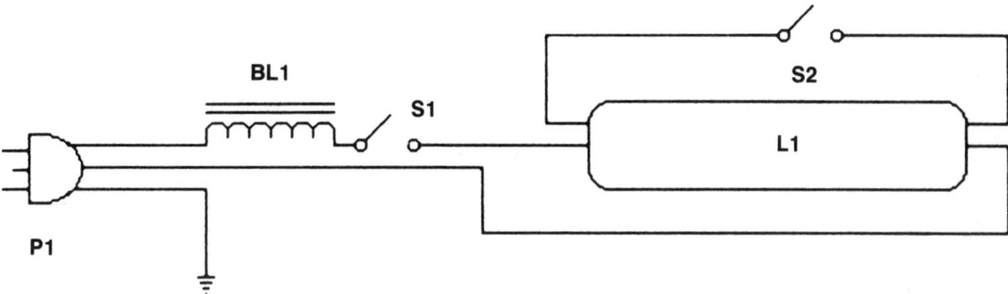

Fig. 9-4. Schematic diagram for the 8-watt EPROM eraser.

A durable metal enclosure should be used for holding the UV lamp and its ballast. The Radio Shack metal cabinets Part #270-25X are excellent for holding this project. Make sure that the final enclosure is *completely* light tight. This requirement will prevent the optically dangerous UV light from escaping from the eraser into the surrounding room. A cushioning foam is an excellent material for eliminating any light leaks. Place this foam over and around any and all surfaces that lack a tight fit. Foam with an adhesive backing makes this application even easier.

The enclosure's floor that holds the EPROMs must be less then two inches from the bulb. This distance permits the 8-watt bulb to rapidly erase the target EPROMs. When positioning the floor make sure that the quartz window of the EPROM is approximately one inch away from the UV light source. Multiple layers of conductive foam are the best material for elevating the EPROM to this necessary level.

When the construction of the 8-watt eraser has been completed, several tests should be performed before operation. Figure 9-5 and Table 9-4 show the test points and list the results for checking the assembly of the eraser. If

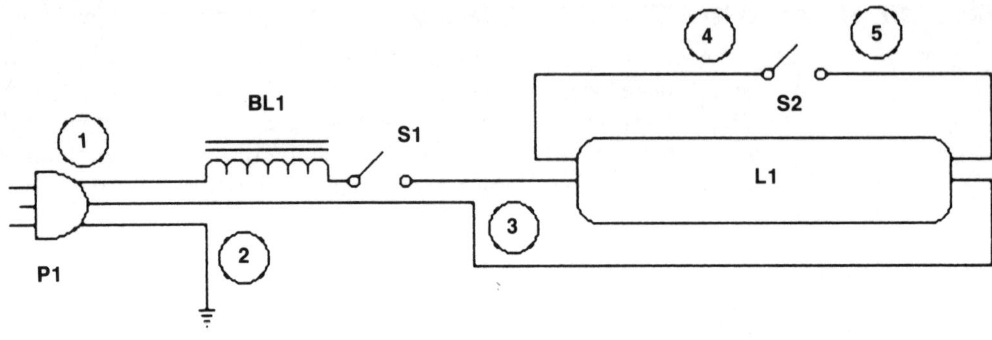

Test 1 Infinity ohms
Test 2 0 ohms
Test 3 Infinity ohms
Test 4 Infinity ohms
Test 5 >75 ohms

Fig. 9-5. Voltage test locations for the 8-watt EPROM eraser.

all of these tests produce good results, then the EPROM eraser is ready for operation.

Five steps are required for the proper operation of this EPROM eraser:

- Unplug the eraser from its voltage source and turn both switches off.
- Place the target EPROMs on the enclosure's floor.
- Close the eraser's cover.
- Plug the eraser into its voltage source and turn both switches on.
- Turn off, unplug, and remove the erased EPROMs after the correct erase time has expired.

CAUTION: UV light from this eraser is harmful to *all* human eyes and optic centers. Avoid any visual contact with this light source.

Under normal operating conditions, this eraser should be able to provide approximately 2000 hours of erase time. Replacing the 8-watt UV bulb after this time will ensure complete EPROM erasure.

10

Commercial Programmers and Erasers

Commercially marketed EPROM programmers and erasers fall into two general categories: pre-wired and kit. Within these two broad brushstrokes, there are in excess of 43 different models to choose from (this figure is based on a 1987 census of the EPROM programmer and eraser market). In general terms, a pre-wired model is a factory-assembled and tested unit that requires only a handful of EPROMs and support software (this requirement is for computer-based programmers) for operation. A kit model, on the other hand, places different demands on the user.

A kit EPROM programmer and/or eraser must be assembled by the user prior to the subsequent writing and erasing of EPROMs. A recent survey of the programmer and eraser kit market produced a wide range in the ease with which these kits can be assembled. At the simplest end of this assembly spectrum are the serial EPROM programmers. These programmers require very little digital circuitry for their operation. Therefore, the prospective kit builder is left with only a modest soldering requirement. Usually, 15-to-20 gate, buffer, and inverter ICs form the backbone of this kit. Additionally, a UART and an occassional personality ROM complete this modest serial kit. The assembly time for this kit ranges between 1 and 5 hours, based on the level of expertise of the user.

At the other, more complex end of this kit assembly spectrum is the intelligent or "smart" EPROM programmer. These kits feature a supervisory MPU for directing the writing, verifying, and reading operations of the programmer. In this case, the main circuit board may hold up to 40 digital and linear ICs. An excellent example of this form of EPROM programmer is the Heath EPROM Programmer. As an introduction and guide to the assembly and operation of an EPROM programmer kit, the remainder of this chapter will outline the construction of a sophisticated intelligent EPROM programmer. Based solely on its universal availability, the Heath EPROM Programmer is used as an illustration of this kit building process.

THE HEATH ID-4801 PROGRAMMER

Heath Company's EPROM Programmer is equipped with its own Z80 MPU operating at a clock speed of 2 MHz. A six-digit LED display is used for indicating both the current address location and its respective data, both in hexadecimal notation. A 16-key hex keypad provides a manual interface for feeding data into the target EPROM. In order to simplify this data entry process, the ID-4801 also sports an RS-232C serial interface. This standard DB-25 port is a direct read/write (R/W) channel between the host computer and the target EPROM.

The Heath programmer's 2K bytes of on-board RAM are expandable up to a maximum of 16K bytes. This RAM serves as a buffer for receiving data from the keypad, the host computer, or another source EPROM. Once this data transfer is complete, several edit functions can be performed on the RAM-stored data. While in this RAM buffer, individual bytes can be searched, inserted, and deleted. There is also a verify edit function, which compares the RAM buffer's contents against the data of the resident EPROM. All of these powerful commands and features can be accessed through six top-panel pushbuttons with their status displayed on the six LEDs.

EPROM to RAM
RS-232 Transmit
RS-232 Receive
Simulate
Insert RAM Data
Delete RAM Data
Byte Search
Program EPROM
Verify EPROM

The final physical landmark on the Heath Programmer is the EPROM interface. This ZIF socket operates smoothly and is intelligently isolated from the rest of the EPROM programmer's control panel.

Assembly of the Heath Programmer

Construction of the EPROM Programmer begins on page five of the Heath manual, found with the unpacking instructions (see Fig. 10-1). Careful attention at these early stages will ensure a flawless performance during the operational testing procedures on the Manual's page 39 (see Fig. 10-2). The circuit board's

Fig. 10-1. Heath's documentation for the Heath ID-4801 EPROM Programmer kit.

Fig. 10-2. The Heath main circuit board and three items that will ensure success: a PanaVise circuit board holder, a pencil for notetaking, and enough room for both instruction and illustration manuals to open simultaneously.

support components are soldered into place following the typically thorough Heath parts checklist (see Fig. 10-3). This assortment of parts includes resistors, capacitors, and glass diodes. Installing glass diodes is a delicate matter in kit construction, but if you should break one of these diodes during assembly, a plastic replacement diode can be found at Radio Shack (part #1N4002).

After all of the support components have been soldered into place, the IC sockets (see Fig. 10-4), resistor packs, transistors, and the clock crystal are added. Rounding out the component side of the Programmer's circuit board is the installation of the pushbutton switches (see Figs. 10-5 and 10-6), function LEDs (see Fig. 10-7), ZIF socket, and personality module socket (see Fig. 10-8).

The power supply components are attached to the solder side of the circuit board. Several power capacitors, a heat sink, and a voltage regulator IC must all be added in this inverted position (see Fig. 10-9).

With the circuit board completed, the construction now swings to the chassis assembly. This step is divided into the cabinet bottom and cabinet top subassemblies. The wire preparation requires the stripping and tinning

Fig. 10-3. Sequenced part tape strips make the soldering of these support components a snap.

Fig. 10-4. Use masking tape to hold IC sockets in place when you flip the board over for soldering.

Fig. 10-5. Add the pushbuttons after the IC sockets have been soldered in place.

Fig. 10-6. Install the pushbutton key-caps on the soldered pushbuttons before final assembly.

Fig. 10-7. A cardboard spacer ensures that all of the LEDs are at a proper angle and height for the fitting into the cabinet top.

Fig. 10-8. IC sockets U101, U116, and U115 hold the Z80 MPU, personality module, and target EPROM, respectively.

Fig. 10-9. All power capacitors, including the 22 mF modification, are soldered to the foil side of the main circuit board.

Fig. 10-10. Inside the cabinet bottom. The AC filter board, fuse holder, and DB-25 port are all located upside down under this panel labeled, "Caution."

of 19 pieces of supplied wire. Following this wire routine, the transformer assembly, AC line filter board (see Fig. 10-10), line cord, and DB-25 port (see Fig. 10-11) are all positioned in the cabinet bottom. The cabinet top work consists of pushing sixteen brass inserts into screw ports located on the inside of the cabinet top and installing the main power switch, power status LED, and associated labels.

NOTE: During this assembly, a difference in Heath's documentation and the actual construction can be found in Heath Pictoral 2-4. This power transformer illustration labels the red colored pin 6 with an incorrect green color. *This point should be corrected and incorporated into the final assembly.*

Assembly Testing

Before the EPROM Programmer is powered up, several wiring and circuitry tests should be made. Using a multimeter, inspect each of the primary power wires for shorts and/or erroneous connections. Heath supplies extensive multimeter charts that illustrate all of the probe test points along with suggested solutions to incorrect readings. Following these wiring checks, the circuit board's resistance and voltage levels are tested through the help of similar troubleshooting charts.

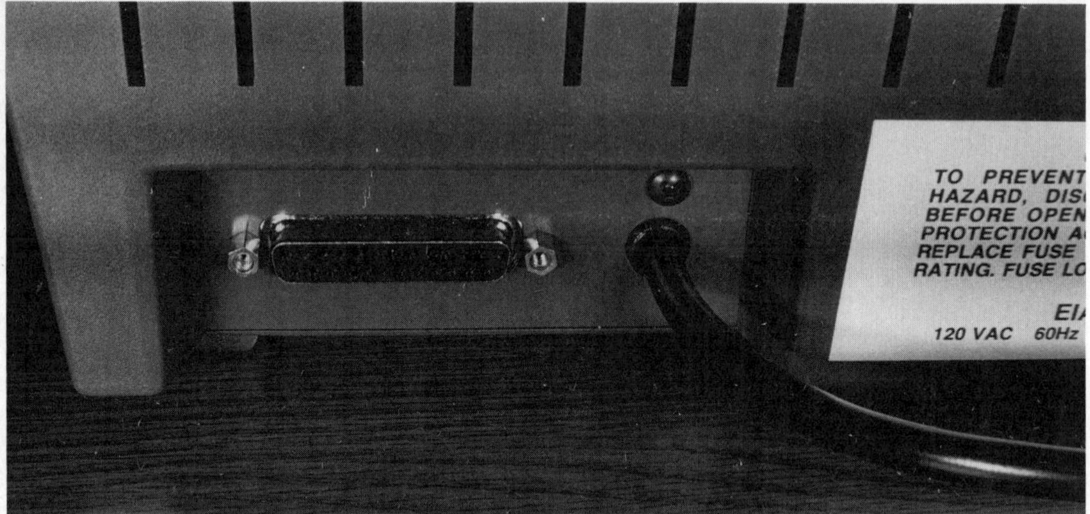

Fig. 10-11. The RS-232C port that enables a host computer to program and read data from a target EPROM.

Once you have completed all of these tests, the final assembly can begin. Each of the designated ICs and display LEDs are pushed into their proper sockets (see Fig. 10-12) and the cabinet top and bottom pieces are joined together. Now the first operational test can be conducted. A 07FF address will be displayed on the LEDs when the 2K bytes Programmer is initally powered up (see Fig. 10-13). The total elapsed construction time is about six hours.

BUILDING THE HEATH ID-4803 ERASER

The Heath EPROM Eraser is a simple kit that serves as an ideal complement to the EPROM Programmer. Unlike the Programmer kit, the Eraser has no ICs or support components and very little soldering. Most of the Eraser's actual building time involves hardware assembly. Once the lamp panel is assembled and nestled into the snug fitting cabinet bottom (see Fig. 10-14), all that remains is securing the cabinet top and bottom together (see Fig. 10-15). The total elapsed construction time for the Eraser kit was 1.5 hours.

HEATH EPROM PROGRAMMER

Several hardware improvements can be made to the Heath EPROM Programmer that enhance its versatility. Furthermore, each of these improvements cost several dollars less than purchasing the comparable Heath upgrade kits.

The first cost-reducing improvement involves the construction of the personality modules for the ID-4801. Virtually any 24-pin IC carrier and cover

Fig. 10-12. The fully populated main circuit board.

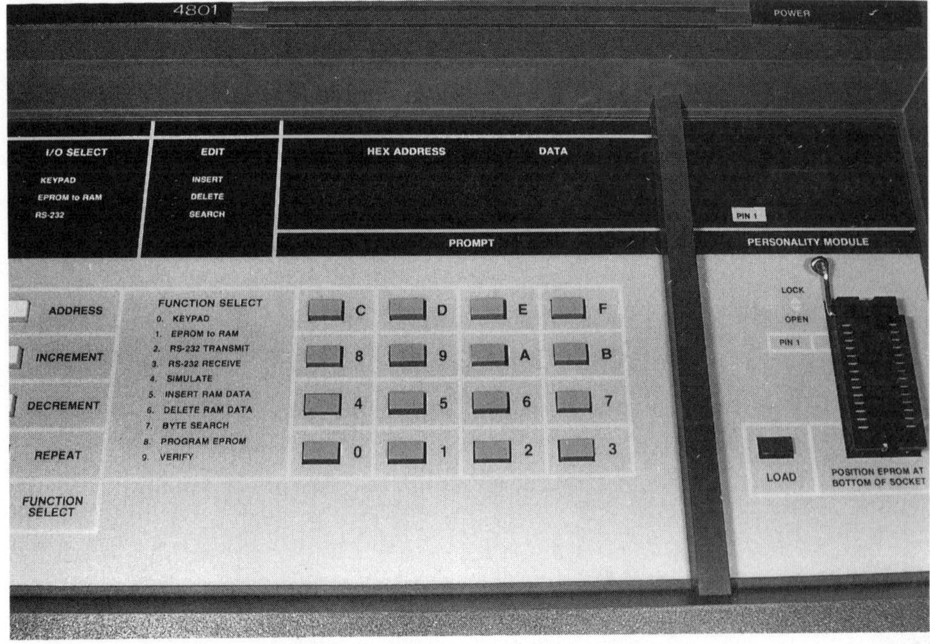

Fig. 10-13. A completed and assembled Heath EPROM Programmer.

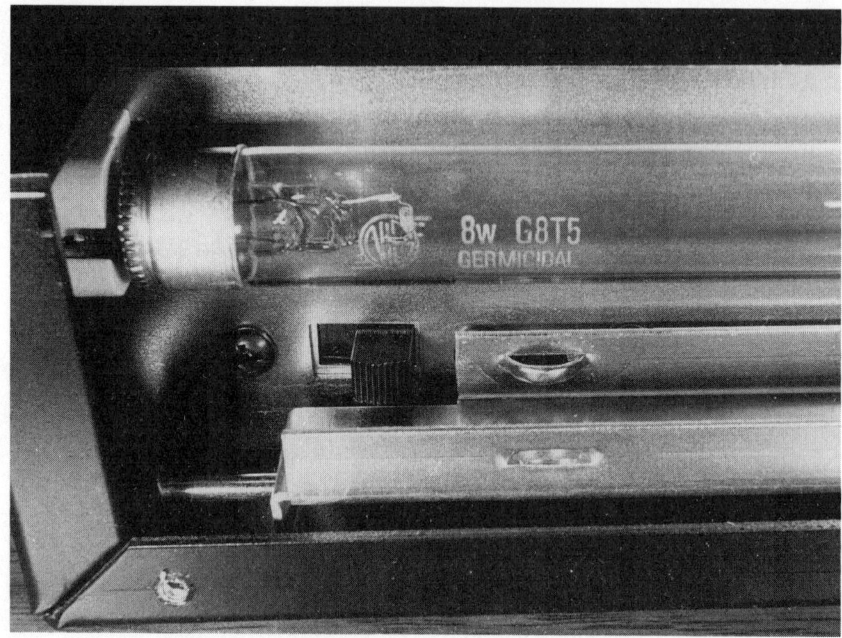

Fig. 10-14. The Heath EPROM eraser's lamp panel holds a UV lamp near the EPROM tray.

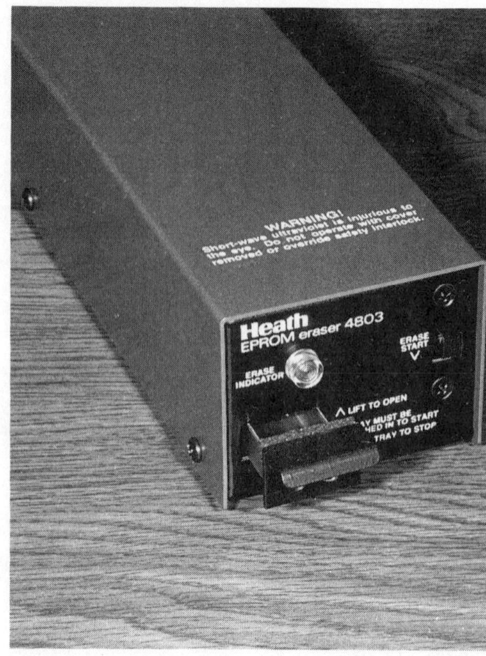

Fig. 10-15. A completed and assembled Heath EPROM Eraser.

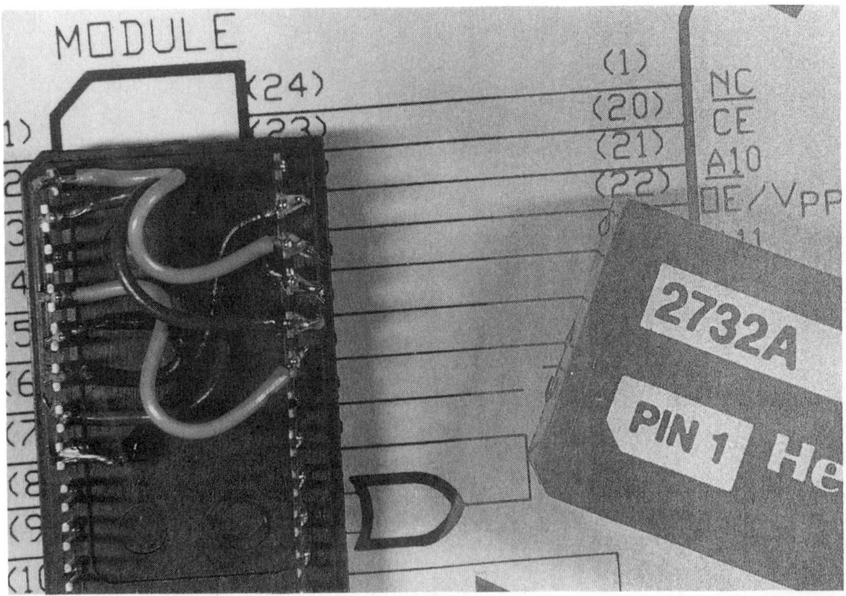

Fig. 10-16. A wired 2732A personality module ready for use with the Programmer.

can be used in the construction of these system configuration jumpers (see Fig. 10-16). The module can then be wired with the necessary components following Heath's instructions (see Fig. 10-17).

As another improvement, by purchasing a handful of static RAM ICs, the memory of the Heath Programmer can be expanded by a factor of 8. In order

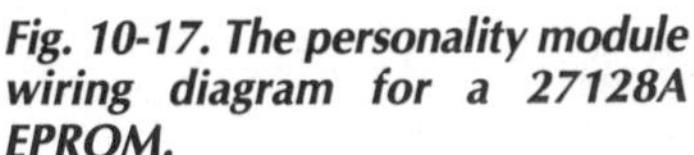
Fig. 10-17. The personality module wiring diagram for a 27128A EPROM.

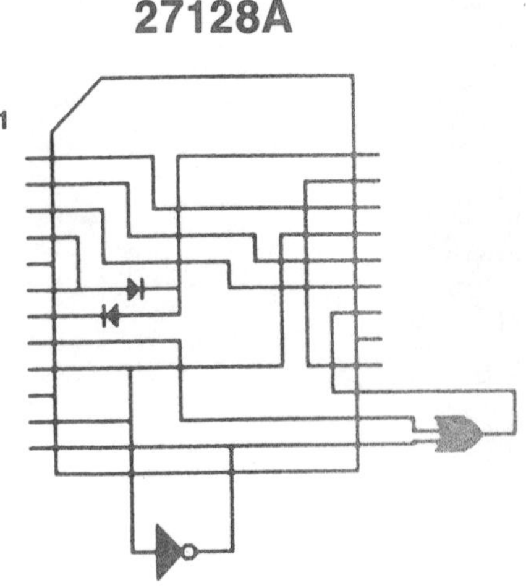

to perform this memory upgrade, the following static RAM chips must be purchased:

6116 2K × 8 bit (3)
6164 8K × 8 bit (1)

All memory chips must have a 150 nS access time.

The installation of these memory ICs requires that the EPROM Programmer be disassembled. After the cabinet top and bottom have been separated, sockets U109, U111, U112, and U113 must be located along the lower edge of the main circuit board (see Fig. 10-18).

Each of the memory expansion chips must then be prepared for insertion into their respective socket. This preparation involves the careful binding of each chip's pins. A preliminary test fit of each IC will confirm when the pins have been bent sufficiently for easy insertion. These prepared RAM chips are then inserted into their designated RAM sockets on the main circuit board. Sockets U109, U111, U112 hold one 6116 IC, each, and socket U113 is the site for the 6164 static RAM. When all of the chips have been inserted, the EPROM Programmer cabinet pieces are assembled. A 3FFF address display on the LEDs upon power up signals the completion of a successful memory expansion.

Certain host computers could have difficulty transmitting and receiving data through the EPROM Programmer's RS-232C interface. This problem could

Fig. 10-18. Five static RAM sockets filled with one 6264 and four 6116 ICs increase the total memory of the Heath EPROM Programmer to 16K bytes RAM.

stem from pin 6 on the DB-25 port. Some computers require that this line be held high (a +15V) during operation. Two modifications to older EPROM Programmer kits (Heath is now supplying this modification with the kit) are required for obtaining this high-voltage pin 6.

First, disassemble the Programmer's cabinet top and bottom. Locate socket U134 and header P101 (see Figs. 10-19 and 10-20). Solder a jumper wire between pin 11 of socket U134 and pin 2 of jumper P101. Second, attach a 12-inch wire, with the appropriate connectors on each end, between hole 2 of socket S101 (this is the connector for jumper P101) and hole 6 of the DB-25 connector (S1). When both of these connections have been completed, assemble the cabinet top and bottom together, again. The EPROM Programmer will now be able to transmit and receive data from your host computer. This modification is necessary when using the Heath-supported Upload/Download Software package (SDA-4801-10).

Fig. 10-19. The component side of socket U134 and header P101.

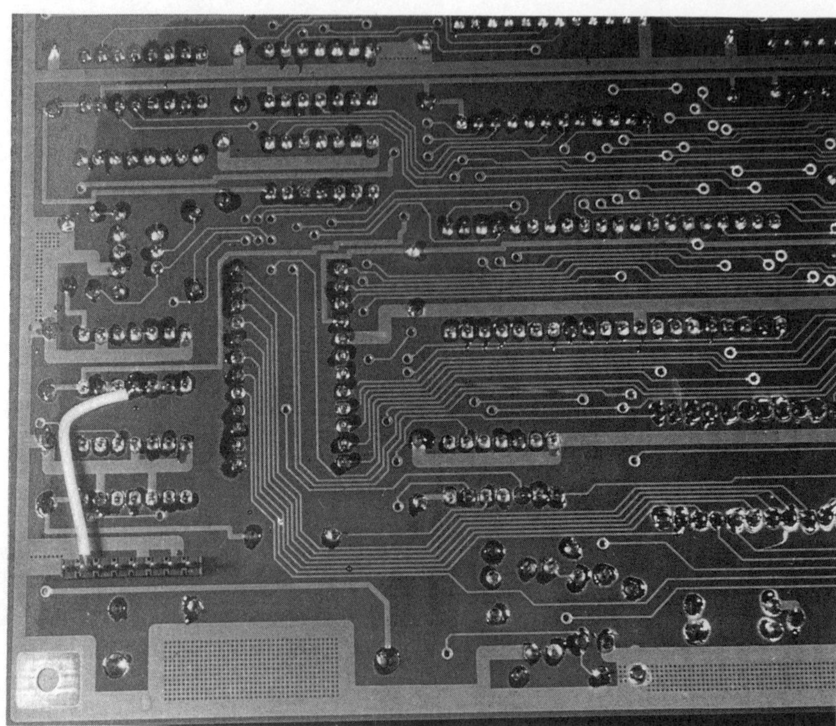

Fig. 10-20. The solder side of socket U134 and header P101 with the jumper wire installed.

11

SAM Technology

Sequential Access Memory (SAM) devices differ significantly from their Random Access Memory counterparts (this designation includes both RAM (RWM) and ROM devices). The major differences between these two memory categories concerns SAMs high data density and variable access time. In terms of a high data density, SAMs are able to hold more information in a given space than are RAMs. For example, a 1M-×-1-bit bubble memory SAM can fit into a 16-pin DIP IC package. This compact construction makes the SAM an exciting alternative to more conventional mass storage devices (e.g., floppy disks).

The second SAM difference, variable access time, is a noteworthy design consideration. Using the above bubble memory SAM example, the access time for this device is not constant for all memory registers. Instead, an average access time, derived from all of the address register access times, is given for this SAM. Therefore, SAMs can not be used in systems were a constant and rapid access time is important.

There are four SAM device types in current production and development: shift registers, charge-coupled devices, bubble memories, and Josephson Junction devices. Of these four SAMs, shift registers are the most common (see Chapter 1). The other three devices are either under development or available in limited quantities. As an introduction to this technology, the remainder of this chapter is devoted to a brief overview of these last three SAM devices.

CHARGE-COUPLED DEVICE

A charge-coupled device (CCD) is a volatile memory manufactured as a serial access MOS shift register. Inside the CCD, data is stored as numerous charged groupings that is moved through a vast network of storage cells via a controlled voltage pulse. This controlling voltage pulse is represented as a phase in the CCD. CCDs are manufactured in two, three, and four phase packages.

A typical "X" phase CCD has the same metal gate, silicon dioxide, p-type substrate construction form that is used in MOS transistors—except for one major difference. This difference is the elimination of the source and drain diffusions from the CCD design. In this design, the charge is retained within a storage cell when a positive charge is applied to the metal gate. This positive voltage forms holes in the p-type substrate, thereby making areas with a depleted charge under the gate. These areas are called a depletion region. A storage cell formed in this manner will hold its charge only for a limited time. Therefore, this volatile memory must be refreshed periodically for complete data retention.

Data in these storage cells are shifted through the CCD in a serial fashion. The charge of these data are transferred from one storage cell to another on the leading edge of the clocked voltage pulse. In other words, all data bits prior to the required data must be accessed first. This non-random or sequential data search greatly reduces the average access time of a CCD. As a result, access times for a CCD can range between 15 and 100 mS.

BUBBLE MEMORY

A more viable alternative to CCDs are bubble memories. Bubble memories are thin garnet magnetic films housed on non-magnetic substrates. When a magnetic field is applied to this magnetic film a magnetic domain or bubble forms. The formed bubble becomes a data bit and is then transferred to a storage area in a serial loop traffic pattern (see Fig. 11-1). Patterns in the magnetic film made from nickel-ferrite permalloy specify the path that the bubbles will travel within the magnetic film. A rotating magnetic field moves the formed bubbles through the defined polarities of the pattern.

While CCDs are volatile memories, bubble memories are non-volatile. This permanence in memory, even when the bubble memory device has had its power source removed, is achieved through a permanent magnet sandwich that holds the magnetic layers of the bubble memory (see Fig. 11-2). These magnets stabilize the highly polarized environment of the bubbles and their substrate. Therefore, no outside magnetic fields are able to disrupt the bubble memory's data.

The non-volatile nature of bubble memories makes them commercially important as an alternative to the mechanical mass storage devices (e.g., floppy disk drives). In addition to their reliable operation, bubble memories are also able to function in harsh environments (e.g., dust, moisture, and vibration) which would limit the application of other, more sensitive, magnetic media. Both the high data density and non-volatile features of the bubble memory must be weighed against several negative points, however.

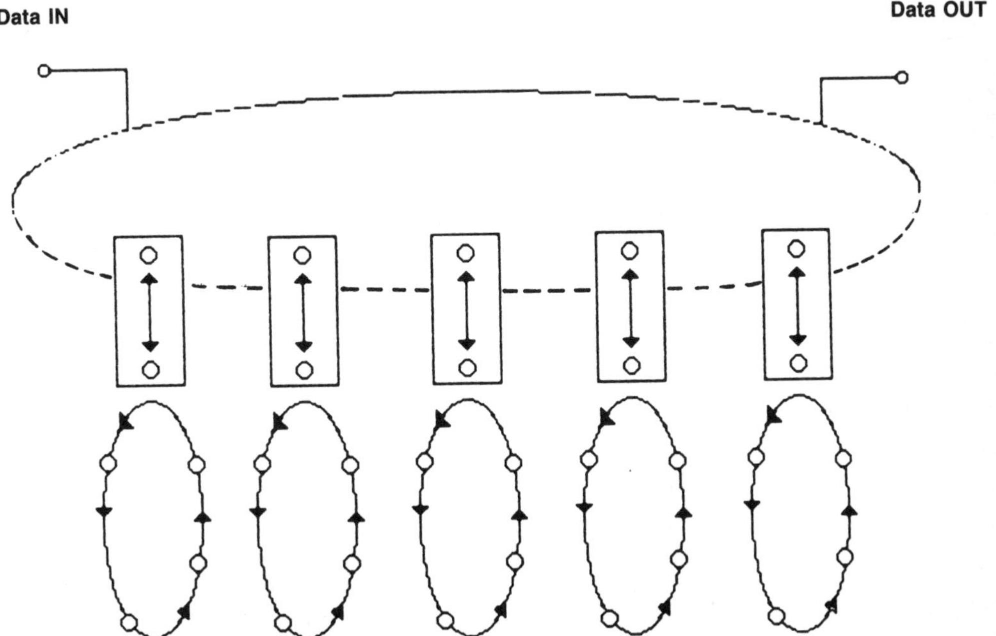

Fig. 11-1. An example of a travel route for a memory bit inside a bubble memory module.

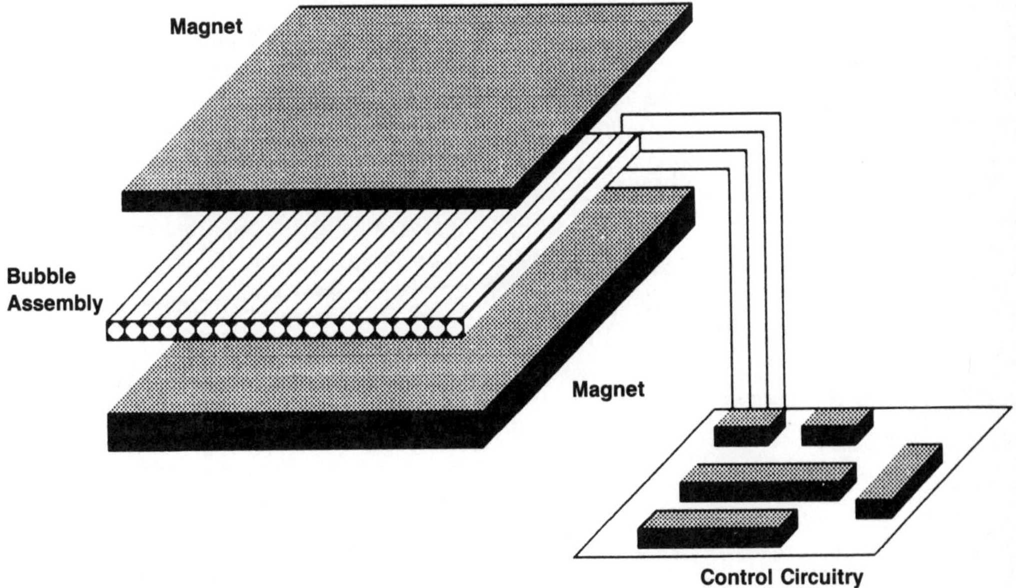

Fig. 11-2. A bubble memory module remains stable due to this magnet sandwich.

High cost, slow access times, and complex support circuitry are negative aspects that have hampered the widespread acceptance of bubble memories in the microcomputer marketplace. A typical complete bubble memory system can cost in excess of $1000. This prohibitive cost includes the bubble memory device and all of its associated support components (memory controller, sense amplifier, operation driver, coil predriver, and coil driver). Additionally, this bubble memory has an average access time of 2 to 11.5 mS. These three factors serve to greatly negate the advantages of the bubble memory.

JOSEPHSON JUNCTION DEVICE

One memory device in current development is the Josephson Junction device. Operating in a cryogenic environment at −460°F, the Josephson Junction device is being tested in fast supercomputer designs. The liquid helium design of this memory device provides it with a *superconductivity* potential.

The current in this superconductor is forced to travel in a closed loop under a determined magnetic charge. This charge is then used to represent a data bit. Due to the zero resistance found in superconductors, the current retains its charge and flow within its storage cell with little reduction in access time and no charge leakage. In this condition, superconductor storage cells can be packed into high density formations with rapid access times.

Even with the serial data access of this device, average access times of 1 to 2 nS are possible at extremely low power levels. Advances in this technology, however, have been made in several countries, most notably Switzerland, China, and the United States. Within the United States, two teams are refining the design of cryogenic memories. These teams located at Stanford University and the IBM Research Laboratory (in conjunction with a similar group in Zurich, Switzerland) have developed superconductors that are able to operate in a balmy liquid nitrogen bath of −320°F. In response to this breakthrough, a research team from China increased the operation temperature up to −280°F. As these temperature barriers continue to decrease, the design of faster supercomputers will proliferate, eventually leading to parallel memory advances in the microcomputer market.

A

Building an EPROM Project

Building your own EPROM programmer (or eraser, or EPROM-based circuit) is an exciting project that has been carefully detailed in this book's preceding chapters. By combining a few dollars worth of parts with an EPROM circuit's schematic diagram, an intelligent design is born. Unfortunately, several factors are bound to block the successful implementation of digital memory. There are financial, mental, and physical reasons that might prevent the introduction of EPROMs into your computer's life. While I can't satisfy either your financial or physical difficulties, I can try to lessen the severity of your naiveté to electronics construction techniques.

Whether you are a seasoned electronic project builder, or a casual computer user, you need to learn a few construction basics. Most of these building techniques center around the most effective means for translating an EPROM circuit from paper into a wired, operating unit. Two specific areas in which this construction education is stressed are the manner in which the circuit is built and the enclosure in which it is placed.

Seasoned electronics project builders may be experienced hands at soldering and printed circuit board (PCB) etching (if you aren't, read further in this appendix), but use of the modular IC breadboard, universal PC boards, and E-Z Circuit boards are three methods of project wiring that are available to all levels of project builders. EPROM circuits are easily transferred from the printed schematic onto a breadboard by using easily cut jumper wires and no soldering. Circuit builders desiring more stability for their projects can quickly translate the breadboard circuits onto either a solderable universal PC board or an E-Z Circuit board. Radio Shack's Modular IC Breadboard

Sockets (Radio Shack's #276-174 and #276-175) and Experimenter's PC Boards (Radio Shack #276-170), Vector's Plugboards (Vector's #4609, #4610, and #4613), and Bishop Graphics' E-Z Bus Boards (Bishop Graphics' #EZ7472, #EZ7464, #EZ7402, and #EZ7475), are all well suited to EPROM construction.

Once you have finalized your EPROM design, it is time to place your circuit inside a housing. As a rule, a housing will only be necessary for stand-alone and parallel or serial port connection computer-based EPROM programmers. For example, if your final EPROM project is for an internal expansion slot of an IBM PC, then you will not need to worry about a housing. Conversely, if your memory circuit uses a parallel port for interfacing with microcomputers, then you will need to consider the design of a circuit housing. In some ways, the familiar, boxy metal or plastic electronics project cabinet has turned into an antiquated relic. For the majority of the constructed EPROM programmers, however, the purchased storage cabinet is the ideal project housing solution.

PLUG 'N PROGRAM

A great breakthrough in the electronics design community has been the introduction of the modular breadboard socket (see Fig. A-1). This tool will be totally alien to those of you who have never before designed an electronics project. But electronics enthusiasts have long employed these reusable boards for testing circuits prior to committing the design to a final, soldered board. The reason behind this pretesting is really quite simple: why solder expensive components to a board when the project's resultant design might contain performance flaws?

The design of a modular breadboard is fairly straightforward: a hard plastic board provides a gridwork of connection slots into which the leads of electronics components are inserted. Electrical connection points are located underneath this surface grid. Without using any soldering, component leads are pinched in place by the underlying contacts. The connection slot spacing of IC compatible breadboards is situated so that integrated circuit chip pins fit neatly into the slots without being bent. Therefore, an additional benefit of the modular breadboard is its ability to accept ICs plugged directly into the board without needing an IC socket. If the builder then decides to discard or alter a project's design, the ICs are easily extracted and remain ready for use in another project.

Modular breadboard sockets are sold by a wide variety of manufacturers, but one particularly accessible type of breadboard is that sold by Radio Shack. This board comes in two sizes: the Modular IC Breadboard Socket (Radio Shack #276-174), measuring 2 inches by 6 inches, and the Modular IC Breadboard Socket (Radio Shack #276-175), which measures 2⅛ inches by 3⅝ inches. These two breadboards are designed so they can be joined together in many different combinations and fit virtually any project size. The modular nature

Fig. A-1. A modular breadboard socket holding the Boole's Box in its initial testing stage.

of these boards permits one to be linked to another through a tight fitting rim that runs around the edge of every board.

When an EPROM circuit is constructed on a Modular IC Breadboard Socket, the underlying pattern of connection points must be remembered. The two strips of connection points, labeled X and Y, located along the left and right sides (in reference to the Radio Shack boards) each form a completely interconnected strip. These strips form a jumper bus along which component connections can be made. An ideal use for these strips is to designate one as the power bus and the other as the grounding bus. Therefore, any circuit connection requiring power can be connected into the most convenient slot on the power bus strip.

Other connection points on each breadboard are united with their neighbors in strips of five horizontal connection points. These sets of connection points are numbered down the length of the breadboard. A separation running down the center of the breadboard creates a no connection "dead" zone between the five connection point strip on the right and the similar strip on the lefthand side of the board. This dead zone facilitates the placement of an IC onto the board across this gap without connecting the opposing pins of the IC.

Component leads are connected on the breadboard by making use of adjacent connection points; in other words, by placing the appropriate component leads next to each other on the breadboard (these leads can even be placed within the same slot). Alternatively, jumper wires can be used for connecting from one component to another over the surface of the board. Small pieces of wire-wrap wire, with their ends stripped (approximately ¼ inch of the insulation is removed from each end), are perfectly suited for such jumper applications.

The use of Modular IC Breadboard Sockets for initial circuit design preparation is ideal for the electronics neophyte. Even the more experienced project builder will find cause for using these breadboards. An EPROM design is tested, and, if the final results are not suitable, modifications are made to the flexible breadboard. This technique reduces parts cost and saves the builder in final construction time. If, on the other hand, the builder decides that the EPROM circuit is worthy of a permanent implementation, the breadboard project can be translated in its exact form onto either a universal PC board or an E-Z circuit board by using the same component placement and the identical jumper wire locations.

UNIVERSAL PC BOARDS

When purchasing a universal PC board for soldering your EPROM circuit's components onto, four considerations are in order. First, a pre-drilled board is an absolute necessity; no one wants to drill dozens of holes to stick component leads into. Not just any pre-drilled PC board will do, however, because the chosen board must have IC spacing between its holes. This type of spacing permits IC sockets, or even an IC, to be soldered directly onto the board. Second, the board must have solder- ringed, or pre-tinned holes. This feature simplifies the soldering process by helping the solder to stick to the board and the component lead. Third, both sides of the universal PC board should be examined before purchase to ensure that the board does not have a specialized solder tracing pattern that will make transferring a breadboard design to the PC board difficult, if not impossible. Fourth and last, if the final EPROM circuit is going to be connected to a microcomputer's internal expansion slot, then make sure that the PC board has an edge connector with the proper number of pads. A mistake at this point could jeopardize your Apple

II project that needs a 50-pad edge connector, that is, if you accidentally placed this EPROM project on a universal PC board with only 44 pads.

Despite these four warnings, universal PC board selection is really quite simple. EPROM programmer builders, using the Radio Shack Modular IC Breadboard Socket, will find the translation of their circuits to a hardwired, soldered state easier than expected, thanks to two manufacturer's products: Radio Shack's Experimenter's PC Board (Radio Shack #276-170) and Vector's Plugboards (Vector #4609, #4610, and #4613).

The Experimenter's PC Board is specifically designed to imitate the function and connection points of Radio Shack's Modular IC Breadboard Socket. This means that specialized tracings *do* appear on one side of the Experimenter's PC Board. But these tracings correspond to the same vertical and horizontal connection strips that are found on the Modular IC Breadboard Socket. Because of this direct emulation, a breadboarded circuit can be exactly copied, component for component, jumper wire for jumper wire, onto the Experimenter's PC Board.

Because some computer-based EPROM programmers must be interfaced with a computer via its internal expansion slot, direct circuit translation with the Experimenter's PC Board is not practical. In these cases, the Vector Plugboards should be used (see Fig. A-2). Three types of computer expansion slots are represented by Vector Plugboards: Apple II family (Vector #4609), IBM PC family (Vector #4613), and Standard Bus (Vector #4610). Each of these boards is made from high-quality glass epoxy with gold-plated edge connector

Fig. A-2. Vector plugboard #4609 is an Apple IIe bus-compatible expansion card.

pads. There is also a helpful tracing arrangement that won't pose too difficult of a conversion chore when translating your design from a breadboard onto one of these plugboards.

Because some EPROM circuits are not large enough to occupy an entire Modular IC Breadboard Socket, they can be planned on the smaller Radio Shack version (Radio Shack #276-175). In this situation, it would not be practical to use an entire Experimenter's PC Board or Vector Plugboard. It is far more economical to cut one of these boards (either the Experimenter's PC Board or the Vector Plugboard) into two pieces and use the halved pieces for constructing two separate circuits. A small handsaw, such as X-Acto's RAZOR SAW BLADE (X-Acto's #234), is the perfect tool for this purpose. A careful cutting job, followed by a light sanding of the board's rough edges, will result in two ready-to-use miniature universal PC boards.

IF IT'S E-Z, IT MUST BE EASY

Custom circuit boards used to be the exclusive domain of the acid-etched PCB. Now Bishop Graphics has introduced a revolutionary concept that could become the next dominant circuit board construction technique. E-Z Circuit, what Bishop Graphics calls it, takes a standard, pre-drilled universal PC board and lets the builder determine all of the tracing and pad placements. A special adhesive copper tape is the secret to this easy miracle in PCB fabrication.

The E-Z Circuit system is both an extensive set of these special copper tape patterns and several blank universal PC boards. The blank boards serve as the mounting medium for receiving the copper patterns. There are general-purpose blank boards (Bishop Graphics' #EZ7402 and #EZ7475) and Apple II family blank PC boards (Bishop Graphics' #EZ7464). Each of these boards is made from a high-quality glass epoxy and pre-drilled with IC spaced holes. There is also a blank edge-connector region on each board for attaching one of E-Z Circuit's copper edge connector strips.

Complementing the blank boards is a complete set of copper patterns. Each pattern is supplied with a special adhesive that permits minor repositioning, but holds firmly once its position is determined. This adhesive also has heat resistant properties that enable direct soldering contact with the pattern. Only an extensive selection of patterns and sizes would make an E-Z Circuit design worthy of consideration for EPROM project construction. Once again, E-Z Circuit satisfies all of these requirements with edge connector, IC package, terminal, test point strip, tracing, donut pad, elbow, TO-5, power and ground strip, and power transistor patterns. Additionally, each of these patterns is available in several sizes, shapes, and diameters.

Only four simple steps are needed in the construction of an E-Z Circuit EPROM project. In step one, you determine which pattern you need and prepare it for positioning. Step two is for placing the selected pattern on the blank PC board. This is a simple process that involves the removal of a flexible release layer from the back of the copper-clad pattern. During Step three, you insert all of the components into their respective holes. Finally, in step four, you solder the component's leads to the copper pattern. This step should be treated just like soldering a coventional copper pad or tracing. If you use a reasonable soldering iron temperature, anywhere from 400 to 600 degrees Fahrenheit, you won't need to worry about destroying the adhesive layer and ruining the copper pattern.

Making a slight digression on the issue of soldering irons, be sure to use an iron with a rating of 15 to 25 watts. Soldering irons that are matched to the demands of working with E-Z Circuit include: ISOTIP 7800, 7700 (the specifications for these two irons "border" the stated E-Z Circuit requirements, but they will work), and 7240, UNGAR SYSTEM 9000, and WELLER EC2000.

The result of this four step process is a completed EPROM circuit built in less time than a comparably prepared acid-etched PCB. Incidentally, the cost of preparing one EPROM circuit with E-Z Circuit versus the etched route is far less. Of course, this cost difference is skewed in the other direction when you need to make more than one PCB. This is because E-Z Circuit is geared for one-shot production and not assembly-line production. The bottom line is, before you decide on your circuit board construction technique (Experimenter's PC Board, Vector Plugboards, or E-Z Circuit), read the remainder of this appendix for the latest advances in acid-etched PCB design. Then evaluate your needs and resources and get to work on your EPROM programmer.

TAMING THE SOLDER RIVER

Before the first bit of solder is liquefied on your PC board, an overall concept must be organized for fitting the completed EPROM project into an enclosure. Small enclosures are usually preferred over the larger and bulkier cabinets simply because of their low profile and discreet appearance. Space is limited within the narrow confines of such a sloped enclosure, however.

It's quite easy to envision a two-dimensional EPROM circuit schematic diagram and then forget that the finished, hard-wired circuit will actually occupy three dimensions. Capacitors, resistors, and ICs all give a considerable amount of depth to a finished project PC board. Fortunately, the effects of these tall components can be minimized through some clever assembly techniques (see Fig. A-3).

It is strongly recommended to leave all component leads at their full length while they remain on a breadboard. These ungainly components, however, do not permit the smooth translation of a project into a narrow enclosure if they are soldered to the PC board in this same manner. With only a few exceptions, all components must be soldered to a PC board as closely as possible. One exception to this rule is in leaving adequate jumper wire lengths for external, enclosure-mounted components, such as switches and speakers.

Both component selection and their mounting methods directly affect an EPROM project's PC board depth. For example, the selection of a horizontally

Fig. A-3. Soldering EPROM project components onto a PC board can result in a nightmare of tangled wires and crowded components.

oriented, miniature PC mountable potentiometer over a standard vertically oriented potentiometer can save up to ½ inch off of a board's final height (see Fig. A-4). Likewise, flat, rectangular metal film capacitors offer space savings whenever capacitors of their value are required (usually .01 mF to 1.0 mF).

If a disc or monolithic capacitor is used on a circuit board, the lead can be bent so that the capacitor lies nearly flat against the PC board. The capacitor can be pre-fitted before soldering it into place and the required bends can be made with a pair of needle-nosed pliers. Be sure the leads of every component are slipped through the PC board's holes as far as possible before soldering them into place. Excessive leads can be clipped from the back side of the board *after* the solder connection has been made. At this point a precautionary note pertaining to overly zealous board compacting is necessary. Do not condense a board's components so tightly that undesired leads might touch; a short circuit is the inevitable and unwanted result for this carelessness. Also, some components emit heat during operation. Therefore, some component spacing is mandatory for proper ventilation.

One way to minimize PC board component crowding is by using a special mounting technique with resistors and diodes. The common practice for

Fig. A-4. This prototype of an EPROM-based message center shows how careful planning and "height-reducing" components, like the resistor DIP, can clean up the final construction.

mounting resistors and diodes is to lay them flat against the PC board. This technique is impractical (and occasionally impossible) on the previously described PC boards. A superior technique is to stand the resistor or diode on its end and fold one lead down until it is parallel with the other lead. The component leads can then be placed in virtually adjacent holes.

One final low-profile component that is an absolute necessity on any PC board that uses ICs is the IC socket. An IC socket is soldered to the PC board to hold an IC. Therefore, the IC is free to be inserted into or extracted from the socket at any time. Acting as a safety measure, the IC socket prevents any damage that might be caused to a chip by an excessively hot soldering iron if the IC were soldered directly to the PC board. IC chips are extremely delicate and both heat and static electricity can damage them. After the EPROM project board has been completely soldered, the ICs are added last.

THE FINISHING TOUCH

The most easily acquired enclosure for your finished EPROM programmer is a metal or plastic cabinet that can be purchased from your local electronics store. Radio Shack makes a stylish, wedge-shaped enclosure (Radio Shack #270-282) and two styles of two-tone cabinets (Radio Shack #270-272 and #270-274), all three of which are perfect for holding your EPROM project. Another slightly less attractive, but still useful, project enclosure that is also available from Radio Shack is the Experimenter Box (Radio Shack #270-230 through #270-233 and #270-627). The Experimenter Box comes in five different sizes for holding any size of EPROM programmer.

If none of these enclosures fit your requirements, you can also build your own EPROM project cabinet. The best material for building your own enclosure is with one of the numerous, inexpensive types of sheet plastics that are currently available. Materials such as Plexiglas are easy to manipulate with the right tools and adhesives. Plexiglas sheeting can be cut with a hand saw or a power jig saw. Just remember not to remove the protective paper covering from the Plexiglas while cutting it; this prevents the sheet from splitting or becoming scratched.

Construct all sides of the enclosure by adjoining sides together and laying a thin bead of a liquid adhesive along the joint. A powerful cyanoacrylate adhesive, such as Satellite City's SUPER "T" will bond two pieces of Plexiglas together immediately. Be sure that all panel edges are perfectly aligned before applying the adhesive. One side of the final enclosure design should not be joined with the adhesive but with screws so that it is easily removed for future access to your EPROM circuit.

Hopefully, you have finished reading this portion of Appendix A before you have started your EPROM project's actual construction. If so, good; you have saved yourself several hours of headaches and, quite probably, several dollars in wasted expenses. If not, all is not lost. Just review your current construction in light of what you have learned in this appendix and make any needed changes in your construction procedures. At least when you make your next EPROM programmer, you will know all of the secrets to successful circuit construction.

PCB DESIGN WITH CAD SOFTWARE

For the most part, if you own either an Apple Macintosh or an IBM PC family microcomputer, then you have the potential for designing your own printed circuit boards (PCBs). This potential is only realized after the purchase of some specialized design software, however. A rather general term is applied to this type of software—computer-aided design or CAD software. CAD is a relatively young field with true dominance already present in the IBM PC arena. This definitive CAD software product is called AutoCAD 2 and it is manufactured by Autodesk, Inc. Don't be fooled by other CAD products that are designed for IBM PCs and their clones and cost less than AutoCAD's roughly $2000 price tag. These cheaper programs are totally inferior to AutoCAD. Without question, the AutoCAD environment is the most powerful CAD software that is currently available for microcomputers and yet it remains flexible to every users' demand. All of this means that if you own an IBM PC (or equivalent) and need to design PCBs, then buy AutoCAD. You will never regret your investment.

One fault that is frequently attached to CAD software like AutoCAD is the lack of a dedicated PCB template formulation application. In other words, programs like AutoCAD must be customized with user-created symbol libraries before PCB templates can be expertly designed in a minimal amount of time. If you think that there's got to be a better way, then let Wintek Corporation show you the path to this ideal solution. Two professional pieces of CAD software, smARTWORK and HiWIRE, are vertical applications with specific PCB template fabrication virtues. These programs sport an impressive list of PCB template design features:

- a silkscreen layer
- text lettering for every layer
- variable trace width
- user-definable symbol libraries
- automatic solder mask generation
- 2× check prints
- numerous printer/plotter drivers
- AutoCAD *.DXF file generation

The bottom line for these Wintek Corporation PCB CAD products is that they will aid you in the design of custom PCB templates for less than half the cost of AutoCAD and with double the creative power.

But what are PCBs anyway? PCBs are vital for the mass production of circuit designs. The printed circuit board serves as the substratum for building an electronics circuit like an EPROM programmer. The board itself is usually constructed from glass epoxy with a coating of copper on one or both of its sides. By using a powerful acid etchant like anhydrous ferric chloride, all of the copper that isn't protected by a resist (a substance that isn't effected by the action of the acid) is eaten away and removed from the PCB. This process leaves behind a copper tracing and/or pad where there should be an electrical connection. The leading method for placing the areas of resist on a PCB is with a photographic negative technique. Kepro Circuit Systems, Inc. markets a full range of pre-coated circuit boards for this purpose. These boards are excellent for PCB fabrication and some, like the KeproClad Dry Film KC1-46B, come with their own developer and stripper.

Basically, this technique acts exactly like its paper-based photographic cousin. In other words, parts of the PCB that are protected by the black portions

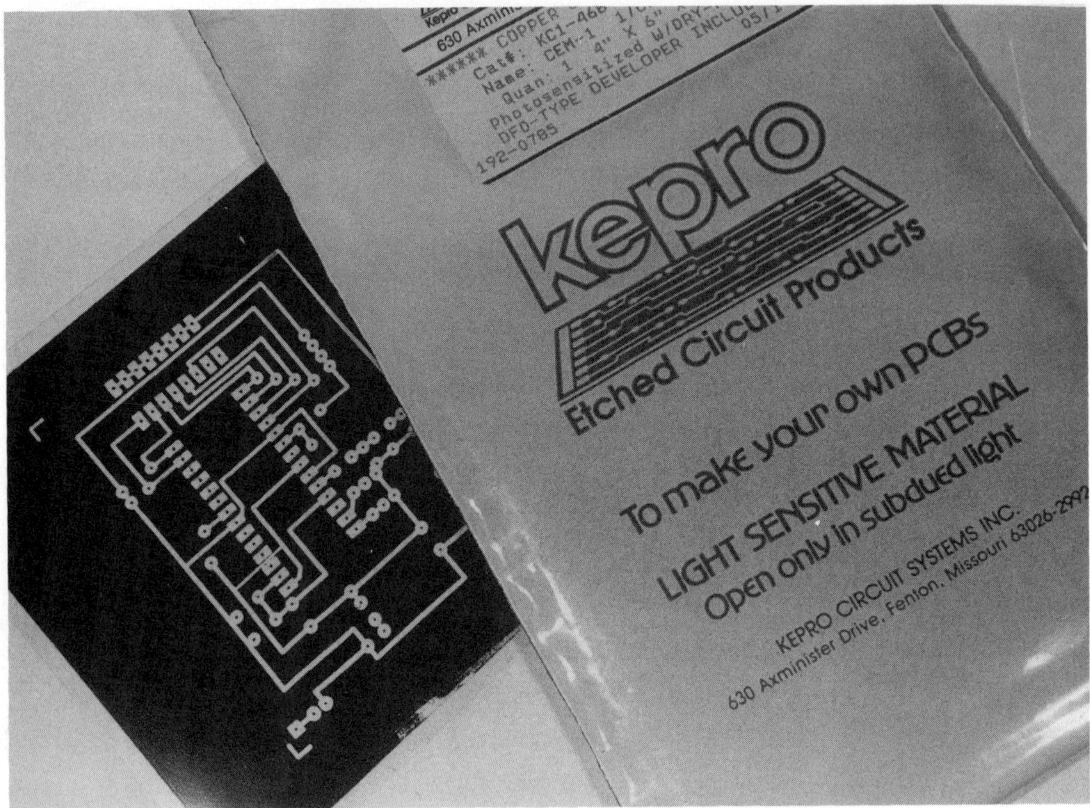

Fig. A-5. Quick and easy PCBs can be created with Kepro materials and the appropriate high-contrast negative.

of the negative are covered with a resist, while those regions that are exposed to the clear portions of the negative are removed by the acid. Figures A-5 through A-7 show this process with a Kepro KC1-46B board and the Bit Smasher PCB template.

Now that you know how a PCB is made, your next step is learning how to make a PCB negative. Until recently, your only CAD route was with the previously described AutoCAD. The cost in the IBM hardware alone was prohibitive to many designers. Most of this need for costly hardware changed with the introduction of the Macintosh. This graphics-based computer seemed ideally suited to the tasks of CAD. Apparently, two different manufacturers shared this same opinion and they each have created a breakthrough product for PCB design. Quik Circuit by Bishop Graphics (see Fig. A-8) and McCAD P.C.B. from VAMP, Inc. (see Fig. A-9) are full-featured CAD programs that utilize a graphics environment for preparing PCB layouts.

Fig. A-6. A carefully timed exposure of the sensitized circuit board with the template negative is the most crucial step in PCB fabrication.

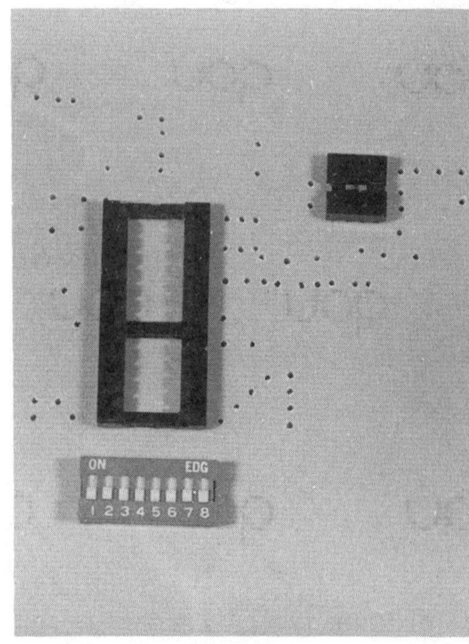

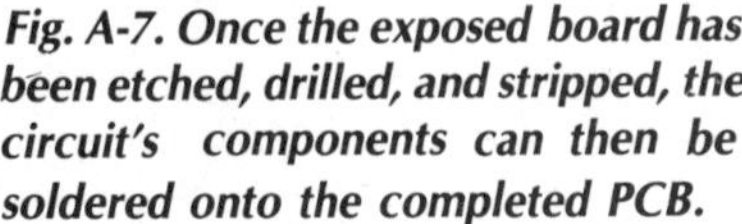

Fig. A-7. Once the exposed board has been etched, drilled, and stripped, the circuit's components can then be soldered onto the completed PCB.

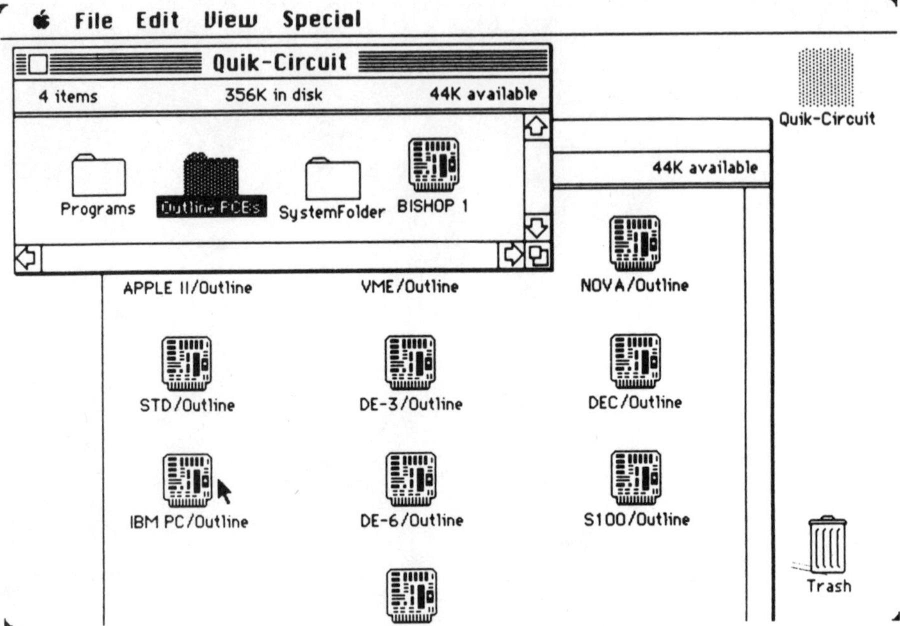

Fig. A-8. Quik Circuit disk catalog. There are a total of 10 different PCB templates ready for immediate use.

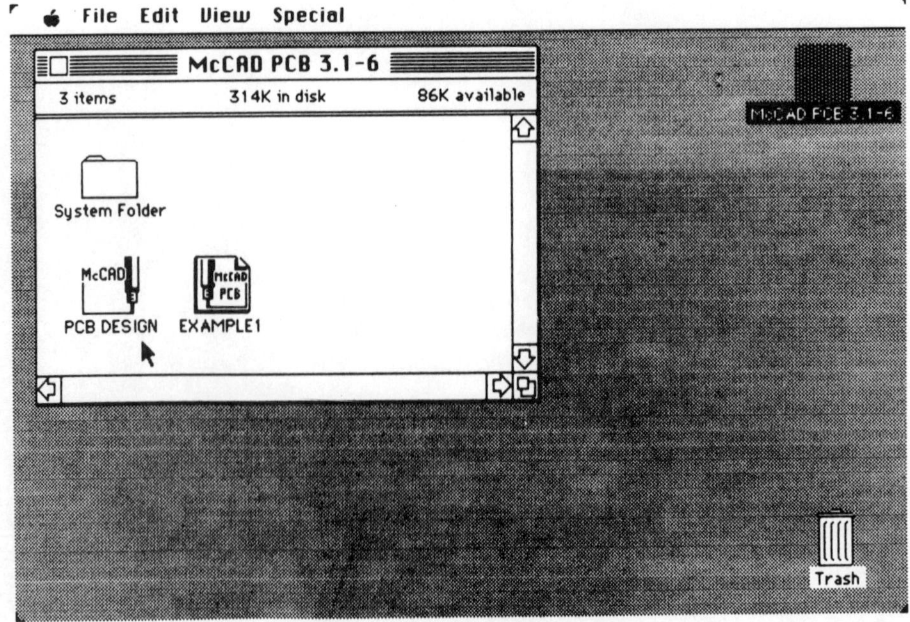

Fig. A-9. McCAD P.C.B. disk catalog.

QUIK CIRCUIT

The operation of Quik Circuit follows the standard Macintosh user interface. You start the program with a system boot and proceed through the Mini-Finder menu to the Layout program (see Fig. A-10). Along the way to the actual Layout program, a dialog box appears and requests the name of your current work file. At this point you can either specify a file that is in progress or start an entirely new layout.

Once inside the Layout program, you will notice that Quik Circuit does use an elaborate menu bar. There are eight menus containing all of the tools, scaling, and patterns that are needed for PCB design. Additionally, there are two work area instruments—the Edit indicator and the Locator box. The Edit indicator is used for providing a visual indication of the current mode. For example, when you are in edit mode, an "X" will fill the Edit indicator. Otherwise, an empty Edit indicator signals that you are in the active mode. The other work area instrument, the Locator box, displays the current coordinates of the cursor.

The procedure for creating a PCB with Quik Circuit begins with the setting of the grid size and magnification. You can now select your pattern from the Patterns menu. There are five unique Pattern menu selections. Each one, however, can be modified for any design need. These customized patterns are

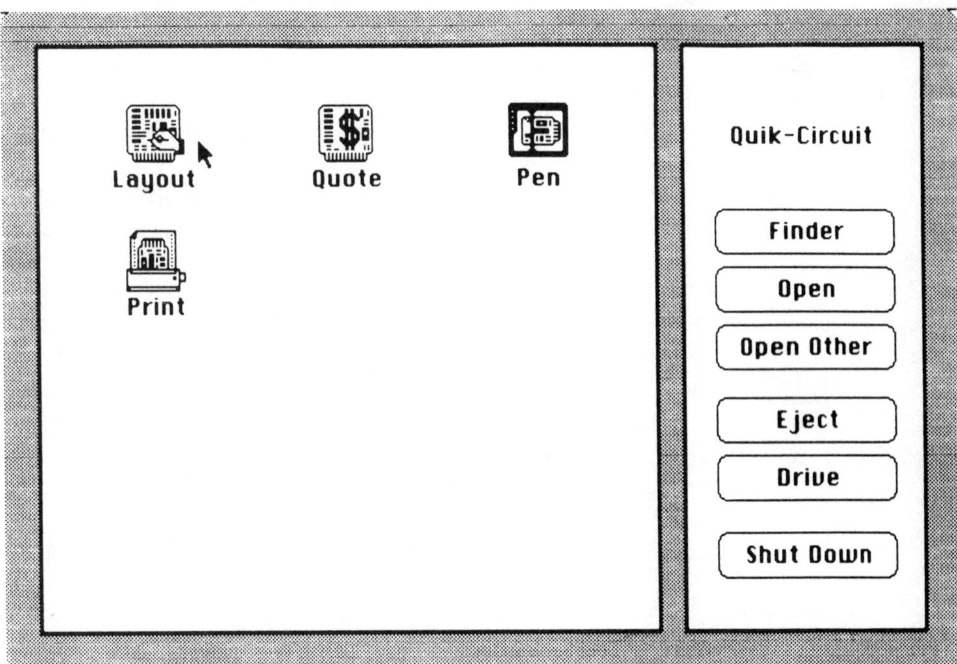

Fig. A-10. Quik Circuit's Mini-Finder menu. Layout is for PCB design, while Quote, Pen, and Print are used for making hardcopies of the complete design.

then saved with the Group and Store selection on the Edit menu. This modification function is a large bonus in Quik Circuit's favor. In practice, you could create a file that holds up to 21 different pin-size IC pad patterns. Then when your PCB needs an IC pattern, you can just access this custom file for the needed pattern.

One excellent beginner's feature is the online Help menu. This menu offers five different selections of help while you are in the layout environment. Each selection has a short summary of the major points that are important to its topic. For example, the grid size, view size, and zooming feature are all discussed under the Scale & Size selection. Even though you will quickly outgrow this assistance feature, it will be a definite plus in your initial PCB design stages.

When you are finished with your PCB layout, it is time to save and print your work. The Close & Put Away selection saves your PCB onto the specified disk and returns you to the Mini-Finder. At this point, you are able to make a printout of your PCB design. If you have an Apple IMAGEWRITER printer connected to your Macintosh, select the Print icon. If, on the other hand, you have a plotter attached to your computer, double click on the Pen icon. After the dialog box prompts you for the file to print or plot, you must pull down the File menu on the main screen.

Select the menu choice that is appropriate for your printer or plotter and begin the printout setup procedure. This procedure establishes the parameters that will be used during the subsequent printing (or plotting). For the best results, you should use a high magnification during the printing. This large printout will then have to be photo-reduced to the required dimensions of the final PCB. This technique ensures the highest possible quality in the PCB negative.

The Quik Circuit package itself is an anomaly in Macintosh software products. First, Quik Circuit is supplied in a handsome binder with an accompanying slipcase. Conversely, almost all other Macintosh documentation is wirebound with thin cardboard covers. Second, and most important, Bishop Graphics ships two disks with Quik Circuit. This little bit of insurance doesn't make up for Bishop Graphics' disagreeable use of copy protection, but it does eliminate system "down time" should the master disk fail.

Making it With Quik Circuit

In order to provide a clearer picture of the operation of Quik Circuit, Figs. A-11 through A-20 illustrate the major steps involved in the design of a PCB. This representative design is the template for the Bit Smasher.

McCAD P.C.B.

McCAD P.C.B. is a PCB design environment with numerous similarities to Quik Circuit. There are differences, however, and the biggest one is McCAD

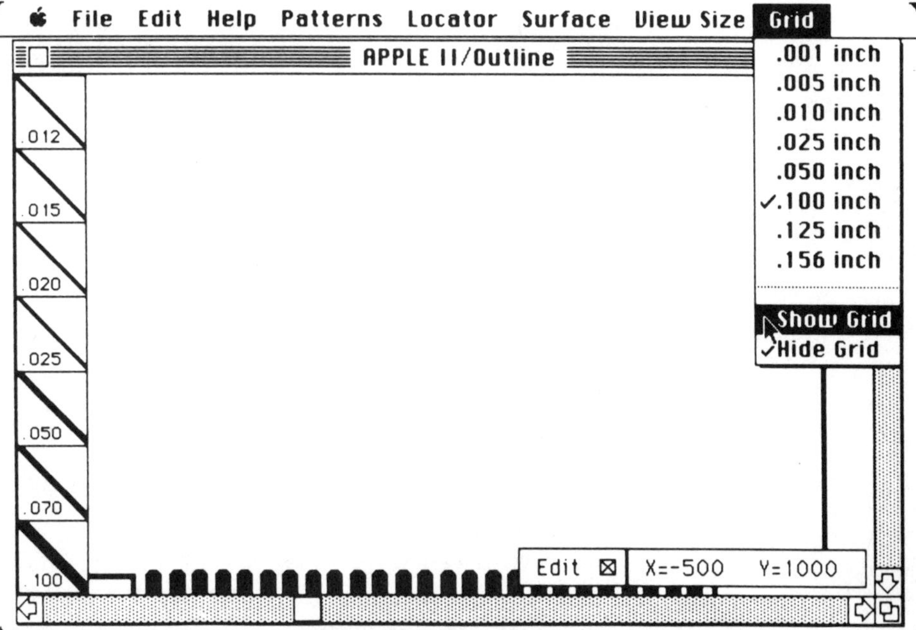

Fig. A-11. Step 1: Place a .100-inch grid over the work area.

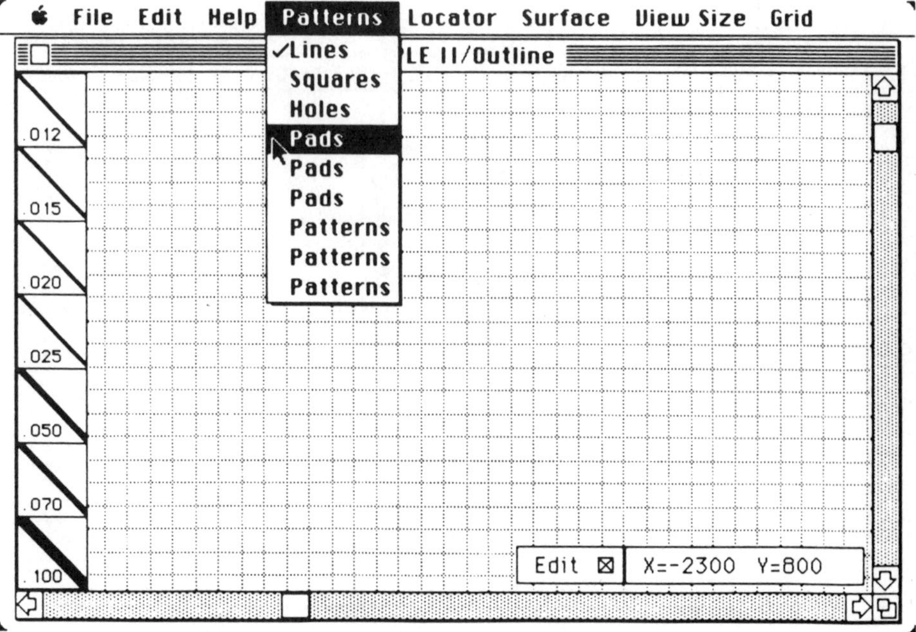

Fig. A-12. Step 2: Select IC pads from the Patterns menu.

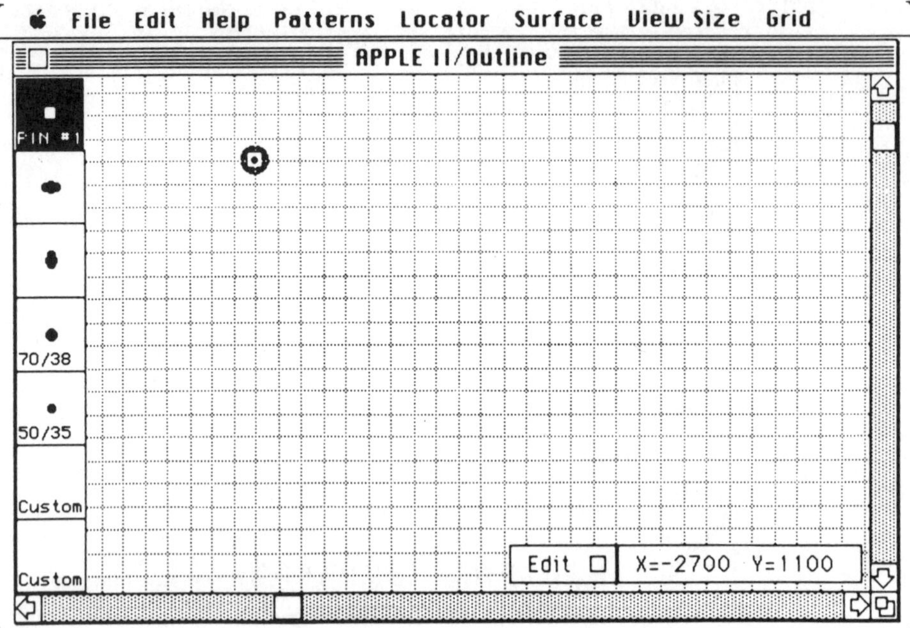

Fig. A-13. Step 3: Use the Pin #1 tool for marking the position of your IC's pin #1.

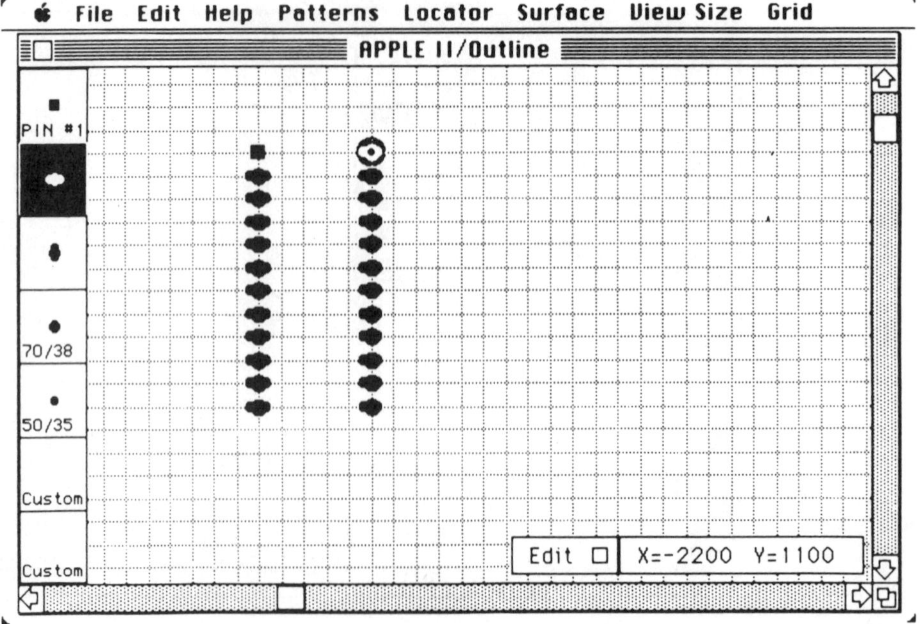

Fig. A-14. Step 4: Draw the other pins on the work area with the horizontal pin pad tool.

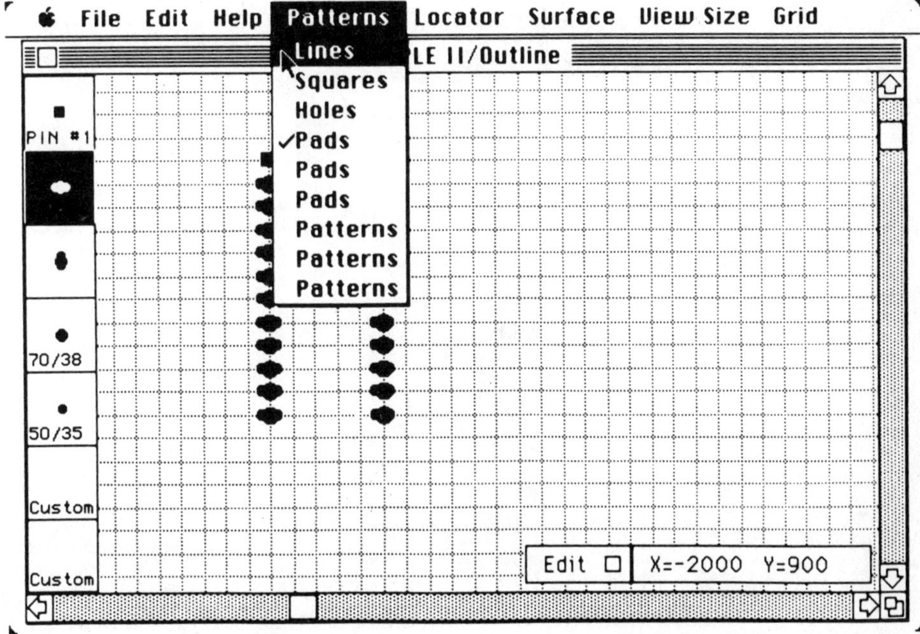

Fig. A-15. Step 5: Select trace lines from the Patterns menu.

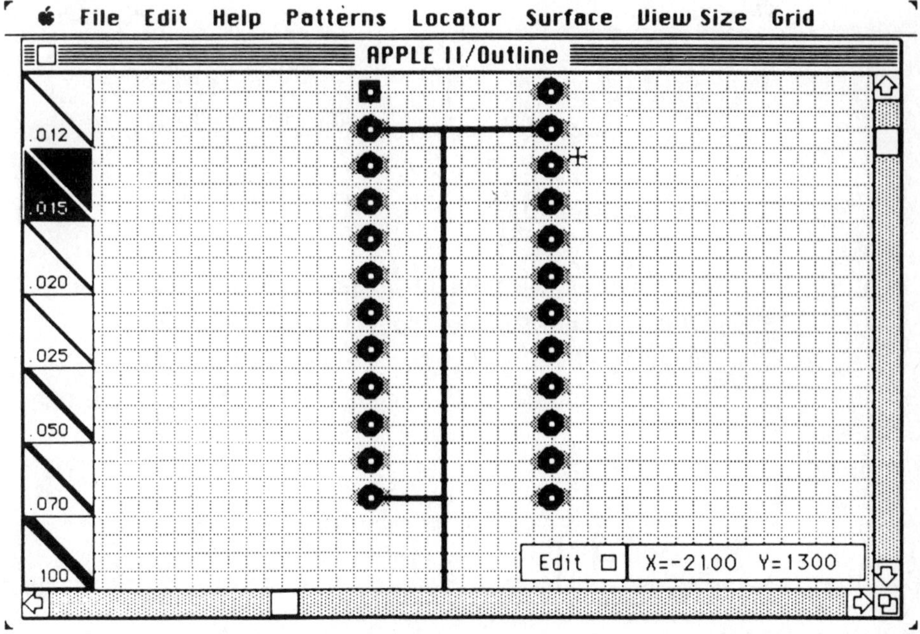

Fig. A-16. Step 6: Use the .015 tool for drawing all circuit traces.

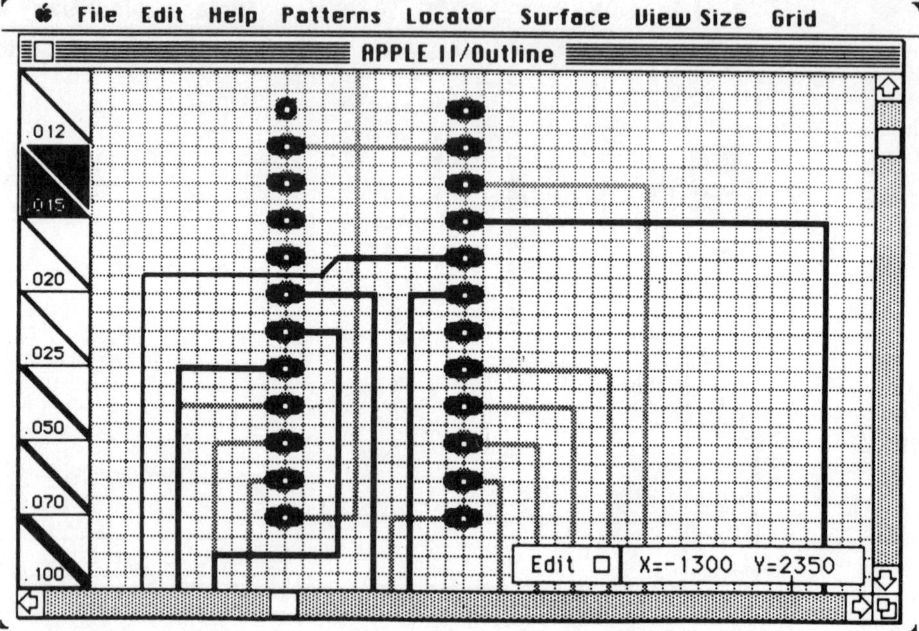

Fig. A-17. Step 7: Place overlapping traces on different sides of the PCB.

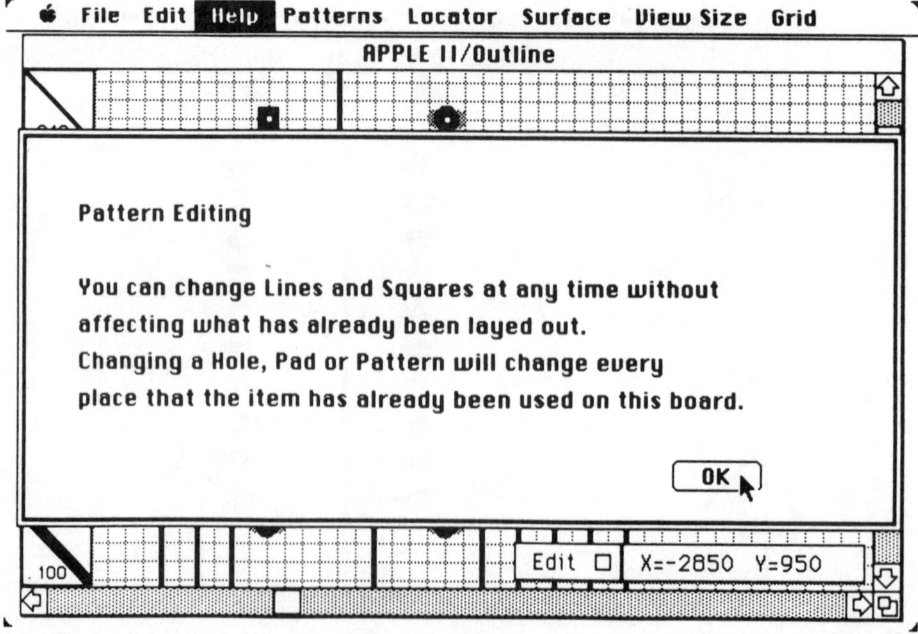

Fig. A-18. Step 8: Refer to the online reference Help menu for answers to any design questions.

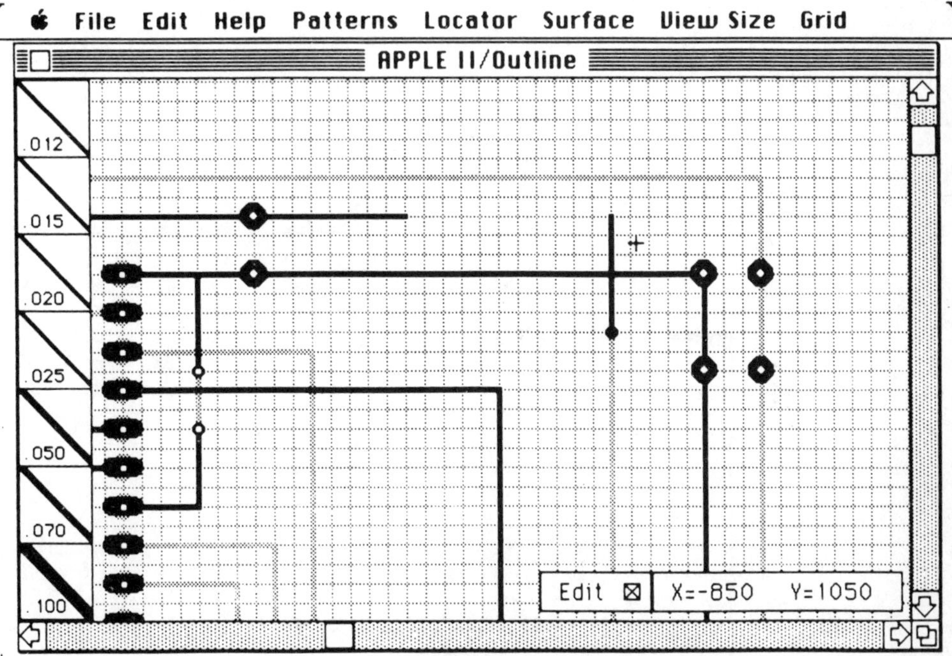

Fig. A-19. Step 9: Remove unwanted traces through selective editing.

P.C.B.'s elaborate use of menu selections for tracings, pads, and patterns (see Fig. A-21). In short, you don't customize with McCAD P.C.B., you just design. Additionally, McCAD P.C.B. has the ability to output to an Apple LASERWRITER, as well as the ImageWriter and assorted plotters.

When beginning McCAD P.C.B., you start at Finder, not Mini-Finder as with Quik Circuit, and double click on the McCAD P.C.B. icon. Before you reach the McCAD P.C.B.'s work area, you can select either a previous layout file or start a new design. These selections are made through the File menu. After you have made your selection, you are placed in the work area.

There are three tools that will make your design life much easier. First, there is a ruler that is located along both the top and the left-hand edge of the active window. This ruler can also be printed on your final printout. You will find this to be a valuable feature during your preliminary design stages. Second, there is a variable grid that can be spread over the entire work area. The grid's size is determined through the Layout menu. This grid is essential for the exact placement of tracings, pads, and patterns. The third and last tool is a selectable magnification. There are seven different magnifications, from 20 to 1000 percent, that can be activated from the Scale menu. Most of these magnifications are used during an average design session. For example, when you are doing detail work, the higher magnifications are selected, whereas the lower magnifications are used in the beginning layout work.

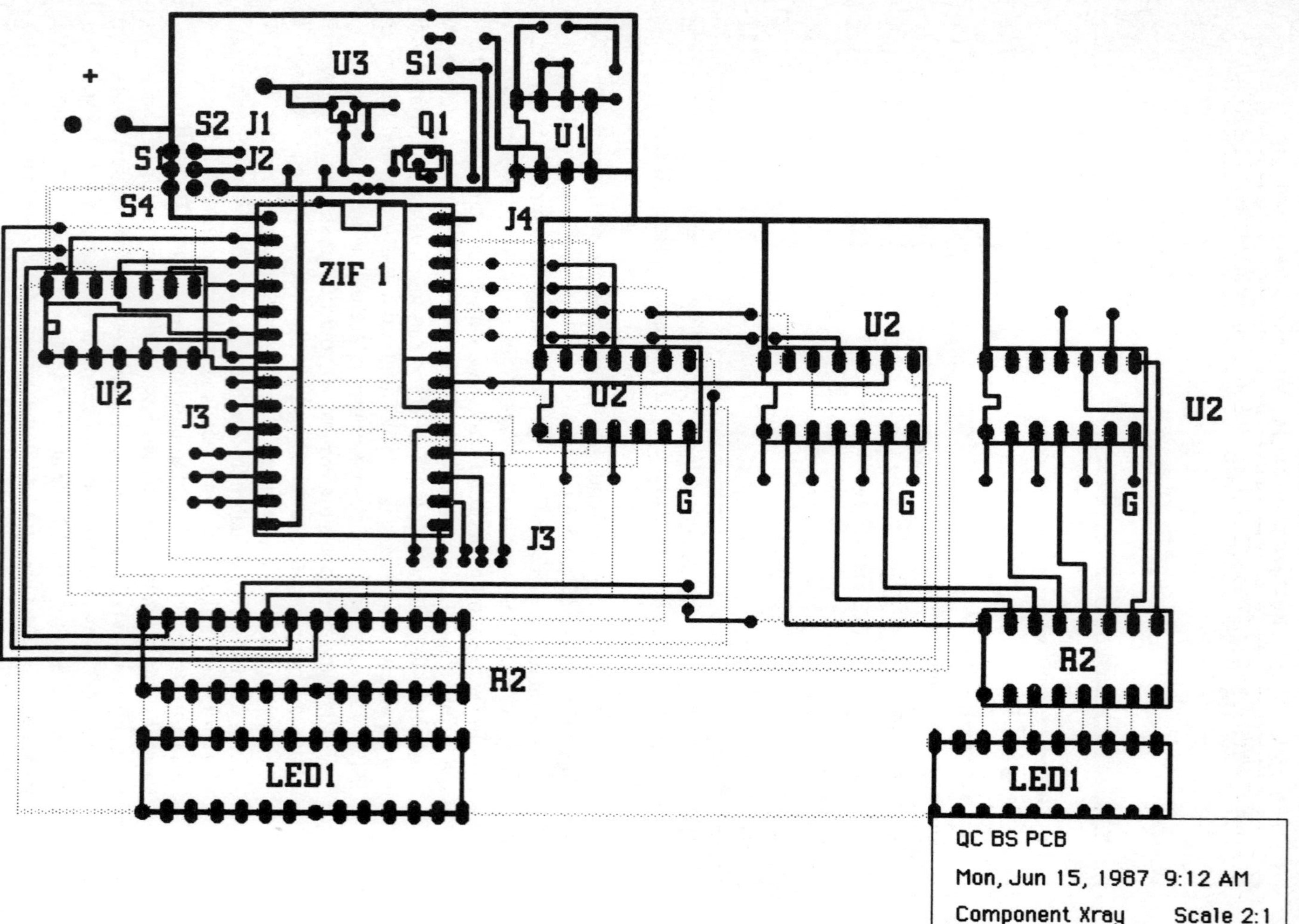

Fig. A-20. Step 10: A completed Quik Circuit-created Bit Smasher PCB.

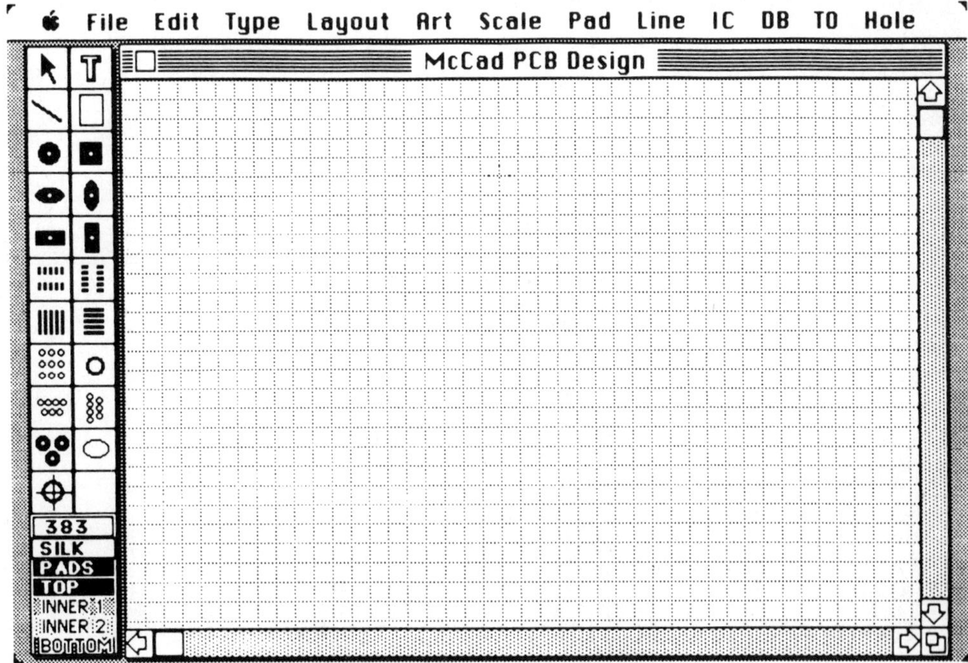

Fig. A-21. McCAD P.C.B.'s "busy" work area is vastly different from the Spartan Quik Circuit one.

Like its other Macintosh CAD relative, McCAD P.C.B. is supplied in a utilitarian, hardbound, three-ring binder. The unique (some might call odd) design of this binder excludes the need for a complementary slipcase. This comprehensive manual can be difficult to wade through in search of a solution to a design problem. Thoughtfully, VAMP has provided a short "five minute manual" for helping you quickly learn the basics of PCB design. On the issue of the software, McCAD P.C.B. comes on both a master disk and a backup disk. Like Quik Circuit, these disks are copy-protected.

A major point in the favor of these two Macintosh PCB design programs is their low cost. Remarkably enough, you could purchase an entire Macintosh CAD system (i.e. 512K Mac, ImageWriter, and either Quik Circuit or McCAD P.C.B.) for the same cost as AutoCAD 2. Now don't misinterpret this statement as a proclamation of equivalence between these Macintosh CAD packages and AutoCAD 2. This just isn't so. The superiority of AutoCAD 2 (or, now, Wintek's smARTWORK and HiWIRE) over both of these Macintosh programs is clearly definable. This cost factor, however, is important to some designers and serves as a yardstick for measuring their solutions. A better and more easily defensed argument that favors all PCB design software is with regard to the time saved over conventional circuit design methods.

Making It with McCAD P.C.B.

In order to provide a clearer picture of the operation of McCAD P.C.B., Figs. A-22 through A-31 illustrate the major steps involved in the design of a PCB. This representative design is also a PCB template for the Bit Smasher.

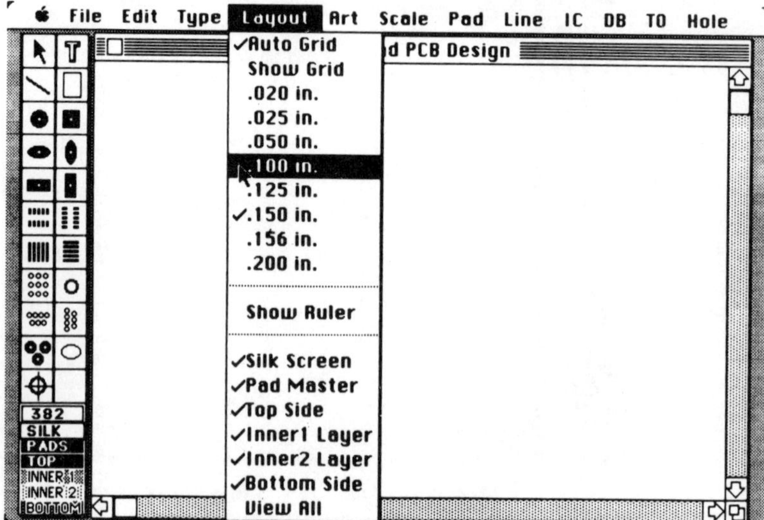

Fig. A-22. Step 1: Place a .100-inch grid over the work area.

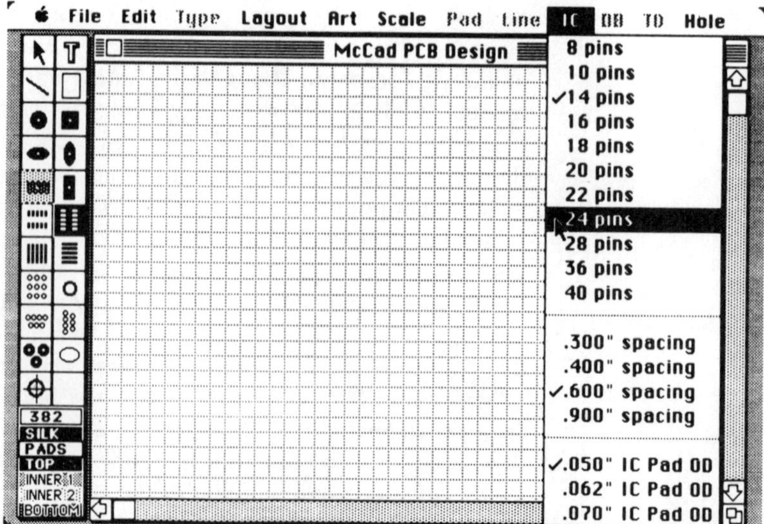

Fig. A-23. Step 2: Select an IC pattern from the IC menu.

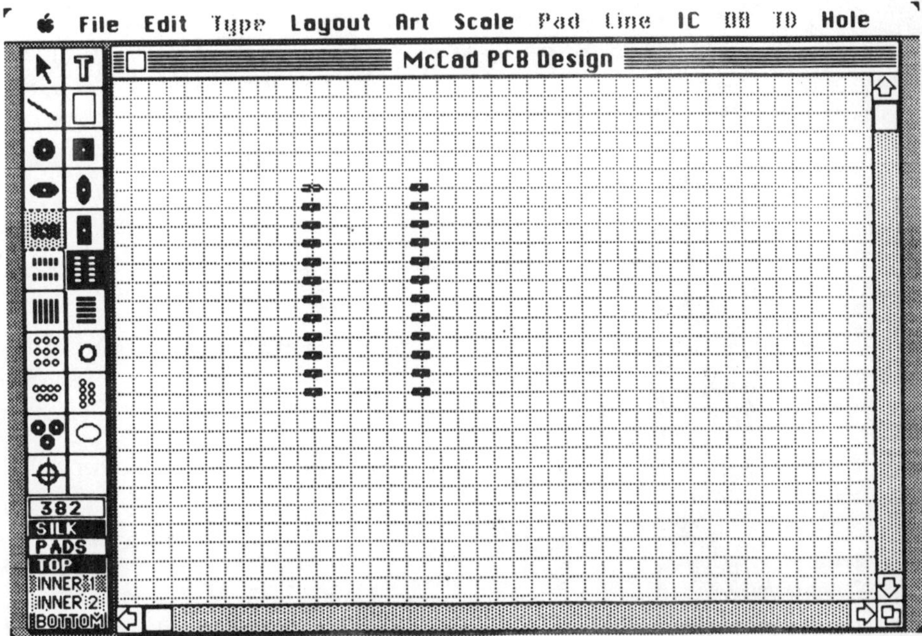

Fig. A-24. Step 3: Use the horizontal pad tool for marking the position of your IC's pin #1.

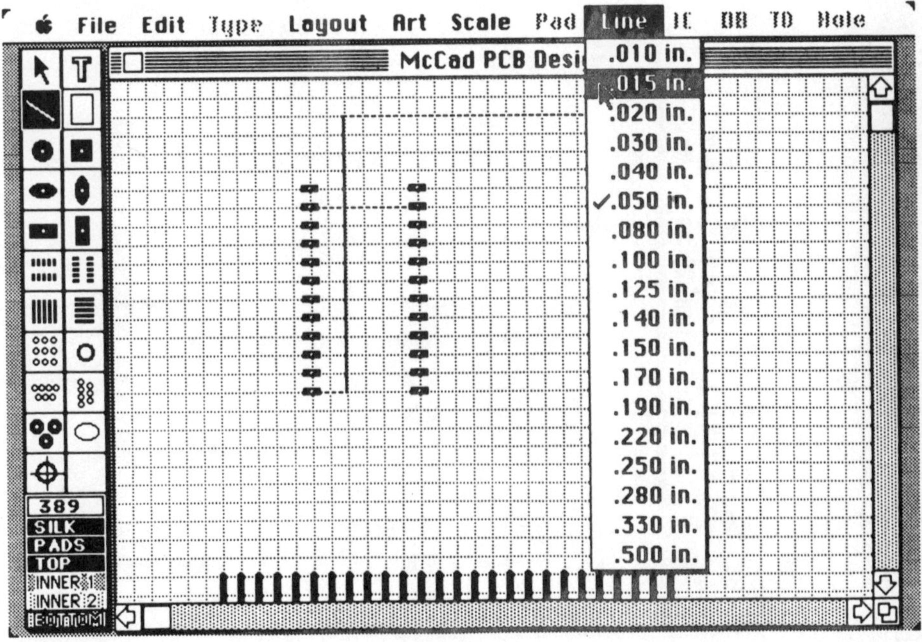

Fig. A-25. Step 4: Select the .015 trace from the Line menu.

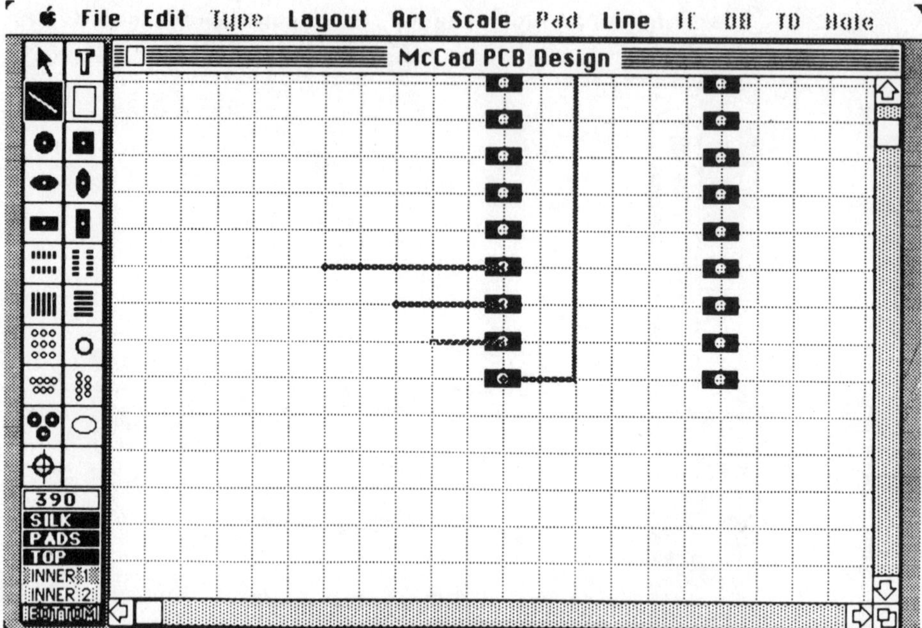

Fig. A-26. Step 5: Use the trace tool for drawing all circuit traces.

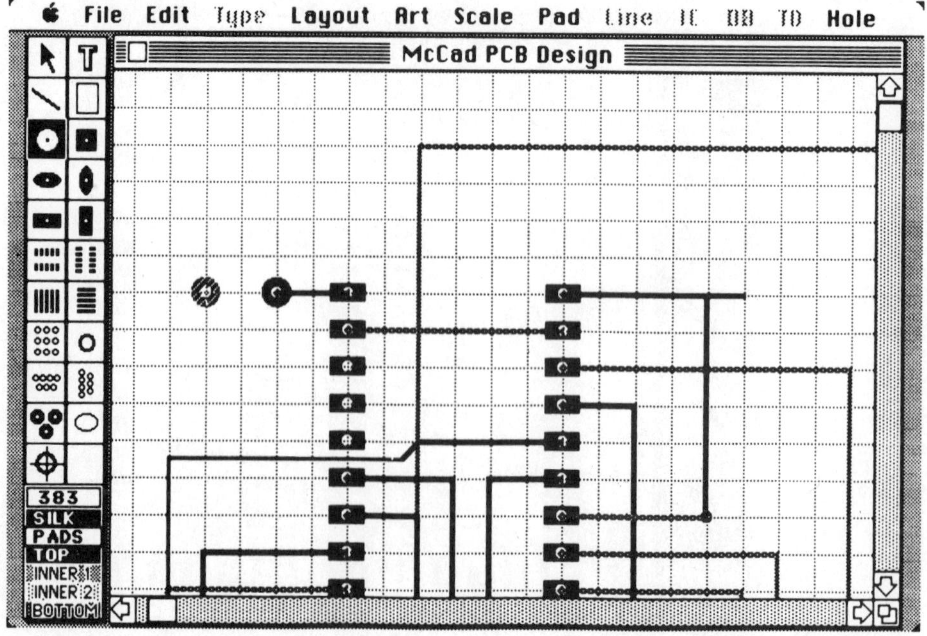

Fig. A-27. Step 6: Place overlapping traces and pads on different sides of the PCB.

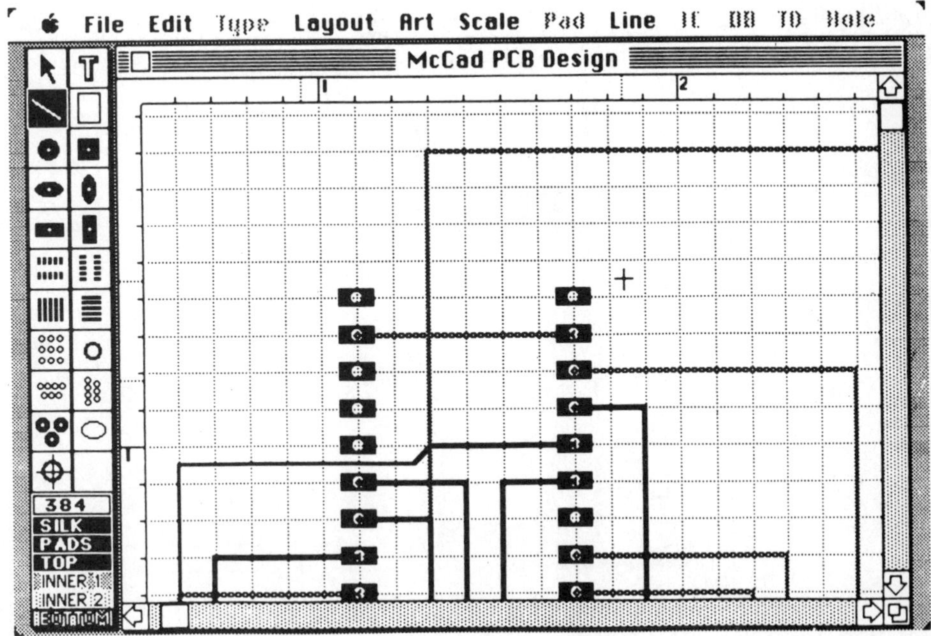

Fig. A-28. Step 7: Use the ruler option for greater precision in PCB design.

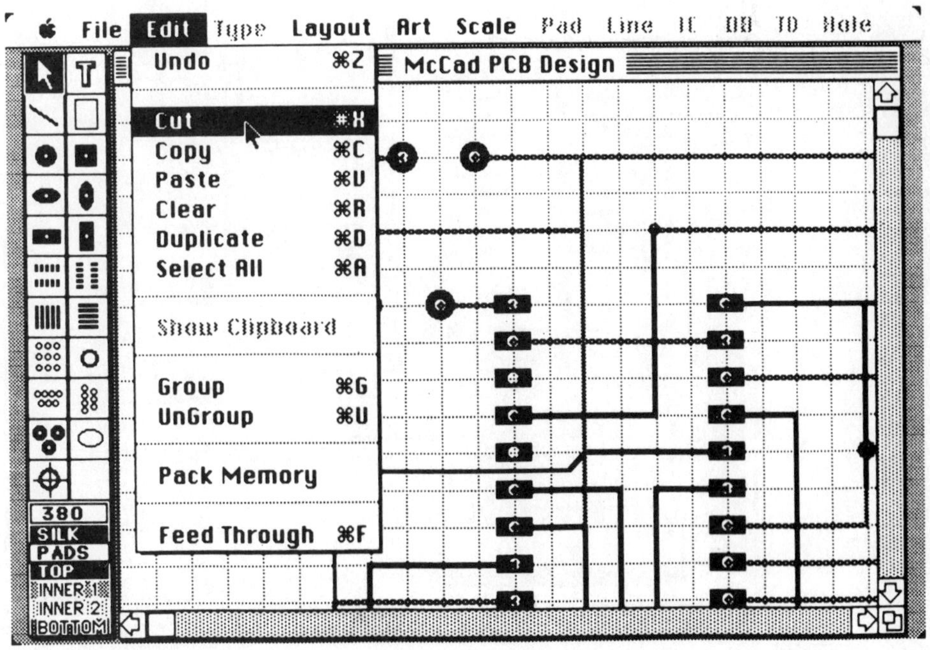

Fig. A-29. Step 8: Remove unwanted traces through selective editing.

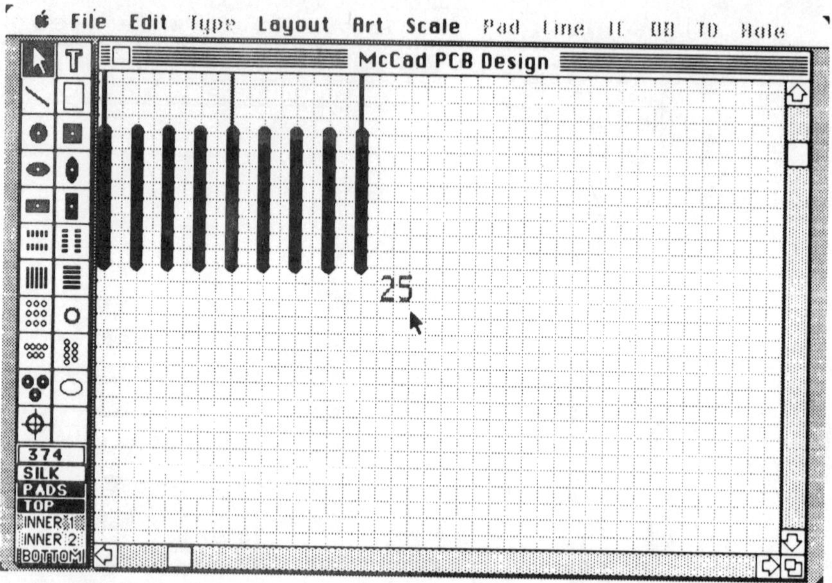

Fig. A-30. Step 9: Add lettering with the text and pointer tools.

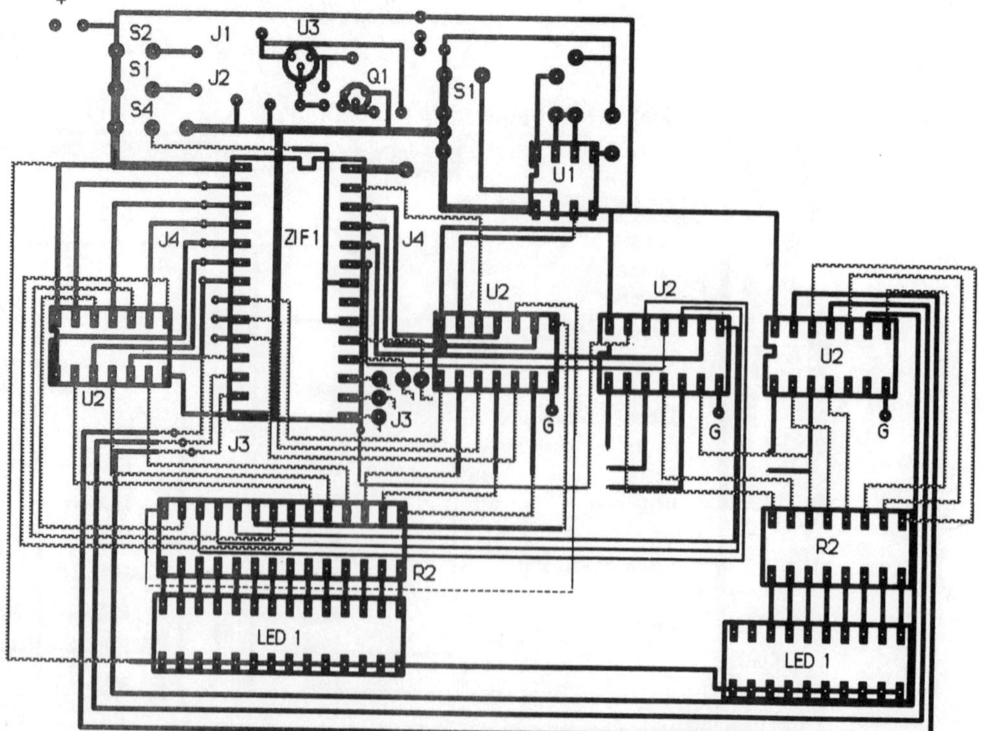

Fig. A-31. Step 10: A completed McCAD P.C.B.-created Bit Smasher PCB.

B
IC Data Sheets

555

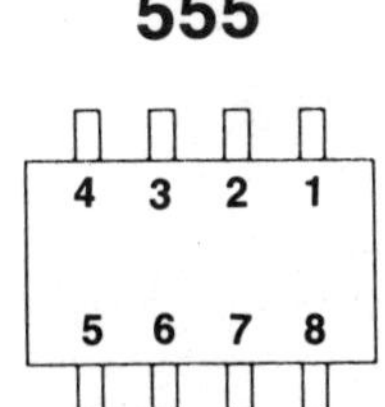

Pin Assignments	
Pin Number	**Function**
1	GND
2	TRIGGER
3	OUTPUT
4	RESET
5	CONTROL VOLTAGE
6	THRESHOLD
7	DISCHARGE
8	V_{CC}

74LS00

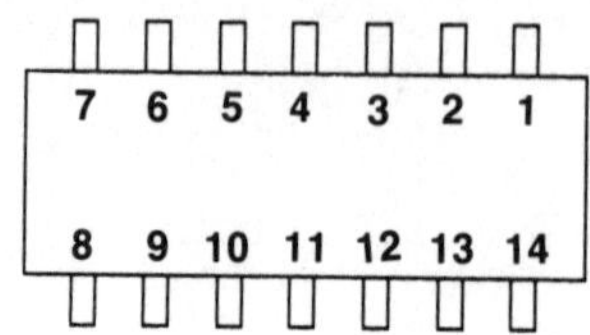

Pin Assignments			
Pin Number	Function	Pin Number	Function
1	1A	8	3Y
2	1B	9	3A
3	1Y	10	3B
4	2A	11	4Y
5	2B	12	4A
6	2Y	13	4B
7	Gnd	14	V_{CC}

7406

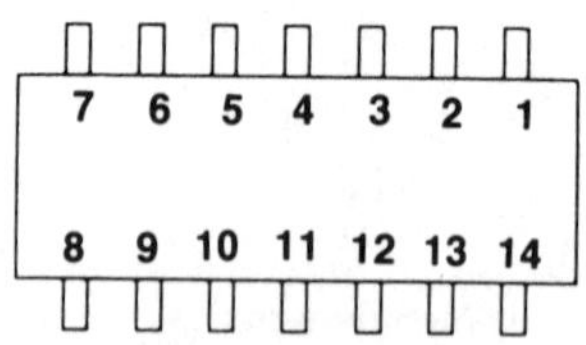

Pin Assignments			
Pin Number	Function	Pin Number	Function
1	1A	8	4Y
2	1Y	9	4A
3	2A	10	5Y
4	2Y	11	5A
5	3A	12	6Y
6	3Y	13	6A
7	Gnd	14	V_{CC}

7417

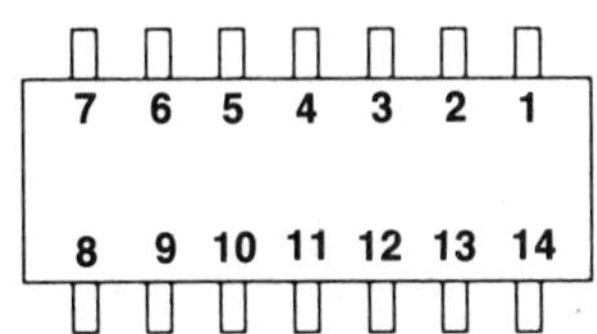

Pin Assignments			
Pin Number	Function	Pin Number	Function
1	1A	8	4Y
2	1Y	9	4A
3	2A	10	5Y
4	2Y	11	5A
5	3A	12	6Y
6	3Y	13	6A
7	Gnd	14	V_{CC}

74LS74

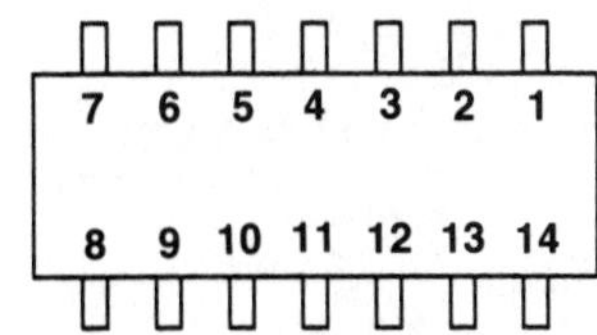

Pin Assignments			
Pin Number	Function	Pin Number	Function
1	1CLR	8	$2\overline{Q}$
2	1D	9	2Q
3	1CK	10	2PR
4	1PR	11	2CK
5	1Q	12	2D
6	$1\overline{Q}$	13	2CLR
7	Gnd	14	V_{CC}

74LS175

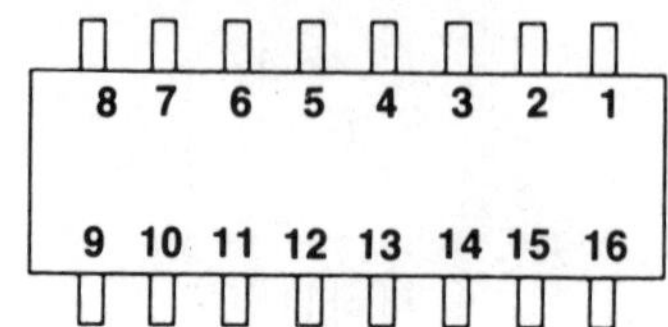

Pin Assignments			
PinPin Number	Function	Pin Number	Function
1	CLEAR	9	CLOCK
2	1Q	10	3Q
3	$1\overline{Q}$	11	3Q
4	1D	12	3D
5	2D	13	4D
6	$2\overline{Q}$	14	$4\overline{Q}$
7	2Q	15	4Q
8	GND	16	V_{CC}

74LS244

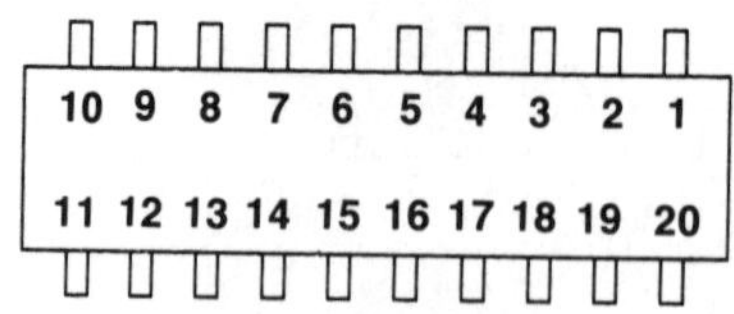

Pin Assignments			
Pin Number	Function	Pin Number	Function
1	$1\overline{G}$	11	2A1
2	1A1	12	1Y4
3	2Y4	13	2A2
4	1A2	14	1Y3
5	2Y3	15	2A3
6	1A3	16	1Y2
7	2Y2	17	2A4
8	1A4	18	1Y1
9	2Y1	19	$2\overline{G}$
10	Gnd	20	V_{CC}

74LS367

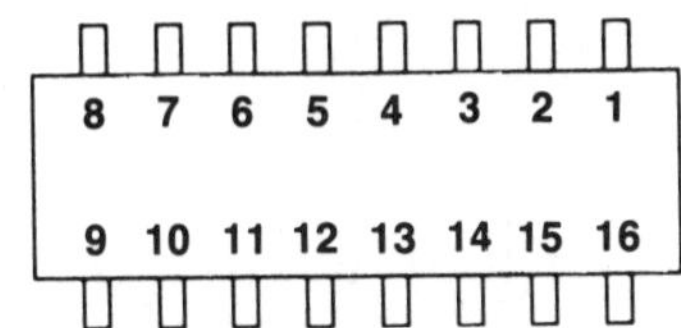

Pin Assignments			
Pin Number	Function	Pin Number	Function
1	$\overline{G1}$	9	4Y
2	1A	10	4A
3	1Y	11	5Y
4	2A	12	5A
5	2Y	13	6Y
6	3A	14	6A
7	3Y	15	$\overline{G2}$
8	GND	16	V_{CC}

74LS374

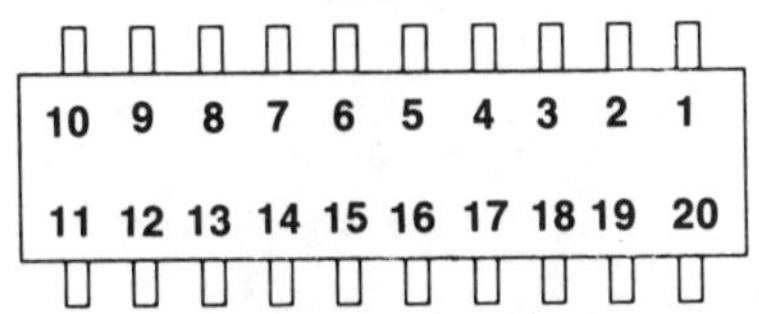

Pin Assignments			
Pin Number	Function	Pin Number	Function
1	Out Control	11	Enable G
2	1Q	12	5Q
3	1D	13	5D
4	2D	14	6D
5	2Q	15	6Q
6	3Q	16	7Q
7	3D	17	7D
8	4D	18	8D
9	4Q	19	8Q
10	Gnd	20	V_{CC}

ICL232

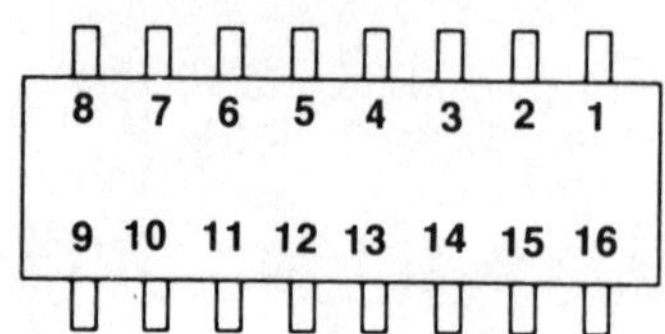

Pin Assignments			
Pin Number	Function	Pin Number	Function
1	C1 +	9	$R2_{OUT}$
2	V +	10	$T2_{IN}$
3	C1 −	11	$T1_{IN}$
4	C2 +	12	$R1_{OUT}$
5	C2 −	13	$R1_{IN}$
6	V −	14	$T1_{OUT}$
7	$T2_{OUT}$	15	GND
8	$R2_{IN}$	16	V_{CC}

IM4702

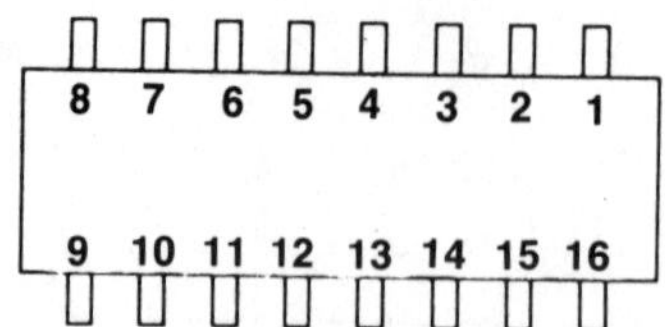

Pin Assignments			
Pin Number	Function	Pin Number	Function
1	Q0	9	CO
2	Q1	10	Z
3	Q2	11	S3
4	E_{CP}	12	S2
5	CP	13	S1
6	Ox	14	SO
7	Ix	15	IM
8	V_{SS}	16	V_{DD}

LM386

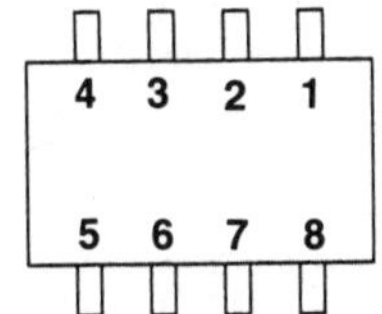

Pin Assignments	
Pin Number	Function
1	Gain
2	– Input
3	+ Input
4	Gnd
5	V_{out}
6	V_s
7	Bypass
8	Gain

MCI488

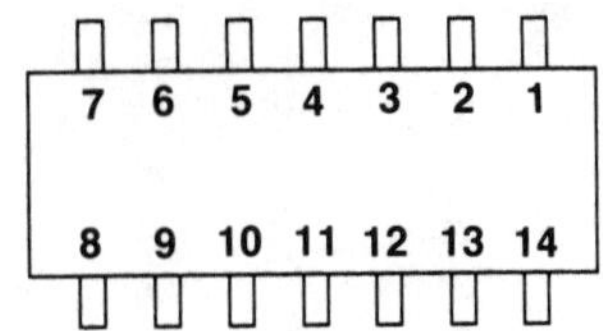

Pin Assignments			
Pin Number	Function	Pin Number	Function
1	V_{EE}	8	Output C
2	Input A	9	Input C_2
3	Output A	10	Input C_1
4	Input B_1	11	Output D
5	Input B_2	12	Input D_2
6	Output B	13	Input d_1
7	Gnd	14	V_{cc}

MC1489

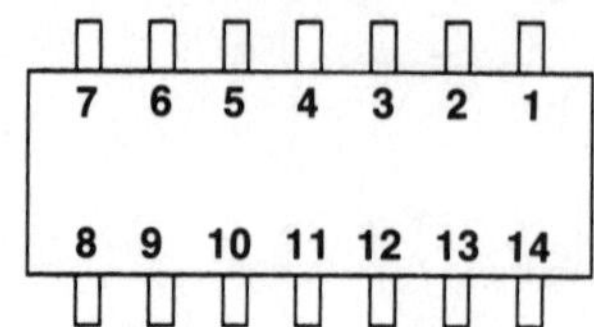

Pin Assignments			
Pin Number	**Function**	**Pin Number**	**Function**
1	Input A	8	Output C
2	Control A	9	Control C
3	Output A	10	Input C
4	Input B	11	Output D
5	Control B	12	Control D
6	Output B	13	Input D
7	Gnd	14	V_{CC}

IM6402

Pin Assignments			
Pin Number	**Function**	**Pin Number**	**Function**
1	V_{DD}	21	MR
2	NC	22	TBRE
3	V_{SS}	23	TBRL
4	RRD	24	TRE
5	RBR8	25	TRO
6	RBR7	26	TBR1
7	RBR6	27	TBR2
8	RBR5	28	TBR3
9	RBR4	29	TBR4
10	RBR3	30	TBR5
11	RBR2	31	TBR6
12	RBR1	32	TB67
13	PE	33	TBR8
14	FE	34	CRL
15	OE	35	PI
16	SFD	36	SBS
17	RRC	37	CLS2
18	DRR	38	CLS1
19	DR	39	EPE
20	RRI	40	TRC

C

Supply Source Guide

References to a number of unusual materials for constructing EPROM projects have been made throughout this book. Because some of these materials might be difficult to find in many remote areas, this appendix provides a list of mail order houses through which these items can be purchased. Additionally, the names and addresses of specific product manufacturers are included.

Apple Computer, Incorporated
20525 Mariani Avenue
Cupertine, CA 95014
ImageWriter
LaserWriter
Apple II family of computers, including the II+, IIe, and IIc
Macintosh Computer

Autodesk, Incorporated
2658 Bridgeway
Sausalito, CA 94965
AutoCAD 2 software

Bishop Graphics, Incorporated
P. O. Box 5007
5388 Sterling Center Drive
Westlake Village, CA 91359
E-Z Circuit PC Boards (#EZ7402, #EZ7475, and #EZ7464)
E-Z Circuit Pressure-Sensitive Copper Patterns
Quik Circuit

Borland International
4585 Scotts Valley Drive
Scotts Valley, CA 95066
Turbo BASIC

Bytek Corporation
1021 South Rogers Circle
Boca Raton, FL 33431
System 125 PROM Programmer
WRITER-I
BUV-3 EPROM Eraser

CAD Software, Inc.
P.O. Box 1142
Littleton, MA 01460
PADS-PCB

Heath/Zenith
Benton Harbor, MI 49022
ET Trainer
ID-4801 EPROM Programmer
ID-4803 EPROM Eraser

Intersil, Inc.
10600 Ridgeview Court
Cupertino, CA 95014
IM4702
IM6402
ICL232

Jameco Electronics
1355 Shoreway Road
Belmont, CA 94002
ICs
EPROMs
EPROM Programmer & Eraser

Kepro Circuit Systems, Inc.
630 Axminister Drive
Fenton, MO 63026
Kepro Pre-sensitized Circuit Boards

Newark Electronics
500 North Pulaski Road
Chicago, IL 60624
ICs
EPROMs

Radio Shack Stores
64K 2764 EPROM
General Instrument SPO256-AL2
Modular Breadboard Socket

Scott Electronics Supply Corporation
4895 F Street
Omaha, NE 68117
Ungar System 9000
Weller EC2000 Soldering Station

Sig Manufacturing Company, Incorporated
401 South Front Street
Montezuma, IA 50171
Aeroplastic ABS plastic sheeting
Clear Plastic Sheets
X-Acto Saw Blades (#234)

Tower Hobbies
P. O. Box 778
Champaign, IL 61820
Satellite City's Super "T" cyanoacrylate adhesive

VAMP, Inc.
6753 Selma Avenue
Los Angeles, CA 90028
McCAD P.C.B.

Vector Electronics Company, Inc.
12460 Gladstone Avenue
Sylmar, CA 91342
Vector Plugboards

Wahl Clipper Corporation
2902 Locust Street
Sterling, IL 61081
Isotip Soldering Irons (#7800, #7700, and #7240)

Wintek Corporation
1801 South Street
Lafayette, IN 47904-2993
smARTWORK
HiWIRE

Glossary

access time—the delay time interval between the loading of a memory location and the latching of the stored data.

address—the location in memory where a given binary bit or word of information is stored.

allophone—two or more variants of the same phoneme.

alphanumeric—the set of alphabetic, numeric, and punctuation characters used for computer input.

analog/digital (A/D) conversion—a device that measures incoming voltages and outputs a corresponding digital number for each voltage.

ASCII—American Standard Code for Information Interchange.

assembly language—a low-level symbolic programming language that comes close to programming a computer in its internal machine language.

binary—the base-two number system, in which 1 and 0 represent the ON and OFF states of a circuit.

bit—one binary digit.

byte—a group of eight bits.

CCD—charge-coupled device; a SAM with slow access times.

chip—an integrated circuit.

chip enable—a pin for activating the operation of a chip.

chip select—a pin for selecting the I/O ports of a chip.

CPU—central processing unit; the major operations center of the computer where decisions and calculations are made.

CMOS—a complementary metal oxide semiconductor IC that contains both P-channel and N-channel MOS transistors.

data—information that the computer operates on.

data rate—the amount of data transmitted through a communications line per unit of time.

debug—to remove program errors, or bugs, from a program.

digital—a circuit that has only two states, ON and OFF, which are usually represented by the binary number system.

disk—the magnetic media on which computer programs and data are stored.

DOS—disk operating system; allows the use of general commands to manipulate the data stored on a disk.

EAROM—electrically alterable read only memory; also known as read mostly memory.

EEPROM—electrically erasable programmable read only memory; both read and write operations can be executed in the host circuit.

EPROM—an erasable programmable read-only memory semiconductor that can be user-programmed.

field-programmable logic array—a logical combination of programmable AND/OR gates.

firmware—software instructions permanently stored within a computer using a read only memory (ROM) device.

floppy disk—see disk.

flowchart—a diagram of the various steps to be taken by a computer in running a program.

hardware—the computer and its associated peripherals, as opposed to the software programs that the computer runs.

hexadecimal—a base sixteen number system often used in programming assembly language.

input—to send data into a computer.

input/output (I/O) devices—peripheral hardware devices that exchange information with a computer.

interface—a device that converts electronic signals to enable communications between two devices; also called a port.

languages—the set of words and commands that are understood by the computer and used in writing a program.

loop—a programming technique that allows a portion of a program to be repeated several times.

LSI—large scale integration; refers to a layered semiconductor fabricated from approximately 10,000 discrete devices.

machine language—the internal, low level language of the computer; binary language.

memory—an area within a computer reserved for storing data and programs that the computer can operate on.

microcomputer—a small computer, such as the IBM PC AT, that contains all of the instructions it needs to operate on a few internal integrated circuits.

mnemonic—an abbreviation or word that represents another word or phrase.

MOS—a metal oxide semiconductor containing field-effect MOS transistors.

NMOS—an N-channel metal oxide semiconductor with N-type source and drain diffusions in a P substrate.
nonvolatile—the ability of a memory to retain its data without a power source.

octal—a base-eight number system often used in machine language programming.
opcode—an operation code signifying a particular task to be performed by the computer.

PLA—see field-programmable logic array.
parallel port—a data communications channel that sends data out along several wires so that entire bytes can be transmitted simultaneously, rather than by one single bit at a time.
peripheral—an external device that communicates with a computer, such as a printer, a modem, or a disk drive.
phoneme—the basic speech sound.
PMOS—a P-channel metal oxide semiconductor with P-type source and drain diffusions in an N substrate.
program—a set of instructions for the computer to perform.

RAM—random access memory; integrated circuits within the computer where data and programs can be stored and recalled. Data stored within RAM is lost when the computer's power is turned off.
ROM—read-only memory; integrated circuits that permanently store data or programs. The information contained on a ROM chip cannot be changed and is not lost when the computer's power is turned off.
RS-232C—a standard form for serial computer interfaces.

serial communications—a method of data communication in which bits of information are sent consecutively through one wire.
software—a set of programmed instructions the computer must execute.
statement—a single computer instruction.
static—a RAM whose data is retained over time without the need for refreshing.
subroutine—a small program routine contained within a larger program.

terminal—an input/output device that uses a keyboard and a video display.

volatile—the inability of a memory to retain its data without a power source.

word—a basic unit of computer memory usually expressed in terms of a byte.

For Further Reading

BOOKS

Mastering the 8088 Microprocessor, 1984, DAO, L.V.
TAB BOOKS, CATALOG #1888
A thorough examination of the 8088 MPU and its command set.

Automatic Translation of English Text to Phonetics by Means of Letter to Sound Rules, 1976, ELOVITZ, H.S., R.W. JOHNSON, A. MCHUGH, AND J.E. SHORE
United States Naval Research Laboratory Report 7948
This is the original study that is the basis for most of today's text-to-speech algorithms.

Interfacing & Digital Experiments with Your Apple, 1984, ENGELSHER, C. J.
TAB BOOKS, CATALOG #1717
All of the elemental electronics that you will need to know for plugging an EPROM circuit into your Apple computer.

How to Use Special-Purpose ICs, 1986, HORN, D.T.
TAB BOOKS, CATALOG #2625
An interesting assortment of component data sheets for numerous digital and linear chips along with a brief look at EPROMs.

30 Customized Microprocessor Projects, 1986, HORN, D.T.
TAB BOOKS, CATALOG #2705
Thirty different Z80-based projects are described along with an EPROM programmer.

101 Projects, Plans, and Ideas for the High-Tech Household, 1986, KNOTT, J. AND D. PROCHNOW
TAB BOOKS, CATALOG #2642
Over one hundred circuit designs and ideas for conversion into EPROM projects.

Microprocessors and Logic Design, 1980, KRUTZ, R. L.
JOHN WILEY & SONS, NEW YORK, NY
A functional introduction into MPU and memory interfacing theory.

Microprocessor Architecture and Programming, 1977, LEAHY, W. F.
JOHN WILEY & SONS, NEW YORK, NY
A beginning text on implementing digital microcomputer designs.

The Handbook of Microcomputer Interfacing, 1983, LEIBSON, S.
TAB BOOKS, CATALOG #1501
An excellent introduction to the electronics of parallel and serial connections.

Troubleshooting and Repairing the New Personal Computers, 1987, MARGOLIS, A.
TAB BOOKS, CATALOG #2862
This book's odd title doesn't adequately convey the wealth of information on general microcomputer circuit design that is contained inside.

Science and Epilepsy: Neuroscience Gains in Epilepsy Research, 1976, O'LEARY, J.L. AND S. GOLDRING
RAVEN PRESS, NEW YORK, NY
An informative examination into the science of the human brain, from the nature of the neuron to the discovery of electrical impulses.

Chip Talk: Projects in Speech Synthesis, 1987, PROCHNOW, D.
TAB BOOKS, CATALOG #2812
The definitive source on digital speech synthesis theory and speech synthesizer design.

Digital Processing of Speech Signals, 1978, RABINER, L.R. AND R.W. SCHAFER
PRENTICE-HALL, INC., ENGLEWOOD CLIFFS, NJ
A technical look at the formulas of the different speech synthesis techniques.

The Thinking Computer: Mind Inside Matter, 1976, RAPHAEL, B.
W.H. FREEMAN & CO., SAN FRANCISCO, CA
For those who think that the brain is a computer.

The Brain: The Last Frontier, 1979, RESTAK, R.M.
WARNER BOOKS, INC., NEW YORK, NY
The biology and psychology of the human brain presented in an elementary fashion.

Mastering the 68000 Microprocessor, 1985, ROBINSON, P.R.
TAB BOOKS, CATALOG #1886
Complete data on the structure and command set found in the 68000 family of MPUs.

Microprocessors and Programmed Logic, 1981, SHORT, K. L.
PRENTICE-HALL, INC., ENGLEWOOD CLIFFS, NJ
All of the theory of MPU and memory interfacing that you'll ever need.

101 Projects for the Z80, 1983, TEDESCHI, F. P. AND R. COLON
TAB BOOKS, CATALOG #1491
Hardware and software projects geared for the SD-Z80 System.

Handbook of Semiconductor and Bubble Memories, 1982, TRIEBEL, W. A. AND A. E. CHU
PRENTICE-HALL, INC., ENGLEWOOD CLIFFS, NJ
An introduction to memory technology.

MAGAZINE ARTICLES

ADAMS, "Intelligent EPROM Programmer, Part 1," *Computer Smyth*, Sep 1986, p. 14.

ADAMS, "Intelligent EPROM Programmer, Part 2," *Computer Smyth*, Nov 1986, p. 28.

ADAMS, "Intelligent EPROM Programmer, Part 3," *Computer Smyth*, Feb 1987, p. 30.

BALL, "Another PROM Programmer?," *Microcomputing*, Jul 1984, p. 106.

CIARCIA, "Build a Serial EPROM Programmer," *BYTE*, Feb 1985, p. 105.

CIARCIA, "Build an Intelligent EPROM Programmer," *BYTE*, Oct 1986, p. 103.

NATHANSON AND GREENGARD, "Second Messengers in the Brain," *Scientific American*, Aug 1977, p. 108.

SAWKIN, "EPROM Programmer, Part 1," *Radio-Electronics*, Oct 1986, p. 61.

SAWKIN, "EPROM Programmer, Part 2," *Radio-Electronics*, Nov 1986, p. 55.

SCHOPP, "A Stand-Alone EPROM Programmer, Part 1," *Modern Electronics*, Feb 1987, p. 50.

SCHOPP, "A Stand-Alone EPROM Programmer, Part 2," *Modern Electronics*, Mar 1987, p. 44.

SHEPHARD, "Microcircuits in the Nervous System," *Scientific American*, Feb 1978, p. 93.

TENNY, "EPROM Eraser," *Modern Electronics*, May 1987, p. 40.

Index